Psychic Phenomena of Jamaica

By

Joseph J. Williams

First published in 1934

Published by Left of Brain Books

Copyright © 2023 Left of Brain Books

ISBN 978-1-397-66844-8

First Edition

PUBLISHER'S PREFACE

About the Book

"The authorship of this book (by a Jesuit ethnologist) makes some of the editorial content suspect. However, the author spent time in the field in Jamaica. His library research was extensive and used rare and unique sources such as contemporary newspapers, legal archives and early accounts. Williams keeps his skepticism active while remaining open-minded. On the downside there are some passages which could be interpreted as racist (in hindsight), so the usual disclaimers apply. All that said, this book remains a good introduction to the outlines of this subject. If you've ever listened to a Reggae song about 'Duppies' and wondered what they were talking about, now you'll know. -jbh"

(Quote from sacred-texts.com)

CONTENTS

INTRODUCTION-WEIRD HAPPENINGS

EARLY in December, 1906, I first visited Jamaica, where I planned staying a couple of months. On January 14th, the day of the disastrous earthquake, I was returning from the north side of the island, driving by way of Mount Diabolo, and I arrived at the Ewarton Railway Station about an hour before the starting time of the train that was to carry me back to Kingston.

The day was unusually tropical for that season of the year in Jamaica, with a cloudless sky, and what was really strange, at a time when the Trade Winds should have been at their height, not a breath of air was stirring. One could almost feel the stillness, and the brightness of the sunshine was simply dazzling. As I reached the station platform, a gentleman and a young lady were attracting much attention. They were brown people of the mulatto type, well dressed and with every indication of refinement. But the young lady, who, I should judge, was about twenty-five years of age, had become hysterical. She was wringing her hands, and between convulsive sobs kept repeating: "Father, we should never have left home to-day. I told you that something dreadful is going to happen."

The gentleman naturally showed great embarrassment as he vainly strove to quiet his daughter who kept repeating in a mechanical sort of way that she knew that something dreadful was going to happen. Finally, her father led her away and I saw nothing more of either of them. But just about half an hour after their departure, suddenly the ground began to tremble and to run in waves with a crackling, sputtering sound similar to the disruption of a gigantic Leyden jar--an earthquake was upon us. Then as the tremors ceased, I glanced at my watch, the time was exactly eighteen minutes past three.

It was the following morning before I reached Kingston, and I found the city a mass of ruins with a ravaging fire still sweeping over the débris. More than a thousand persons had been killed outright and many hundreds of others were succumbing to their injuries.

Amid the general confusion and excitement, I repeatedly heard stories of a weird prophet who, it was said, had passed along the city's streets some hours before the disaster, sounding a cry of warning that had gone unheeded by the populace who had only laughed at him.

Ordinarily, I would not have given any credence to these rumors which I would have classified with those numerous after-fact delusions to be expected on such occasions. But the memory of the strange scene at the Ewarton Station haunted me as it had baffled any explanation that I could offer. Consequently, I made it a point to inquire carefully from the least imaginative of my confrères and they were in agreement that they had heard the rumor many hours before the earthquake had happened.

Years later, this incident was reported in The Times of London for January 13, 1921, as follows: "It is noteworthy that in the forenoon of January 14, 1907, a man wearing a red mantle, who was regarded as an irresponsible person, made his appearance in Kingston warning the people that before evening Kingston would be destroyed. At 3:30 p.m. Kingston, and in fact the entire island, was visited by an earthquake of great magnitude which not only laid a large area of the capital in ruins but killed at least 2,000 persons."

Needless to say, the following days in Kingston were filled with rumors of prophecies of new disasters that never eventuated, and which drove the distraught people to an emotional frenzy of despair. Even the revivalist Bedwardites, clothed in white, as they paraded the city in single files, with that peculiar hip-movement which is so characteristic of myalism,[1] adapted their hymns to the spirit of the occasion. Over and over again, in seemingly interminable reiteration, they sang with a distinctively myalistic lilt to their tune: "It is a warning! It is a warning! On the dreadful judgment day, Heaven and earth will pass away. It is a warning! It is a warning! On the dreadful judgment day there'll be no warning." At first I could not catch the words, but the air itself seemed to burn into my very soul.

I asked a youngster to find out for me what they were saying with the result that I have here set down.

Since that fateful day, about twenty-seven years ago, I have made three other visits to Jamaica and I have spent there in all nearly six years. It has been my good fortune to penetrate to some of the least accessible parts of mountain and "bush" and I have lived for considerable time in those remote districts where superstitious practices are most prevalent. It has been my constant purpose to forward a scientific study of such unusual phenomena as might be regarded as psychic, both by discussing the incidents with natives of every class and colour, and by seeking out those who were reputed as practitioners of the black man's witchcraft.

Time and again I sought to draw out in conversation the professional obeah-men, but I invariably found them evasive and non-committal. As occasion offered, I closely questioned youngsters who, according to common report, were apprenticed to obeah-men as disciples to acquire the art, but they had already learned their lesson of secrecy and I could make no impression on them. I repeatedly watched a black boy whom I knew well, the son of a notorious obeah-woman, as he stood motionless for long periods staring straight at the sun,--a sure indication in itself that he was in preparation for the practice of obeah, yet despite the fact that I remunerated him generously for trifling errands and otherwise strove to win his confidence, I never succeeded in gaining from him any information of value.

It was only from disillusioned clients of obeah-men who shame-facedly made admissions connected with their own experiences, that I was really able to gather directly any reliable facts. Chance, however, occasionally favoured my effort. At rare intervals I stumbled on nocturnal workings of the obeah-man, but even here there was no prearrangement--I am extremely sceptical of all stories of surreptitious rendezvous--and even what I did see usually savoured rather of myalism than of obeah proper, as we shall see in the course of the narrative.

Meanwhile, however, I have carefully studied the works of others and I have searched diligently for every scrap of information on the subject, making it my great objective to sort out judiciously to the best of my ability, what appears to be authentic facts from the mass of fiction that has been written on the subject.

At the Congrès International des Sciences Anthropologiques et Ethnologiques, held in London, July 30 to August 4, 1934, I presented a paper to the Section on Religions bearing the title "Psychic Phenomena in Jamaica." Over a thousand delegates had assembled from forty-two different countries, and it was my purpose to place dispassionately before the learned gathering the results of more than a quarter of a century of intensive research.

After a brief description of the various forms of local belief in Jamaica regarding duppies, shadows, and the like, I then proceeded:--

Without attempting to classify the various phases, we may now take up some particular instances of "Psychic Phenomena in Jamaica". No idle rumors are to be reported. Almost without comment, I purpose citing a series of cases, as far as possible quoting the very words of witnesses for whom I can personally vouch, and also giving an incident or two that actually came under my own observation. The Reverend A. J. E. to whom repeated reference will be made was the Reverend Abraham J. Emerick,[2] a Jesuit Missionary who took up work in Jamaica in 1895, at first in Kingston, and subsequently in the heart of the mountains where for ten years, as he expressed it himself, he "lived in an atmosphere impregnated with obeah and other superstitions."

CASE 1. (BY REV. A. J. E.)

One of the favourite pastimes of the duppies is stone-throwing. Reports of persons and places being stoned by duppies are very common. My first experience of stone-throwing duppies was rather startling and trying. It happened soon after my undertaking the mountain missions on the north side of the island, and before I was acquainted with the habits of the people and knew anything about their superstitions and occult practices. One evening after dark, I was on my way to Alva mission, situated at a lonesome spot on a hill in the Dry Harbour Mountains. I was met by a crowd about a mile away from the mission. They got around me and warned me in an excited way against going up to the mission. They said that duppies were up there at night throwing stones; that the duppies had stoned the teacher away from the Alva school. It seems that the stone-throwing had been going on for a week or more before my arrival. For several nights crowds went up to the old Alva school, not far from the church on a mountain spur partly surrounded by a deep ravine covered with thick bush. The teacher of the school, a certain Mr. D. lived in two rooms that overlooked the declivity. Every night the crowd was there, stones were thrown from various directions, but most of them seemed to come from the bush-covered ravine. What mystified the people most and made them believe and say, as did the teacher and the most intelligent store-keeper in the district, that the stones were thrown not by human hands but by spirits, was that those who were hit by the stones were not injured, and that some of the stones which came from the bushy declivity, after smashing through the window turned at a right angle and broke the teacher's clock, glasses, etc. on a sideboard. In spite of the dreadful stone-throwing duppies, I went up to the hill followed by a crowd. I found the school building littered with stones, broken windows and a generally smashed-up, sure-enough ghost-haunted place. The story of the stone-throwing, which I afterwards put together, amounted to this. On a Saturday night Mr. D. and a hired girl noticed a suspicious person lurking around the premises. They became frightened, left the place, and returned later with a man by the name of H. who brought a gun with him. They were not long in the school building before stones began to fall here and there in different rooms, at first one by one but gradually very plentifully. They ran away in fright with the stones pelting after them as they ran. H. turned around once and fired, pointing his gun in the direction from which the stones were coming. As he did so, a stone flying from the opposite direction hit him in the back of the neck. The stone-throwing followed them into the house to which they fled for refuge about a quarter of a mile away. They, with the family living in the house, made a gathering of six or seven or more. Stones were fired into this house and broke a number of things on the sideboard, but no one could tell from where the stones were coming. Some of them seemed to come in the open door, turn around and fall at the teacher's feet. One of the persons marked a stone and threw it out saying: "If him be a true duppy, him will throw this stone back." This marked stone was said to have been thrown back, proving that the stone-thrower was a true duppy. A while after they went to bed, the stone-throwing ceased.

CASE 2. (BY REV. A. J. E.)

Strange to say the old mission house at All Saints, with a history and location as weird as that of the "House of the Seven Gables," was said to be haunted. A strange coincidence in connexion with its being haunted happened to one of our Fathers. The Father, who had come to the country for a change, was to stop in this house on Saturday night and say Mass at All Saints on Sunday, while I went on to Falmouth about eight miles away to say Mass there. Before going I said to the Father, "As you are not accustomed to sleep alone in a house, you had better have a boy remain in the house with you." "Do you think," he asked, "that I am afraid to sleep alone in the house?" "No," I said, "but I think it more prudent that you have the boy in the house in case anything should happen."

The next day the Father seriously asked me why I warned him against sleeping alone in the house. He said that during the night the boy who was sleeping in the hall called him and said that a lady and gentleman were there and wanted to see him. The Father, having dressed hurriedly and come out of his room into the hall, asked the boy where were the lady and gentle- man. The boy pointed to the corner where he said he had seen them; but when the lady and gentleman were not there, the boy was so frightened that he could not be persuaded to remain alone in the hall.

So much for Father E's account. In January, 1907, On the occasion of my first visit to Jamaica and just a few days before the earthquake to which reference has been made at the opening of this Introduction, I myself spent a night at All Saints in this very mission house which was supposed to be haunted. At the time, however, I was absolutely in ignorance of its ill-repute, and it was only later that I heard of other incidents similar to the one I have just related. I should note, too, that Father E. knew nothing whatever of my experience when he wrote his own account some time later. After we had both committed the facts to paper we met and talked them over.

All Saints mission is located in a mountain district, looking out over the Caribbean towards Cuba. The night that I spent there found my sleeping accommodations restricted to a sofa in the front room which was of unusual size. It was this very room which in Father E's account is called the hall where the boy was sleeping and where the lady and gentleman so unceremoniously disappeared.

On three sides of this room there were windows and on the fourth a passage led to the rear of the house. This passage was cut off from the room by a pair of swinging doors. It was a bright moonlight night and as there were no curtains on the windows I might easily have read without artificial light. As I put out the lamp, the doors of the passage began to swing back and forth in unison. When I touched them, the motion ceased. But while I felt no pressure of any kind, as soon as I withdrew my hand they immediately began to swing again. I could feel no draft of air and examining all around the doors I found no explanation of the movement. After about three-quarters of an hour, the doors ceased of their own accord.

Going over to the sofa, I lay down and tried to sleep. While I could see nothing out of the ordinary, I was disturbed by all kinds of sounds. First it was as if someone came tramping across the floor in my direction. That might easily have been imagination. Then a hand or something similar, I could see nothing, seemed to press heavily against various parts of my head and arms. That, too, might possibly have been imagination. But this was no imagination: while the rest of my body was burning hot with fright, the parts touched were left not merely clammy but actually wringing wet with water which I mopped up with my handkerchief in sufficient quantities to be squeezed out. And that, I repeat, was no imagination.

CASE 3. (BY REV. A. J. E.)

One day a man living about a mile away from Alva mission, came to me and said that he was in trouble and asked me to help him out of it. He said that the spirits had been troubling him and his family for a long time, and that it had become unbearable. "The duppies," he said, "come every night and knock from sunset to sunrise, frightening the life out of my wife and children. I tried to shoot one the other night but I could not. I put a cap on the pivot ammunition in my gun and fired at the place from which the knocking came, but the gun would not go off. I went into the house, opened the pivot with a pin and tried to fire at the ghost again, but again the gun would not go off. I felt something shaking in my hat rim, which turned out to be the cap I had put on the pivot of my gun. I tried the gun again, firing in another direction, and it went off." I told him that I would go to his house and bless it.

At the appointed time I went to the house. After closing the door, I heard the knocking and all in the room heard it. It was a slow dull knock. The man went out and knocked at the place from which the sound seemed to come, but it was not the same sound at all. I listened to the knocking for awhile but could come to no conclusion as to the source of the sound. I was not in the least afraid or nervous but rather indifferent, having become habituated to sleeping alone in lonesome, outlandish places and hearing at night all sorts of creepy sounds, rappings, knockings, clankings, crawlings, etc., so that this knocking made very little impression on me. I thought to myself, I will bless the house and by so doing I will not commit myself to passing any judgment as to the source of the knocking. When I pulled out my ritual to read the blessing of the house, I was, as far as I remember, trying in my mind to account for the knocking by some kind of insect concealed somewhere in the house. While reading the prayer I suddenly became excited and with great difficulty finished it. I felt as if I had been put under some kind of an exhaust pump that drained me of all my supernatural energy. I felt as if I were injuring someone and tears, or a feeling of tears, came to my eyes. I tried to conceal what happened to me by saying in a joking way, "Now duppy him gone." My embarrassment left me. I sprinkled holy water in the house and out in the yard and especially in the place from which the sound seemed to come. When I returned into the house I raised my hand to give the common blessing, "Benedictio Domini Nostri Jesu Christi descendat super hanc domum et maneat semper." ("May the Blessing of Our Lord Jesus Christ descend on this house and remain forever.") I found the same excitement come over me and the same difficulty in finishing the blessing, but it was not so strong as the first time. I was told that after I left, the duppy gave two hard bangs and then stopped knocking. Sometime afterwards, I heard the people speaking of its return,--this time it was outside of the house,--and that crowds went up to see it, and some claimed that they saw it. It left shortly after, not to return. I learned later that the wife of the man whose house was troubled by the duppy was a revivalist, one of a religion which is nothing but a form of myalism. If they are not

possessed by the devil at times, there is no lacking in appearances of their being possessed.

CASE 4.

The following incident was related to me by both parties
concerned and their accounts agreed in all details As they are
still alive I do not feel free at present to disclose their identity
even by initials or to fully identify the locality itself. It all
happened at a particularly lonely spot on a mountain overlook-
ing the sea where a priest made his headquarters in a house
that was since demolished by a hurricane. A brother priest who
came to visit him was spending the night in a room concerning
which weird stories were told, although the occupant knew
nothing of the fact at the time.

On retiring, finding that there were no matches in the room, the
visitor went in quest of a box and left it with a candle on a table
near the door of the room. Three times during the night he was
awakened by someone entering the room, striking a match and
lighting the candle. Each time he could just make out the figure
of a man withdrawing from the room with face averted and
closing the door behind him. Knowing that he and his host were
alone in the house, he naturally concluded that it was all a
practical joke that was being played on him.

On the first two occasions he got up, extinguished the candle
and retired again to bed. But on the third perpetration he felt
that the joke had been carried far enough. Quickly he sprang
from the bed and rushed to the door just as it closed behind the
figure. When he reached the hall, the figure had vanished, and
going to the far end to his host's room, he found the occupant
sleeping soundly, with the door of the room securely locked. On
being aroused, the host vainly protested and strove to persuade

his guest that he had been playing no tricks, and that the whole incident must have been a dream. But, on returning to his own room again, the visitor counted on the table three partially burnt matches where there had been no loose matches at all when he retired. Next morning he made his departure from the house as early as possible.

CASE 5. (BY REV. A. J. E.)

It sometimes happens that the duppy's attacks upon human beings resemble possession by the devil. One day I was asked to come and see some sick children. When I arrived, I found two young girls under a peculiar spell which came about, I was told, in the following manner. Mrs. D. said she was sitting in a room with a girl named J., when three slow raps came upon the jalousies, then came three more slow raps, followed by three more slow raps; then a warm wave passed through the room. At the same time J. leaped into the air crying out, "Old man come," and from that time up to my arrival she had been acting queerly. When I arrived, about three days after the event, she was much better, I was told, than she was at first. While under this strange influence she said, "Old man catch M." The M. in question was a quiet, shy, modest girl of about seventeen years whose father was a Portuguese and whose mother was a slightly brown woman. When she came home she started laughing and kept it up for two or three days. When I came she was hoarse from laughing. The people of the house told me that a peculiar mutual sympathetic influence controlled J. and M. If one laughed the other laughed, if one had a headache the other had a headache, and so on. I was told that similar occurrences had been going on in this family for years, and that it was attributed to the malicious black-art working of a family enemy.

Some of the effects of this possession, if I may use the word, was that those affected spoke in an unknown tongue. I read

Latin at them and they thought the unknown tongue sounded like Latin. Another strange effect of this possession was the impulse to run wild in the woods, climb trees, etc. I was told that in past years those attacked had to be constantly watched, and that at times it was difficult to hold them down, and that they would even work themselves loose from ropes with which they were tied.

I asked J. what had happened to her. Speaking with difficulty and with a guttural sound she said, "A dooorrrg queeezed me," that is, a dog squeezed me, or a dog jumped up against me. I did not think it a case of diabolical possession, nor, did I attempt to exorcise the children, but I read some of the prayers taken from the form of exorcism, and blessed the two girls, the house, and the yard. I remained around for some time, and on my way home, I met the girls returning from a spring with pails of water on their heads, laughing and chatting as happy as larks, apparently well. I never heard of them being again troubled by duppies.

CASE 6. (BY REV. M. E. P.)

Father p. who died in Jamaica during the "Flu" epidemic, once told me of an experience of his own. He was called to a young woman who was dying. She had been baptized as a Catholic, but had never attended church and had led a notoriously immoral life. He found her unconscious, lying on a couch in a single-room hovel. After sending everybody out of doors, he strove for some minutes to elicit from the dying woman at least some sign of contrition for her misspent life. Failing in his effort, he gave conditional absolution, real zing that possibly the wretched woman, while unable to give any external sign, might still be fully conscious of what was going on. Father p. then prepared to anoint her according to the Catholic ritual which gives even a poor creature like this the benefit of every doubt when eternity is at stake.

Just as he stooped over to begin, a black arm reached around him and struck the woman on the side of the head with such violence that the head was dislodged from the pillow. Father p. turned quickly, but the arm was gone and he was alone in the room with the dying woman. Trying to persuade himself that it was all a trick of the imagination, he started again. Once more the arm reached around and this time it actually threw the woman from the couch to the ground. Father-P. immediately looked for the body to which the arm should have been attached, but as he did so, the arm itself vanished, and he was still alone. Then, as he turned back again, he found the woman, to all appearances, dead at his feet.

This same clergyman, I have heard, on another occasion witnessed the severe flogging of a woman by unseen hands which left cruel welts upon the body. But, as I never received the story from his own lips, I omit it here, as I am now confining myself strictly to first-hand information.

CASE 7.

The weirdest happening in my own experience occurred when I took up residence at my first mission with headquarters at M. The house was a spacious one that was intended ultimately for a school. A large double hall passed down the centre with a range of rooms on either hand. On the side that I occupied, my bedroom was the second from the rear. Next came a vacant room with doors on the four sides including an entrance from the yard. The door that connected this room with mine was always left open for purposes of ventilation. The other three doors were kept locked and were bolted on the inside of the room which had formerly been a bathroom. About twenty minutes past eleven one night, shortly before the Hurricane of November, 1912, I was awakened by a loud knocking at the side entrance. My first thought was that I was needed for a sick-call. Calling to my supposed visitor to wait a minute, I began to dress hurriedly. When I was about half-clad, the knocking changed to a series of crashing sounds as if someone was forcing an entrance with a crowbar. At this I concluded that thieves were breaking in. Being alone in the house, I flung my shoe against the door and saw it bounce back a couple of feet or so, and I then shouted to the marauders to go away. As I did so, the door crashed open towards me and I sprang back to escape being knocked down. It was a dark night and I saw nothing beyond the door. There was an old gun in the corner of my room. I did not know whether it was loaded or not. But as I turned to get it, still thinking that it was thieves that I had to deal with, I could hear a tramp of feet across the room next to mine and it sounded as if the door into the hall had been forced open in the same way as the outer door had been. Opening my own door that led into the hall, I thrust the gun in the general direction that I supposed the thieves must be, and aiming high, I pulled the trigger. There was a snap and that was all. The gun was not loaded. But as all noise had now ceased, I hurried through my room to gain the side entrance, with the purpose of summoning help, only to find that the door that I had seen crash open was now closed and locked and bolted on the inside and nothing was broken. And it was only then that I realized that I was not dealing with thieves, as my hair seemed literally to stand on end, especially when I found my shoe that I had seen fall well in front of the door actually back against the wall where it had been pressed when the door swung open.

And so it is that, as I ponder upon the weirdest stories of the Jamaica "bush," I find the question arising in my mind: Is it then all hallucination? Or is there some mesmeric influence at work, as more than one critic has suggested in connexion with Haitian voodoo? Or, again, have we here a recrudescence of the diablerie found recorded in the Scripture narrative? What must the answer be? The out-and-out materialist will meet my question with a sneer, perhaps even question my sobriety if not my veracity, and dismiss the matter from his mind as unworthy of further consideration. The devotees of spiritual séances, on the other hand, may seek to turn it all to their foolish ends and claim to find here a verification of the potency of spirits who may be used to impose upon the ignorant and superstitious for the entirely unspiritual purposes of material gain.

For my own part, with full realization of the seeming bathos of the confession, as regards the individual cases considered separately by themselves, I must simply say: I do not know. I state the facts. I admit man's proneness to exaggerate and that even by a process of self-hypnotism there is a possibility of his becoming convinced at times that the figments of the imagination have actual objective reality in the material order of things. I acknowledge no less the power and machinations of the evil one, always subordinate, of course, to the limitations set by Almighty God. And so it is, that in each particular case, if considered by itself, I am constrained to shake my head and admit: I am not sure.

But, taking all the cases cited as a group, the collective evidence, I feel, compels us to acknowledge that we are dealing with some preternatural agencies or forces, call them what you will. All the witnesses cannot have been victims of delusions. I knew them individually, and without exception, they were men of mature years, characterized by sound judgment. They were practical men and distinctively unimaginative. In fact, they were rather phlegmatic than otherwise, and had in each case sifted every possible natural cause as an explanation. In consequence of the years of missionary service which they had seen in

Jamaica, they had become accustomed to the creepy sounds of the tropical night in the "bush," that invariably disturb the uninitiated.

However, I do not feel that we have here sufficient data to propound any clearly defined theory as to whether the preternatural forces are influences for good or evil. Consequently, while obeah contacts might seem to imply his Satanic Majesty as the principal agent, I am far from considering this here as an established fact.

So concluded the paper presented at the London Gathering of Anthropologists, and it was so favourably received that I feel constrained to treat the whole matter in more detail since the limited time afforded by the Congress restricted me to a very cursory review of the subject.

It is the aim of the present work, to go more deeply into the question of weird happenings and superstitions in Jamaica; to examine carefully the curious beliefs, still prevalent in the island; to analyze critically the extraordinary manifestations that are reported from time to time; and, to seek some plausible explanation for the various phenomena. It is the purpose, however, to restrict the study to such phenomena as are distinctively Jamaican, and consequently a residue of the days of slavery and so presumably of African origin. Our field of investigation, then, is Negro culture, which precludes such occult practices as have been acquired through contacts with the Whites as well as European superstitions, however they may have been introduced to the island. For these latter cannot be regarded as peculiarly Jamaican, either in origin or practice. They are ingrafts and nothing more.

To understand properly many of the superstitions and practices in Jamaica, it is necessary to trace them back to their origins in Africa whence they were brought in the days of slavery and adapted to the exigencies of new surroundings and varying contacts. Hence we must determine in the first place just what tribal centres exerted the greatest influence in the cultural development of Jamaica, especially as it concerns the "bush" to-day. And here it should be carefully noted that the word "bush" is a colloquial term for the less accessible country districts in Jamaica. For, in the Isle of Springs, there is neither jungle nor forest. Even the most remote parts of the island are well cultivated and provided with schools and local shops where all necessities and even conveniences may be procured.

ASHANTI CULTURAL INFLUENCE IN JAMAICA

THE Reverend William James Gardner, a Congregational Minister, came to Jamaica in 1849, and after nearly a quarter of a century of observation and research published in 1873 A History of Jamaica, which is characterized by its scholarly and dispassionate treatment of the domestic affairs of the island.

We are told in the Preface: "In writing the history of the colony during the days of slavery, the author has availed himself of the labours of those who have preceded him, but the sources from which they derived their information have been carefully investigated. The public records of the colony have been searched, and a great mass of books and pamphlets, published from time to time, examined. In fact, no source of information to which it was possible to gain access has been neglected. Whether the writer has succeeded in eliciting the truth, so often obscured by party strife, his reader must determine. He can honestly say that such has been his endeavour."[3]

Writing of the period that led up to the Anti-Slavery struggle of 1782, in his chapter on "Manners and Customs of the Inhabitants," Gardner describes what he calls the "social life of the slaves", and tells us: "Little can be said with confidence as to the religious beliefs of these people. The influence of the Koromantyns seems to have modified, if not entirely obliterated, whatever was introduced by other tribes. They recognized, in a being called Accompong, the creator and preserver of mankind; to him praise, but never sacrifice, was offered."

Edward Long, the first historian of Jamaica to go into such details, writing in 1774, expresses uncertainty concerning the source of these Koromantyns. Unquestionably they came from the Gold Coast but he finds it impossible to determine whether their tribal habitat was some distance inland or not. Their classification as Akims, Fantis and Ashantis raises a doubt in his mind. It may signify the town of origin or the market where they were bought. However, he insists that the entire group are effectively banded together by their obeah-men who administer the oath or fetish. From our later knowledge, this fact alone would be sufficient to identify their leading spirits with the Ashanti. Long further informs us concerning these Koromantyns: "Their language is copious, and more regular than any other Negro dialects; their music too is livelier, and their dances entirely martial." And again: "Their persons are well made and their features very different from the rest of the African Negroes, being smaller, and more of the European turn."

And finally: "On many estates, they do not mix at all with the other slaves, but build their houses distinct from the rest."

Concerning these same Koromantyn slaves Sir Harry Johnston wrote in 1910: "They were probably derived from the Ashanti and the warlike tribes of the Black and White Volta. The Koromantyn slaves were always the prominent or the sole fighters in the great slave revolts of the West Indies and Guiana during the seventeenth and eighteenth centuries." He adds in a note: "They were also called 'Koffies' from Kofi, a common Ashanti name." As we shall see shortly, Kofi is the Ashanti name given to a male child who is born on a Friday.

Later Sir Harry remarks: "Koromantin was the first and greatest of the British slave-trade depots on the Gold Coast. It was situated about sixteen miles to the east of Cape Coast Castle. Either the larger proportion of the slaves was drawn from the

Gold Coast, where the principal slave-trading depots of the British were established between 1680 and 1807, or this ethnic type (Fanti, Ashanti, and their kindred) prevailed over the others. This is shown by the greater part of Jamaica folklore being traceable to the Gold Coast and its hinterland, and by the fact that the fragments of African speech still lingering in the Negro-English dialect of Jamaica are derived from the Chwi (Twi) language of Ashanti-Fanti. The popular 'Nancy' stories are so called from their taking 'Anansi' the spider, as the chief figure. Anansi is spider in Ashanti."

Lieutenant-Colonel Alfred Burton Ellis, of the lately disbanded West India Regiment, who spent many years in Jamaica and on the Gold Coast, adds his testimony as follows: "The Gold Coast Negroes are termed Koromantees or Koromantyns, in the jargon of the slave-traders, this name being a corruption of Koromantine, whence the British had first exported slaves. They were distinguished from all other slaves by their courage, firmness, and impatience of control; characteristics which caused numerous mutinies on board the slavers, and several rebellions in the West Indies. In fact every rebellion of slaves in Jamaica originated with, and was generally confined to, the Koromantyns; and their independence of character became so generally recognized that at one time the legislature of Jamaica proposed that a bill should be brought in for laying an additional duty on the 'Fanti, Akan and Ashanti Negroes, and all others, commonly called Koromantyns,' that should be imported. The superior physique of the Gold Coast Negroes, however, rendered them very valuable as labourers, and this bill met with such opposition that it was withdrawn; and, notwithstanding their dangerous character, large numbers continued to be introduced to the island."

This agrees with the opinion of Gardner who declares: "The Negroes from the Gold Coast were known generally as Koromantyns. The Ashanti and the Fans described by Chaillu were included in the term. They were strong and active, and on this account valued by planters. The Spanish and French colonists shunned them on account of their ferocious tendencies; but attempts to prohibit their importation into Jamaica failed, though they were the instigators and leaders of every rebellion."

While promiscuous intercourse during the past century has effectively obliterated all physical characteristics which may have been preserved more or less during slavery by the Koromantyn exclusiveness, still there have come down to us certain cultural traits, even now prevalent throughout the island, that were unquestionably of Ashanti origin and which must have been impressed upon the Negro population as a whole by the tyrannical domination of the so-called Koromantyns.

Long assures us that in his day it was customary among the plantation Negroes in Jamaica "to call their children by the African name of the day of the week on which they were born." And he forthwith furnishes us with a list wherein we find the following names for males: "Monday, Cudjoe; Tuesday, Cubbenah; Wednesday, Quaco; Thursday, Quao; Friday, Cuffee; Saturday, Quamin; and Sunday, Quashee."

Captain Rattray, in turn, informs us that "Every Ashanti child born has, as one of its names, a name derived from the particular day on which he or she was born." And J. B. Danquah, a native of the Gold Coast, confirms this statement and gives us a set of Akan names closely corresponding to those met with in Jamaica. Thus we have: "Monday, Kwadjo; Tuesday, Kwabena; Wednesday, Kwaku; Thursday, Yao; Friday, Kofi; Saturday,

Kwame; and Sunday, Kwasi." The Ashanti, of course, belong to the Akan group, and these Akan names in the Ashanti dialect become Kojo, Kobina, Kwaku, Yao, Kofi, Kwame and Kwesi. That this list is substantially identical with that given by Long for Jamaica need not be pointed out. What should be noted, however, is the fact that while the custom was general among the Jamaica slaves and not confined to the descendants of the Ashanti alone, it is the Ashanti terminology that is uniformly followed in the day-names, indicating how complete the ascendancy of the Ashanti became over the entire slave population.

Moreover, the generic term for the black man in Jamaica, in contradistinction to the Bockra, or white man, is even now Quashie, the designation of a male Sunday-child, and I could not help noticing on more than one occasion, that Quaco was a common nickname, and one that was not at all relished by the recipient. But why a Wednesday-child should be a term of reproach, I could not determine, and the more I questioned, the more embarrassed the victim became and the more his tormentors enjoyed his discomfiture. They themselves simply did not know the origin or real signification of the term. Captain Rattray now calls my attention to the fact that in Ashanti folklore, Anansi, the spider, is usually referred to as Kwaku Anansi. He is a roguish sort of a fellow who is constantly overreaching himself and guilty of endless sharp practice. But despite it all, he is a likeable chap of a most amusing character.

Hence one Ashanti will twit another: "O you Kwaku Anansi!" or simply: "O you Kwaku!"

Before leaving the subject, it may be well to call attention to the real significance of this day-name among the Ashanti them-selves, and consequently among their descendants in Jamaica.

According to Ashanti custom, each day of the week is named after a subordinate deity or bosom to whom it is dedicated. Thus Wukuda, Wednesday, is compounded of the name of the bosom Wuku and the word eda, a day. Children, in turn, receive a "soul-name" according to the day of the week on which they are born, pretty much after the custom of many Catholics whereby the name of the child is determined by the Calendar of the Saints. Thus an Ashanti boy receives as a patronymic the name of the bosom of the day of his birth with Kwo, from akoa, a man or slave, prefixed; e.g. a boy born on Wednesday is named Kwaku, literally the man or slave of Wuku, implying that he is dedicated to this bosom. The idea of bosom, plural abosom, is not unlike the Catholic concept of Saint or Angel. For the abosom are tutelary or guardian spirits subordinate to God. They are intermediaries between the Supreme Being and man and in practical life receive veneration though not the formal worship due to the Supreme Being alone. Writers commonly confuse these abosom or spirits with fetishes, a term which should be reserved for charms or amulets, material objects associated in popular belief with preternatural influences.

The Maroons, or fugitive slaves of the Jamaica Mountains, who so long disturbed the peace of the island and who defied even the regular troops that were sent against them, were composed in great part and actively led by Gold Coast Negroes, whether we call them Ashanti or Koromantyns.

On February 1, 1866, Commander Bedford Pim, R. N. read a paper before the Royal Anthropological Society on the Negro and Jamaica, in connexion with the rebellion that had taken place there during the previous year. In the discussion that followed, a Mr. Harris who was speaking from personal observation said in reference to the Maroons of Sierra Leone who had been transported from Jamaica by way of Halifax: "The

Maroons are principally descendants of the Gold Coast tribes; and still retain amongst them the same religious superstitions, customs, and common names, as, for instance, the naming of their children after the days of the week upon which they were born, such as Quamin (Monday), the son of Quacco (Thursday), each day being denoted by the masculine and feminine gender. They boast of being directly descended, or having been concerned in the Jamaica rebellion at the end of the eighteenth century, as partisans of King Cudjoe, their leader."

According to the generally accepted theory, the Jamaica Maroons are to be traced to the Negro slaves of the Spaniards who fled to the mountains when their old masters were driven from the island by the English in the days of Cromwell. The first chief among them who has been recorded in history was Juan de Bolas.

With the importation of slaves by the English, almost from the start irrepressible spirits among the Koromantyn fled to the mountains and found refuge with the Maroons in such numbers that they soon gained control of the entire body. Thus as early as 1693 we find a Cudjoe chosen as a general leader of all the Maroons.

In 1730, another Cudjoe led an uprising in the central part of the island, and Dallas in his History of the Maroons asserts: "The original body of Negroes under Cudjoe was distinguished by the appellation of Kincuffies, in which line the succession of their chiefs continues." This is probably the same as the term Cuffees which according to Sir Harry Johnston, as we have seen, was applied to the Ashanti.

Dallas makes the further statement that while the Negroes of other tribes joined the Maroons, "the Koromantyn language, however, superseded the others and became in time the general one in use." Moreover, it is clear that Cudjoe's domineering influence over the slaves on the plantations was due in great part to the practice of obeah.

It is not surprising, then, to find Dallas recording: "The Maroons continued to believe, like their forefathers, that Accompong was the God of the Heavens, the Creator of all things, and a deity of infinite goodness."

The Supreme Being among the Ashanti is Nyame, and his primary title is Nyankopon, meaning Nyame, alone, great one. Accompong is the white man's effort to transliterate the spoken Nyankopon as heard from the early slaves. As a matter of interest, during the Ashanti War of 1872, one of the Ashanti Chiefs was reported by the English as Akjampong.

When Governor Trelawney of Jamaica concluded a treaty with the Maroons on March 1, 1738, the Articles of Pacification were ratified with Captains Cudjoe, Accompong, Johnny, Cuffee and Quaco. With the exception of Johnny, these are all clearly Ashanti names and as we actually find in the course of the Articles that Johnny was a brother of Cudjoe and Accompong, his appellation must have been only a nickname.

It should be remarked in passing that this use of the name of the Supreme Being by Accompong might look like arrogance. But in the first place, his position was subordinate to that of his brother Cudjoe and we are assured by Christaller that among the Ashanti the Divine Name was frequently given to a slave in acknowledgment of the help of God enabling the owner to buy the slave.

At the very time when Governor Trelawney made peace with Cudjoe, the leader of the Eastern Maroons was Quao, another

Ashanti name. However, these distinctively Ashanti names now begin to disappear among the Maroons who after their pacification took up the plan of "adopting the names of gentlemen of the island." A usage which we are told "was universally practised among them." Thus we find among the Scot's Hall Maroons in 1774, Captain Davy, Sam Grant who later became Major of Maroons at Charles Town, and a personage of the name of Mac Guire. Nevertheless, Ashanti names do turn up at times. Thus when Governor Littleton was attended by a party of Maroons at Montego Bay in 1764, the leader was named Cudjoe. Again, one of the Maroons who stirred up the slaves in 1755 was Quaco, and J. B. Moreton writing in 1793 mentions another Cudjoe as Chief of the Central Maroons at the time of his visit to them.

Finally in the rebellion of 1760, according to Bryan Edwards who was personally familiar with every detail of the uprising, the real leader was "a Koromantyn Negro of the name of Tacky, who had been a Chief in Guiney." This name is also Ashanti where it is written with a final i, Takyi. All this goes to show that the real leaders among the Koromantyns, whether met with as slaves or Maroons, were none other than Ashanti as Gardner and Ellis maintained.

This is further confirmed by an observation made by Sir William Butler who took part in the Ashanti Campaign of 1873, to the effect that in the slave trade "the protected tribes of the coast were the prime brokers. They bought from the black interior kingdoms of Dahomey and Ashanti, and they sold to the white merchant traders of Europe." This statement indicates that the so-called Koromantyn or Gold Coast slaves were not natives of the Coast itself but were brought from the interior; and secondly, it clearly specifies the Ashanti as one of the chief sources of supply.

Consequently, it is not to be wondered at, as Sir Harry Johnston has already assured us, that the vestiges of such words, etc., to be found to-day in Jamaica, as can be traced back to African sources, are almost invariably of Ashanti origin. Let me cite just a few examples that came under my own observa-tion while I was in Jamaica.

Throughout the "bush" there is a peculiar type of fowl with ruffled feathers and half-naked neck as if they had been partially plucked. The "picnies"[4] call them peel-neck, i.e. bald-neck, since peel-head means bald. These are technically known as senseh fowl. Now a writer in Chambers's Journal for January 11, 1902, suggests as an indication of obeah "a few senseh feathers; in one's soup-plate," and mentions in connexion with a particular case of obeah that among the ingredients required were "two white senseh fowls." Moreover, May Robinson, in a contribution to the Folk-Lore Quarterly in 1893 further associates the senseh fowl with the working of obeah especially in the process of "duppy catching" as a cure. Now this Jamaica senseh fowl which is thus closely connected with obeah is identical with the asense fowl of Ashanti, whence, as we shall see later, the Jamaica obeah was derived.

As it is peculiar to the Ashanti to use as a sobriquet of the Supreme Being or Creator Ananse kokroko, the Great Spider, it is significant to find Isabel Cranstoun Maclean in her Children of Jamaica making the complaint: "Most of their beliefs are very depressing, and very degrading. It could not, for instance, help the children to grow into good men and women when they are told the Creator of man was a spider." Both in Jamaica and Ashanti the utterance is connected with fables illustrative of wisdom, and nothing else.

The Jamaica peasant habitually makes use of words that are to him simply meaningless, and yet they are not only pure Ashanti but their signification has been faithfully preserved during the century and a quarter since the importation of slaves was stopped. Thus the staple food of the Ashanti is fufu which consists of mashed yam or plantain, while in Jamaica mashed yam retains the same identical name, fufu. This word fufu is itself the reduplicated form of the Ashanti fu, meaning white, and in the Jamaica "bush" a very superior species of white yam is called fufu yam. While none of the peasants apparently know the origin of the term, this particular usage is clearly distinguished from that already mentioned where it signified yam that had been mashed. Again, the name of the common yellow yam in Jamaica is afu which is presumably a simplified form of nkamfo, the Ashanti name for the same yellow yam. So too, in Jamaica, a yam that has developed spherically, and not in the usual elongated form, is known as pumpun yam, a reduplicated form of the Ashanti word pun, primarily meaning to become swelled or distended.

The fabulous duckano or dumpling-tree which is so frequently met with in Jamaica Anansi stories is derived directly from the Ashanti word dokono, boiled maize-bread.

The Ashanti name of odum for the silk-cotton tree perseveres in Jamaica both as regards its name and its characteristic association in popular superstition with duppies or ghosts who are supposed to make the odum tree their usual abode. The Ashanti word for owl, patu, is still preserved in Jamaica and the Ashanti apakyi, a broad calabash and apakyim, a small calabash recur in the Jamaica name for a small calabash, packy. So too, the Ashanti bonkara, a travelling basket, is the Jamaica bonkra, or as it is sometimes spelt bankra, just as the Ashanti kotokuwo, a small bag or sack, is the Jamaica cutacoo, which is associated with the obeah-man.

The Ashanti nyam, to move quickly, has the reduplicated form nyinnyam, agony pangs of death, and the derivative gyam, to be in the agonies or pangs of death. This is seemingly the origin of the Jamaica nyam, to eat greedily or devour, as we find it in the proverb "darg nyam darg," or as we would express it, "dog eat dog."

Concerning the Koromantyns, Bryan Edwards tells us: "Assarci is the god of earth" who receives the offering of first fruits besides a libation poured out of what they drink. According to Captain Rattray, Asase is the Ashanti earth goddess to whom Thursday is dedicated. "Even now," he declares, "the Ashanti farmer will not till or break the soil on this day." He is of opinion, however, that "when the Ashanti, before partaking of wine or spirits, pours a little on the ground from the cup, he does so, not to the Earth Goddess, but for the shades of his ancestors."

The Ashanti Sasabonsam is well described by Captain Rattray as "a devil or evil spirit" in league with the obayifo or witch who is its servant. That this Ashanti Sasabonsam exercised great influence among Jamaica slaves is evidenced by Herbert G. DeLisser, a native Jamaican, who records their belief that "Sasabonsam's favorite residence is the ceiba, the great silk-cotton tree." True it is, that Bryan Edwards speaks of the Koromantyn Sasabonsam as Obboney. (So) But this is probably due to the fact that the obayifo was confused with its master, Sasabonsam, and Obboney became the object of the obeah cult in the white man's effort to clarify and express the black man's witchcraft. But we shall see more of this in a later chapter.

Finally, there is a tropical skin disease known as yaws, which is characterized by ulcerated tumors of a most contagious form.

The Oxford Dictionary regards the derivation of the word as of unknown origin although the earliest reference connects it with Jamaica, where the distemper is very prevalent. Now it is at least suggestive that the Ashanti word for the same disease is gyato or gyatowa, and that its signification is given as yaws.

As noticed in Hebrewisms of West Africa, a visitor to Jamaica from the States is immediately impressed by the cleanliness of the native peasant in his habits and in his fondness for bathing-- a striking contrast with our Southern Negro, who too frequently seems to have a horror of water. In Jamaica coastal towns, the entire male population as a rule devotes a great part of every Sunday morning to swimming, so much so, that it frequently interferes with divine service, and even on weekdays, wherever water is plentiful, the morning bath is the rule rather than the exception.

In this connexion it is interesting to find A. W. Cardinall writing: "The Ashanti are remarkable for their extreme cleanliness; and they take a pride in themselves, their clothing and their houses, which some of the other tribes do not, and many of the non-African population completely ignore." Bowditch too, had noted the same characteristic of the Ashanti more than a century before: "Both men and women are particularly cleanly in their persons," he wrote of them, and adds that they washed "daily on rising, from head to foot, with warm water and Portuguese soap, using afterwards the vegetable grease or butter, which is a fine cosmetic." Is it a consequence of this use of Portuguese soap that in Jamaica to-day, perhaps no gift is more highly prized, even by the better class of the peasantry, than a cake or two of scented soap? On the occasion of my first Christmas in Jamaica, I was astonished by the number of gifts of soap, which almost seemed a reflexion until I became better acquainted with the native customs.

I was also long puzzled by a custom associated with the "bush" funeral in Jamaica. Before setting out for the burial ground, the coffin was raised and lowered three times. No one could give me any explanation for the practice nor did any local superstition seem to be associated with it in the public mind. It was always done in that way from time immemorial, and that was all there was about it. No one was willing even to make a conjecture regarding its origin or purpose. Strange as it may seem, a similar practice has been in vogue among the Ashanti from prehistoric times. It is thus described by Captain Rattray: "The coffin is now closed, and a hole is knocked in the wall; through this the coffin is carried by the asokwafo: on its arrival outside it is placed on the ground, but not without a pretence being made to set it down twice before it finally comes to rest. The reason for this curious custom is undoubtedly to give Asase Ya (the Earth Goddess) due notice and warning." Then, after a brief ceremony, he continues: "The sextons now raise the coffin to carry it away to burial; the same courtesies are paid to the Earth Goddess as when the corpse was set down." A striking parallel to this formality was concomitant with the enthroning, or rather enstooling, of a new paramount chief among the Ashanti, in comparatively recent times, whereby he was required to feign three times to sit upon the Golden Stool, though actually he might not rest upon it, raising and lowering his body three times to put him in mind that it would be raised and lowered after death.

The Jamaica Anancy Tales, as was remarked by Sir Harry Johnston, bear the impress of Ashanti influence. Not only is the central figure in the stories the Ashanti Anansi or spider, but while in the folklore of the Gold Coast generally the spider's son is called Kweku Tsin, among the Ashanti the name is Ntikuma, and the same individual is never styled anything but Tacooma in the Jamaica "bush".

Incidentally, the Jamaica Anansi stories have been handed down in living tradition by the old Nanas, a word that is pure Ashanti both in form and usage, meaning Granny in general and applicable to grandparents and grandchildren alike with proper qualifications.

Here we may call attention to an account, as it appeared in Voodoos and Obeahs, of the making of an amulet or charm by a Jamaica myal-man which might well have been a description of a similar process as practised among the Ashanti.

"My first experience with an obeah-man in Jamaica was as follows. Accompanied by a native of the district I was returning late one night to my residence high up in the mountains, when suddenly my companion who was leading the way shrank back and pointing a trembling finger through an opening of the coffee walk where we happened to be passing, whispered almost inaudibly: 'Obi, Sah!'

"It was a bright moonlight night, and a short distance off the path might be seen a filthy-looking bedraggled fellow plying his art of obeah for weal or woe. I drew my reluctant companion behind a shrub to watch the process which is so seldom vouchsafed to the eye of a white man.

"The obeah-man had placed on the ground some sticks, feathers, egg-shells and other objects that could not clearly be distinguished. A piece of string was placed on top of the little heap. He then retreated for a short distance and began a mumbling incantation which was accompanied by a rhythmic swaying of the body. With hands behind the back he next approached, crossing one leg over the other as he slowly advanced and drew near the incongruous ingredients of what was evidently intended for a fetish. With legs still stiffly crossed and swaying body he stooped and breathed upon and spat at it, and then gathered up the articles one by one, still mumbling some weird incantation as he placed the sticks together and crushed the egg-shells and other ingredients within them and finally bound all together with the piece of string.

"When the task was accomplished a cringing woman advanced from the shadow of a tree where her presence had not previously been noted. The obeah-man passed her the fetish charm and with fierce injunction charged her to hasten on her way without looking back or speaking to a living soul. She was especially warned to guard her fetish from every moisture. Should river or rain or dew, or even the perspiration of her own body chance to wet it, not only would all efficacy be lost but it would inevitably turn against herself. I could not follow all the words despite my knowledge of the language of the 'bush', but I had been able to gather the general gist of the instructions which were almost in the form of an invocation or curse.

"Strictly speaking what I had been watching was not really the practice of obeah but rather the making of a protective fetish or good luck charm, our friend was working in the rôle of myal-man and cared nothing if he was observed. Had he been really making obi he would have been surer of his privacy and would have squatted on the ground by his paraphernalia."

Compare this with Captain Rattray's account of the making of a nkabere, or good luck charm, among the Ashanti. After specifying the three particular trees that must be represented by twig or root, he says: "These three sticks are placed upon the ground, or sometimes upon an inverted pot, along with some pieces of a sweeping broom. A piece of string is placed on top of all. The medicine man or priest now retires a few paces and then advances towards the charm with his hands behind his back, and stooping down sprays pepper and guinea grain--which he had in his mouth--over the charm, saying: 'My entwining charm Nkadomako, who seizes strong men, mosquito that trips up the great silk-cotton tree, shooting stars that live with the Supreme Being, I have to tell you that so-and-so are coming here about some matter.' Here he takes his arms from behind his back and, stooping down, picks up the sticks and twine. Making a little bundle of the sticks he begins to bind them along with the broom sticks, saying as he does so: 'I bind up their mouth. I bind up their souls, and their gods. I begin with Sunday, Monday, Tuesday, Wednesday, Thursday, Friday, Saturday.' As he repeats each day he gives a twist to the string round the sticks till he has bound them all together, when he knots the string to keep them from unravelling, ending by saying: 'Whoever comes may this be a match for them.'"

If this enumeration of the days of the week, which is really an invocation of the various abosom, was an essential in the making of the suman or charm, the practice might explain how the Ashanti terminology alone remains in the day-names of Jamaica, since the myal-man who monopolized the making of amulets even as the obeah-man who "made obi" were exclusively of Ashanti origin.

Incidentally, this account of Captain Rattray is given in connexion with a description of a gold weight which represents a medicine man sacrificing a fowl to a nkabere charm, and he adds: "From time to time a fowl will be offered to this suman. The medicine man or priest will advance upon it with crossed legs and hands behind the back and perhaps with a whistle in his mouth, to call up the spirits, and will stand over the charm with legs crossed. He then holds the fowl by the neck and blows the whistle. This is what is shown in this weight."

A Jamaica exile, whether he be Jamaican by birth or like myself by adoption, needs only to read Ashanti Proverbs by Captain Rattray to be straightway carried back in spirit to his "Isle of Springs."

Thus the Ashanti "It is the Supreme Being who pounds the fufu for the one without arms," has found its counterpart in the Jamaican "When cow lose him tail, Goramighty brush fly." In both cases the care of Providence is implied.

The Ashanti "The white-tailed one (the black colubus monkey) says: 'What is in my cheek is not mine, but what has gone into my belly that is my very own,'" has become in Jamaica, where incidentally monkeys are not known; "Monkey say, wha' in a him mout' no fe him, but wha' in a him belly a fe him." A variation is even closer, "Monkey say wha' da in him jaw-bone no fe him, but wha' da in him belly a fe him."

The Ashanti "When rain beats on a leopard it wets him, but it does not wash out its spots," becomes paraphrased in Jamaica as "Seben years no 'nough fe wash freckle off a guinea-hen back." The saying usually implies the harbouring of revenge.

The Ashanti "When you have quite crossed the river, you say that the crocodile has a lump on its snout," is the Jamaica "No cuss alligator long mout' till you cross riber."

The Ashanti "When a fowl drinks water, it (first) takes it and shows it to the Supreme Being," is usually amplified in Jamaica into "When fowl drink water him say 'tank God,' when man drink water him say nuttin." Sometimes, however, the Jamaican merely remarks: "Chicken member God when him drink."

The Ashanti "The hen's foot does not kill her chicken," has become in Jamaica "Fowl tread 'pon him chicken, but him no tread too hard," or again, "Hen neber mash him chicken too hot."

The Ashanti "If you are too wise a man, you say 'Good Morning' to a fowl," is explained by Captain Rattray as being said in a sarcastic sense and with the implication that "you will find yourself committing some supreme folly." The Jamaican with like intent observes: "Man lib too well, him tell fowl howdy."

The Ashanti "When the cat dies, the mice rejoice," is the same as the Jamaican "Cat dead, mus-mus fat."

The Ashanti "A sheep does not give birth to a goat," is rendered in Jamaica "Sheep and goat no all one."

The Ashanti "Where the sheep stands its kid stands," has become in Jamaica "Goat and him kid 'tand one place."

The Ashanti "If the horse does not go to war, its tail does," is adapted in Jamaica "Goat no go a war, but him send him 'kin."

The Ashanti "When a great number of mice dig a hole, it does not become deep," is the Jamaican "Too much ratta nebber dig good hole."

The Ashanti "No one begins to twist creepers into a rope in front of an animal (he hopes to catch)," is rendered in Jamaica as "Set tie-tie, no mek bud see you," i.e., in setting a snare don't let the bird see you.

The Ashanti "All animals sweat, but the hair on them causes us not to notice it," is particularized in Jamaica "Darg sweat, but long hair cober i'."

The Ashanti "'Good morning, good morning,' kills an old woman" is explained by Captain Rattray as meaning "The old woman who sitting by the house all day, and having nothing to do but return salutations, is said to be killed eventually by them." The same sentiment is expressed tersely in Jamaica by "Too much si'down bruk breeches."

The Ashanti "When two slaves look after (your) cow, hunger kills it," finds this adaptation in' Jamaica "Too much busher, darg crawney."

The Ashanti "A stranger does not carry the head of the corpse," is clarified by the Jamaican "'Trainger hab no right fe carry coffin if him no know wha de burying grung dey."

The Ashanti "It is the fool's sheep that breaks loose twice," has as a variant in Jamaica "One time fool no fool, but two time fool him de fool."

The Ashanti "The poor man does not get in a rage," is rendered in Jamaica "Poor man nebber bex," which Gardner the Historian explains by saying "he is humble, and cannot afford to take offence."

The Ashanti "Wood already touched with fire is not hard to set alight," is practically unchanged in Jamaica "Ole fire 'tick no hard fe ketch."

The Ashanti "It is the water which stands there calm and silent that drowns a man," appears in the negative form in Jamaica as "Braggin' riber nebber drown s'mody."

The Ashanti "There is nothing that hurts like shame," is found in Jamaica as "Shame no load, but it bruk neck."

The Ashanti "A path has ears," has the Jamaica paraphrase "A bush hab yeye."

The Ashanti "When you do not know how to dance, then you say, 'The drum is not sounding sweetly,'" finds a two-fold expression in Jamaica. "If a man can' dance him say de music no good," and also "If a man can' dance him say de fiddle no good."

The Ashanti folkstory "How it came about that Ananse, the Spider, went up on the Rafters," is referred to by the Jamaica proverb "A fas' mek Anancy dey a house-top," which signifies "An impertinence makes Anancy stay in the house-top."

Admittedly, similar proverbs are to be found throughout Africa. But, since so much of the Jamaica culture is clearly of Ashanti origin and practically nothing can be definitely traced to other tribes, it is but reasonable to conclude that here also the actual introduction to Jamaica is to be ascribed to the Ashanti.

A study of the records of slave arrivals in Jamaica leads to the conclusion that at no time did the Ashanti compose more than 15% of the whole slave population in the island. How this small minority quickly asserted and continuously maintained a mastery over the more numerous and normally antagonistic tribes would be inexplicable were it not for the fact that there is clear evidence that the machinations of obeah terrified all into submission and effectively eliminated those who might otherwise have opposed the dominance of the autocratic Ashanti.

Summing up the present chapter, we may safely accept it as a fact that the Ashanti exercised a paramount influence in the development of the present cultural complex in Jamaica. In consequence we are justified in assuming, that when there is no evidence to the contrary, in the case of Jamaican traits and practices that are not in themselves fully intelligible, in all probability the true explanation is to be sought among the manners and customs of the Ashanti.

When culture diffuses from a centre, it usually radiates in successive waves in ever-widening circles which here and there become retarded. As a consequence subsequent culture-cycles emanating from the same centre occasionally overtake and become confused with those that preceded.

Simultaneously other culture-cycles from vastly divergent sources are spreading out independently, and as the various fields of influence overlap, there is necessarily a coalescing or modification of culture-complexes in constant process of development, until it becomes an extremely difficult task to trace back particular cultural-traits to their true origins.

However, in the case of the Ashanti culture in Jamaica, it reached its new field of influence, thousands of miles from its place of origin, not by a gradual diffusion but by a violent transfer over sea, and its proponents were in sufficient strength and numbers not only to resist all encroachments of other cultural-systems, but to violently suppress whatever Negro trait went counter to their own cultural-complex.

Thus it has come to pass that we have in Jamaica to-day so many of the old-time Ashanti customs as well as Ashanti terminology as little changed in usage as they are in the homeland despite the years that have intervened since their transplanting to new surroundings and conditions.

JAMAICA WITCHCRAFT

IN Notes and Queries, London, January 25, 1851, we find the following communication.

"Can any of your readers give me some information about obeism? I am anxious to know whether it is in itself a religion, or merely a rite practised in some religion in Africa and imported thence to the West Indies (where, I am told, it is rapidly gaining ground again); and whether the obeist obtains the immense power he is said to possess over his brother Negroes by any acquired art, or simply by working upon the more superstitious minds of his companions. Any information, however, on the subject will be acceptable. T. H., Mincing Lane, January 10, 1851."

This inquiry drew forth several replies. In the issue of February 22, 1851, we find: "As our correspondent T. H. desires 'any information' on the subject of obeism, in the absence of more and better, I offer my mite: that in the early part of this century it was very common among the slave-population in the West Indies, especially on the remote estates--of course of African origin--not as either a 'religion' or a 'rite,' but rather as a superstition; a power claimed by its professors, and assented to by the patients, of causing good or evil to, or averting it from them; which was of course always for a 'consideration' of some sort, to the profit, whether honorary, pecuniary, or other of the dispenser. It is by the pretended influence of certain spells, charms, ceremonies, amulets worn, or other such incantations, as practised with more or less diversity by the adepts, the magicians and conjurers, the 'false prophets' of all ages and countries, etc." The writer thinks that obeism is on the decline and simply signs the letter M.

Another reply in the same issue runs as follows: "In answer to T. H.'s Query regarding obeahism, though I cannot answer his question fully, as to its origin, etc., yet I have thought that what I can communicate may serve to piece out the more valuable information of your better informed correspondents. I was for a short time in the island of Jamaica, and from what I could learn there of obeahism, the power seemed to be obtained by the obeah-man or woman, by working upon the fears of their fellow-Negroes, who are notoriously superstitious. The principal charm seemed to be, a collection of feathers, coffin furniture, and one or two other things which I have forgotten. A small bundle of this, hung over the victim's door or placed in his path, is supposed to have the power of bringing ill luck to the unfortunate individual. And if any accident, or loss, or sickness should happen to him about the time, it is immediately imputed to the dreaded influence of obeah! But I have heard of cases where the unfortunate victim has gradually wasted away, and died under this powerful spell, which, I have been informed by old residents in the island, is to be attributed to a more natural cause, namely, the influence of poison. The obeah-man causes a quantity of ground glass to be mixed with the food of the person who has incurred his displeasure; and the result is said to be a slow but sure and wasting death! Perhaps some of your medical readers can say whether an infusion of powdered glass would have this effect. I merely relate what I have been told by others, etc." This letter is signed D. p. W.

In the issue of April 19, 1851, a communication signed T. J. furnishes a number of references to show that "obeahism is not only a rite, but a religion, or rather a superstition." It is further stated that "the influence of the obeist does not depend on the exercise of any art or natural magic, but on the apprehensions of evil infused into the victim's mind."

In Notes and Queries of May 10, 1851, Henry H. Breen writing from St. Lucia insists: "Obeism is not itself a religion, except in the sense in which Burke says that 'superstition is the religion of feeble minds.' It is a belief, real or pretended, in the efficacy of certain spells, and incantations, and is to the uneducated Negro what sorcery was to our unenlightened forefathers. This superstition is known in St. Lucia by the name Kembois. It is still extensively practised in the West Indies, but there is no reason to suppose that it is rapidly gaining ground."

While the interest awakened in the subject by this correspondence was still rife, The Medical Times published a communication from Doctor Stobo of Tortula, in the Virgin Islands, of a peculiar case of child-birth which had been accompanied by symptoms that he seems unable to diagnose although he evidently does not credit the patient's explanation that she was a victim of obeah. The title of the article is "Spasmodic Action of the Uterus.--Obeism," and the main fact in the case is thus stated: "Ann Eliza Smith, aged 50, Sambo, domestic servant, mother of three children; has a miscarriage between first and second, and an interval of seventeen years between second and third child. During that interval was in bad health, and under the delusion that she was (hurted) obeahed, and is now under that delusion."

The Editor of The Medical Times adds this information in a footnote: "Obeism was a species of witchcraft employed to revenge injuries, or as a protection against theft, and is so called from Obi, the town, city, district or province of South (sic) Africa where it originated. It consisted in placing a spell or charm near the cottage of the individual intended to be brought under its influence, or, when designed to prevent the depredations of thieves, in some conspicuous part of the house, or on a tree; it was signified by a calabash or gourd containing, among other ingredients, a combination of different coloured rags, cats' teeth, parrots' feathers, toads' feet, egg-shells, fish bones, snakes' teeth, and lizards' tails. Terror immediately seized the individual who beheld it; and either by resigning himself to despair, or by the secret communication of poison, in most cases death was the inevitable consequence."

The Editor immediately adds: "The following is a description of the superstition as given by a witness in a trial that took place some years ago: 'Do you know the prisoner to be an obeah-man?--Ees massa! shadow-catcher true. What do you mean by shadow-catcher?--Him heb coffin (a little coffin was here produced) him set fe catch dem shadow. What shadow do you mean?--When him set obeah for somebody, him catch dem shadow, and dem go dead.'" This example is really taken from Alexander Barclay, A Practical View of the Present State of Slavery in the West Indies, London, 1828, p. 185f, although no credit is given by the Editor who quotes it in The Medical Times.

From what has been said thus far, it is evident how confused has been the concept of that form of witchcraft which is known as Jamaica obeah even in usually most reliable sources of information. It must be our purpose, then, at the very outset to try and clarify the origin of the name as well as the practice of this intriguing subject, obeah.

The following communication appears in Notes and Queries for July 15, 1899, signed by James Platt, Jun.: "Obi; obeah.--The origin of this well-known West Indian term is not precisely defined in any of our existing dictionaries. We find such statements as 'probably of African origin' (Webster and Chambers); 'said to be of African origin' (The 'Century'); 'said to have been introduced from Africa' (Worcester). The following quotation from the Rev. Hugh Goldie's Dictionary of the Efik Language (of Old Calabar), Glasgow, 1874, p. 300, appears to set the matter at rest, and should interest etymologists and students of folklore; 'Ubio, a thing, or mixture of things, put in the ground, as a charm, to cause sickness or death. The obeah of the West Indies.'"

This little notice had far-reaching effects, or at least its writer's influence quickly made itself felt. For the Oxford Dictionary shortly afterwards accepted Mr. Platt's suggestion and came to describe obeah with its variants obi, obia, obea, obeeah, as "A West African word: cf. Efik ubio, 'a thing, or mixture of things, put in the ground, as a charm to cause sickness or death,'" and quotes as its authority Goldie's Dictionary of Efik, 1874.

Sir Harry Johnston, too, regarded the word as "a variant or a corruption of an Efik or Ibo, word from the north-east or east of the Niger Delta." But as his Preface is dated May, 1910, long after the appearance of Vol. VII of the Oxford Dictionary, it would be only natural to suppose that Sir Harry drew his information from that source, unless perhaps he was originally the authority consulted by the Editor of the Dictionary. In either supposition, we would have overlapping authority for the Efik origin of the word and not independent sources.

Now I am informed by those who are actually working among the Efik speaking people that ubio really means rubbish or dirt, and that the derivative ubi signifies wickedness in general. Further that witchcraft is included under ubi or ubio only in so far as it is a wickedness like any other evil act.

In keeping with this observation, Goldie himself gives the primary meaning of ubio as "anything noxious," and the citation quoted by the Oxford Dictionary is a secondary meaning. However, even here Goldie says nothing about witchcraft which he actually renders as idion. This, in itself, might well imply that obeah is given as a particular illustration of the generic idea of what is noxious or wicked.

All this is supported by tracing historically the introduction of the word obeah into English usage. The first appearance of the word in any dictionary is in An American Dictionary of the English Language by Noah Webster. Revised and Enlarged by Chauncey A. Goodrich; Published by George and Charles Merriam, Springfield, Massachusetts, and Copyrighted in 1847. In this, the Third Edition of Webster's Dictionary-it does not appear in the earlier editions--we find the entry on page 762: "Obeah, n. A species of witchcraft practised among the African Negroes. Encyc. Am."

As will be noticed, the only reference given in the above entry is to the Encyclopedia Americana. The first edition of this work was edited by Francis Lieber and published in thirteen volumes in Philadelphia by Carey, Lea and Carey, 1829-1833. The word obeah appears in volume IX which was issued in 1832: "Obeah; a species of witchcraft practised among the Negroes, the apprehension of which, operating upon the superstitious fears, is frequently attended with disease and death."

There is reason for thinking that the entry in the Encyclopedia Americana is based on one of the Philadelphia editions (1805-6 or 1810) of Bryan Edwards, History, Civil and Commercial, of the British in the West Indies, which was originally published in London in 1793.

Edwards avowedly drew his information from the Report of the Lords of the Committee of the Council appointed for the consideration of all Matters relating to Trade and Foreign

Plantations, which appeared in London in 1789. It is in this same Report of 1789 that we first find the distinction suggested: "The term obeah, obiah, or obia (for it is variously written) we conceive to be the adjective, and the obe or obi the noun substantive."

As noted in that Report, the principal source of information regarding obeah was Edward Long who belonged to an old Jamaica family and who had already been Speaker of the House of Assembly in Jamaica. He had published a History of Jamaica, London, 1774, wherein is the first reference by an historian to obeah as such.

As far as I can ascertain, the first actual record of the word in print is in the Acts of the Jamaica Assembly of 1760, Vol. II, Act. 24: "To remedy the Evils arising from irregular Assemblies of Slaves, prevent possessing Arms and Ammunition, going from Place to Place without tickets, and for the preventing of Obeah, etc."

Up to the Report of 1789, as we find recorded therein, the word was not much in use outside of Jamaica. Thus Montserrat, Nevis, Dominica, St. Vincent, Bermuda and Bahama know nothing about obeah, and in the Barbados, Antigua, Granada and St. Christopher, where obeah is more or less known, there are no restraining Laws mentioned, indicating that it had not yet been recognized as a menace to the public peace.

It was long the Law in Jamaica, even before the real workings of obeah were understood, to transport to other West India Colonies such obeah-men as were convicted of the practice. This would explain the presence of the word and practice in those islands where it was known but only in a less degree.

Hence we may conclude from all this that the earliest acceptation of the word obeah in the English dictionaries must be traced to a Jamaica origin. And when I brought the foregoing facts to the attention of the publishers of the Oxford Dictionary, with characteristic courtesy, they made acknowledgment through the present Editor, Sir William A. Craigie, under date of August 3, 1934: "The Efik etymology of obeah given in the Oxford English Dictionary was no doubt supplied by James Platt, who would have no other authority for it than the similarity of sound and meaning. As the part of the Dictionary containing O to Onomashie was published in July 1902, there was plenty of time for Sir Harry Johnston to get it from that source. In such cases, unfortunately, the evidence of dictionaries is often unsatisfactory, and is of no weight against evidence to the contrary such as you have supplied."

Having definitely established Jamaica as the source of the English usage of the word obeah, the question naturally presents itself, whence was it derived by Jamaica?

It has been shown in Voodoos and Obeahs that strictly speaking, myalism, the direct antithesis of obeah, is the residue of the old religious dance of the Ashanti, just as obeah itself is the continuation of Ashanti witchcraft. Thus obeah is secretive, malicious, and has gradually taken on a form of devil-worship. Myalism, on the contrary, is practised in the open. It is beneficent in its purposes, and it has developed into modern revivalism in Jamaica. In practice, however, the same individual is now frequently an obeah-man by night and a myal-man by day when he "digs up" the very obeah which he has planted while exercising the other rôle.

To explain how all this has come about, a brief review of what has been set forth in detail in Voodoos and Obeahs becomes necessary.

Among the Ashanti of West Africa there was a clearly defined system of religion wherein the Supreme Being, Onyame, was more popularly known under the title Nyankopon, meaning Onyame, alone, great one. Subordinate to this Supreme Being were numerous abosom, minor deities or spirits, acting as mediators between God and man, and claiming a prominent place in religious observances, since God Himself was regarded as so remote, that ordinarily He was to be approached only through His mediaries, except at a time of particular need when He was addressed directly.

Consequently, while the Supreme Being actually had among the Ashanti a temple and a regular priesthood for which a three-years' novitiate was required, in the ordinary daily affairs of life recourse was regularly had through the subordinate abosom who were regarded as more accessible, and in consequence the okomfo, or priest, of these various spirits exercised a dominant influence upon the general life of the Ashanti both as a people and individually. It was the prerogative of the okomfo not merely to lead the service of the shrines of the minor deities but to imbue the good luck charm with its particular potency and this he did by invoking not only the Supreme Being directly but especially through the intermediary spirits since they were regarded as closely associated with the affairs of man. All those rites and practices that characterize the leading events in life, such as birth, marriage, or death, were clearly of a religious character. So, too, were the civic or national celebrations and even preparation for war or the coronation of a paramount chief.

But concomitant with this religious spirit that permeated the very life of the Ashanti there existed, essentially antagonistic to it, a condition of affairs which may be summed up under the single term witchcraft. Of this phase, Captain Rattray, the great authority on all things Ashanti, writes: "Witchcraft was essentially the employment of anti-social magic. The belief in its general prevalence was largely due to the fact that certain forms of illness resulting in death could not otherwise be accounted for. There appears to be considerable logic in regarding killing by witchcraft as akin to murder, even if its classification as such by the Ashanti was not directly due to an acknowledgment of a fact which was in many cases true, i.e. that poison in some form or other was often an important stock-in-trade of the professed witch."

That the Ashanti believed in a personal devil or evil spirit is evidenced by the secondary meaning of obonsam, viz. "The devil conceived to be an evil spirit reigning over the spirits of deceased wicked men."

As a derivative of this word, we have sasabonsam who, according to Christaller, is "an imaginary monstrous being, conceived as having a huge body of human shape, but of a red colour and with very long hair, living in the deepest recess of the forest, where an immense silk-cotton tree is his abode; inimical to man, especially to the priests, but the friend and chief of the sorcerers and witches."

Captain Rattray declares that the power of the Sasabonsam. "is purely for evil and witchcraft," and elsewhere he declares: "The Sasabonsam of the Gold Coast and Ashanti is a monster which is said to inhabit parts of the dense virgin forests. It is covered with long hair, has large bloodshot eyes, long legs, and feet pointing both ways. It sits on high branches of an odum or onyina tree and dangles its legs, with which at times it hooks up the unwary hunter. It is hostile to man, and is supposed to be especially at enmity with the real priestly class. Hunters who go to the forest and are never heard of again--as sometimes happens--are supposed to have been caught by Sasabonsam."

Here then we have a clear theoretical distinction between the Ashanti devil, bonsam, and this fabulous forest monster, Sasabonsam. But, just as in English the term devil represents indiscriminately either Satan or his minions, so in practice the Ashanti Sasabonsam is used as a euphemism for bonsam since it is not well to even mention names of the dead lest their spirits haunt you.

The Ashanti word for witch was obayifo and Captain Rattray furnishes us with the following information on this interesting topic. "Obayifo, deriv. bayi, sorcery (Synonymous term ayen), a wizard, or more generally witch. A kind of human vampire, whose chief delight is to suck the blood of children whereby the latter pine and die. Men and women possessed of this black magic are credited with volitant powers, being able to quit their bodies and travel great distances in the night. Besides sucking the blood of victims, they are supposed to be able to extract the sap and juice of crops. (Cases of coco blight are ascribed to the work of the abayifo.) These witches are supposed to be very common and a man never knows but that his friend or even his wife may be one. When prowling at night they are supposed to emit a phosphorescent light from the armpits and anus. An obayifo in everyday life is supposed to be known by having sharp shifty eyes, that are never at rest, also by showing an undue interest in food, and always talking about it, especially meat, and hanging about when cooking is going on, all which habits are therefore purposely avoided. A man will seldom deny another, even a stranger, a morsel of what he may be eating, or a hunter a little bit of raw meat to any one asking it, hoping thereby to avoid the displeasure of anyone who, for all he can tell, is a witch or wizard."

At the recent Anthropological Congress in London, Modjaben Dowuona, Esq., a native West African and one of the Vice-Presidents of the African Section of the Congress, presented a most interesting and scholarly paper on the subject of witchcraft. According to his view: "There are in the main two forms in which witchcraft is practised. The first takes the form of a power to do harm to other people, especially children, without any physical contact or concrete act of poisoning. Death due to poisoning is considered separate from that believed to be due to witchcraft, though in practice it is not always distinguished from it. The tendency is to ascribe to witchcraft any death which cannot be accounted for on other grounds. It seems that this non-physical way of killing was first directed against children, as is evidenced from the Twi word for witchcraft, 'Bayi' meaning literally 'taking away or removing children.' It is interesting to find that a corrupt form of the word, namely 'obeah' appears in the West Indies, though there it is associated with the worship of various cults."

Again Mr. Dowuona stated: "I think that we may connect the belief in witchcraft of the first kind with the desire to find reason for the heavy infantile mortality which exists in African communities. . . . A saying among the Ga seems to support this view. It is this: 'If you have no witch in your family, your children do not die young.'" And he explained this assumption by the fact that "the power of a witch is limited to the members of her own family and that therefore no witch outside the family can do harm to any one in the family except through the co-operation of a witch inside it."

Mr. Dowuona thus traces back Jamaica obeah through the Ashanti obayifo, a witch, to the term for witchcraft, bayi, meaning literally "taking away children." This view is supported by Christaller who derives bayi, witchcraft, from oba, child, and yi, to take away, and renders obayifo as a witch or wizard. Christaller also gives as a synonym ayen with obaayen, a compound of obaa, woman, and ayen, as the female form. And it is probably from this form obaayen that the Jamaica word obeah was directly derived. For Long in his History of Jamaica at times spells the word obeiah. Incidentally, while examining Long's own copy of his work which is now deposited in the Manuscript Section of the British Museum, I noticed that he had entered a marginal correction: "Here et sequent., for obeah."

As Mr. Dowuona well observed, the primary concept of witchcraft undoubtedly implied among the Ashanti a projection of some personal power whereby even death might be produced without physical contact. But in practice, if the spirit-projection with its customary incantation proved ineffective, it was only natural that the surreptitious administration of poison should be resorted to, so that the reputation of the witch might not suffer in popular esteem. Yet even here, it was claimed that the effect was produced by the spiritual projection alone.

Unquestionably, the Ashanti clearly distinguished religious practices, the rôle of the herbalist and the workings of witchcraft. Thus we are told by Captain Rattray: "From the information at our disposal, we now know that the Ashanti makes a distinction between the following: the okomfo, priest; the sumankwafo or dunseni, the medicine man; and the bonsam komfo, witch doctor. The word okomfo, without any further qualification, refers to a priest of one of the orthodox abosom, gods. We see, however, that a witch doctor is allowed the same name as a kind of honorary title or degree, being known as a bayi komfo, a priest of witchcraft. Again the ordinary medical practitioners are never termed okomfo; they are sumankwafo, dealers in suman; or dunsefo, workers in roots; or odu'yefo, workers in medicine."

It would be well to notice here that Ashanti witchcraft, as a practice of black magic is essentially antagonistic to religion in any form, and that it is as clearly dissociated from the making of a suman, which may be regarded as white magic, as its practitioner, the obayifo, is distinguished from the medicine man, sumankwafo. Nevertheless, the title bayi komfo, a priest of witchcraft, indicates that even in Ashanti there has developed a phase of what might be called devil-worship inasmuch as the sasabonsam, or devil, is so closely associated with witches.

This would help to explain the assertion of J. Leighton Wilson who when writing of that part of West Africa which lies between Cape Verde and the Cameroons, declares: "Fetishism and demonology are undoubtedly the leading and prominent forms of religion among the pagan tribes of Africa. They are entirely distinct from each other, but they run together at so many points, and have been so much mixed up by those who have attempted to write on the subject that it is no easy matter to keep them separated."

Thus it came to pass that as the Ashanti were gradually carried by the slavers in increasing numbers to Jamaica, they naturally brought with them all their old traditions and beliefs which they sought to put in practice in their new surroundings. A strongly religious people, even as slaves in a strange land, they instinctively turned openly to their okomfo for guidance and consolation, while they necessarily feared the secret machinations of the nefarious obayifo. This very fear quickly became accentuated among the slave population generally, and it was this baleful influence more than anything else which tended to give the Ashanti their dominant control over all other tribes in Jamaica. For, secretly administered poison came to play a more and more active part to supplement incantations that might otherwise have remained inoperative. So, too, Nyankopon became the Accompong of Jamaica, just as obeah-man was a transition from obayifo.

Herbert G. DeLisser, a native Jamaican who is now Editor of the Kingston Daily Gleaner, was one of the first writers to differentiate the functions of Ashanti priest and wizard among the early practices of the days of slavery in Jamaica. More than twenty years ago, he wrote: "The West African natives and particularly those from the Gold Coast (From which the larger number of Jamaica slaves were brought) believe in a number of gods of different classes and unequal power. All these gods have their priests and priestesses, but there is one particularly malignant spirit, which, on the Gold Coast, has no regular priesthood. He is called Sasabonsam, and any individual may put himself in communication with him. Sasabonsam's favourite residence is the ceiba, the giant silk-cotton tree. He is resorted to in the dead of night, his votary going to the spot where he is supposed to live, and collecting there a little earth, or a few twigs, or a stone, he prays the god that his power may enter this receptacle. If he believes that his prayer has been heard, he returns home with his suhman, as the thing is now named, and hence forward he has a power which is formidable for injurious purposes, to which he offers sacrifice, and to whose worship he dedicates a special day in the week. By the aid of this suhman he can bewitch a man to death. He can also sell charms that will cause death or bodily injury. . . . A priest, on the other hand, may also sell you charms to scare away thieves, help you to prosperity, or keep away disaster. All this comes within the functions of a member of the West African priesthood. He may even undertake to 'put death on a man,' as the wizard does, if he is sufficiently well paid for the business. But priests do not care to indulge in this sort of thing. Their main function is to propitiate the gods, to unbewitch people; in a word, to prevent disasters from occurring. . . . Both witches and wizards, priests and priestesses, were brought to Jamaica in the days of the slave trade, and the slaves recognized the distinction between the former and the latter. Even the masters saw that the two classes were not identical, and so they called the latter 'myal-men' and 'myal-women'--the people who cured those whom the obeah-men had injured. Of the present-day descendants of these priests or myal-men more will be said later on. It is probable that many of the African priests became simple obeah-men after coming to Jamaica, for the very simple reason that they could not openly practice their legitimate profession. But when known as obeah-men, however much they might be treated with respect, they still were hated and feared. Every evil was attributed to them. The very name of them spread terror."

From the earliest days of legislation in Jamaica, there was recognized to be a growing danger to the peace of the Colony in the assemblies of slaves that were characterized by old tribal dances. These ceremonies were openly accompanied by a system of drumming which evidently aroused the fanaticism of the Africans to such a pitch as to endanger a general uprising. It never occurred to the planters that these dances were really an adaptation of time-honoured religious rites and they made the initial mistake of attributing the danger entirely to the fact that the slaves had gathered from various plantations and considered that while these assemblies were dangerous when attended from without, they might still be harmless enough if allowed to each group of slaves separately in their own plantation. Accordingly in 1696, it was enacted: "And for the prevention of the meeting of slaves in great numbers on Sundays and Holidays, whereby they have taken liberty to contrive and bring to pass many of their bloody and inhuman transactions: Be it enacted by the aforesaid authority, That no master, or mistress, or overseer, shall suffer any drumming or meeting of any slaves, not belonging to their own plantations, to rendezvous, feast, revel, beat drum, or cause any disturbance, but forthwith endeavour to disperse them, by him, or herself, overseer or servants; or if not capacitated to do the same, that he presently give notice to the next commission-officer to raise such number of men as may be sufficient to reduce the said slaves."

In his Ashanti, Captain Rattray has a very illuminating chapter on "The Drum Language." Almost incredible stories are told of the rapidity with which news is passed across Africa by means of the so-called "Talking Drums," and it was more or less taken for granted that something like a Morse Code must be employed for the purpose. We now find that what actually happens is that two drums are set in widely different tones and are known as the male and female drums, the former carrying the low note and the latter the high note. These drums are so manipulated that the musical intonation which replaces articulation, at least in the case of languages like the Ashanti which are distinctively tonal, with sufficient accuracy as to be intelligible to the people generally just as if the spoken word was used.

Space will not permit our going into the question in detail, but so efficiently is the process carried out by the Ashanti that we have recorded, for example, the history of Mampon in a drum recital that has preserved "an accurate record of the migrations of the clan from the far-away days when the Mampon were settled in Adanse, and also the names, deeds, and physical attributes of their former rulers."

Indeed, so exacting is the demand for accuracy in this drum record, that we are told: "A drummer who falters and 'speaks' a wrong word is liable to a fine of a sheep, and if persistently at fault he might in the past, have had an ear cut off." When we remember that the entire audience is checking up every sound at each recital, the drummer must needs be skilful before he attempts publicly to display his proficiency.

What particularly interests us here is the fact that the early Ashanti slaves in Jamaica must have numbered among them some really expert drummers who would naturally exchange messages throughout the island while all their fellow Ashanti could perfectly understand the conversation. And even when the use of the drum was prohibited, native ingenuity made use of barrels, gourds, boards or any other medium of producing notes that would correspond with those of the male and female drums.

This immediately gave rise to a new anxiety among the planters. For, while they seemingly knew nothing of the system of talking-drums, they certainly realized that their troublesome Ashanti were signalling to one another at considerable distances and were actually communicating their designs back and forth.

Hence, in 1717 a new enactment prescribed: "And whereas the permitting or allowing of any number of strange Negroes to assemble on any Plantation, or settlement, or any other place, may prove of fatal consequences to this your Majesty's Island, if not timely prevented: and forasmuch as Negroes can, by beating on drums, and blowing horns, or other such like instruments of noise, give signals to each other at a considerable distance of their evil and wretched intentions: Be it further enacted, That in one month's time after the passing of this Act, no proprietor, attorney, or overseer, presume to suffer any number of strange Negroes, exceeding five, to assemble on his plantation or settlement, or on the plantation or settlement under the care of such attorney or overseer; nor shall any proprietor, attorney, or overseer, suffer any beating on drums, barrels, gourds, boards, or other such like instruments of noise on the plantations and settlements aforesaid."

However, there was no material interference with the purely local gatherings. Even in the Act of December 21, 1781, amusements are permissible to the slaves on the properties to which they belong although the use of "drums, horns, and other unlawful instruments of noise" are, of course, prohibited, and in the Act of December 19, 1816, the restriction is made: "Provided that such amusements are put an end to by ten o'clock at night."

Meanwhile, as a precaution against complete proscription, the Ashanti okomfo began to further disguise what was left of the old religious rites under cover of one of the dances that were permissible in the local amusements, until it was gradually appropriated to his own purposes. This dance in its adapted form became known to the Whites as the myal-dance. Possibly this was its original title, but thus far I have not been able to trace its origin. Certainly the name itself is not Ashanti, since no letter l is included in the Ashanti alphabet, and the only words in which it occurs are foreign proper names.

This subtle appropriation of an alien dance completely disguised the true purposes of the okomfo as far as the Planters were concerned, but as a consequence the okomfo himself gradually lost his own identity until he became known to the Whites as myal-man, or leader in the myal-dance. And myal-man he has remained up to the present time.

Myalism, then, was in reality the old tribal religion of the Ashanti with some modifications due to conditions and circumstances. It substantially featured the veneration of the minor deities who were subordinate to Accompong and included communication with ancestral spirits.

The age-old antagonism to obeah or witchcraft on the part of the priestly class gradually became accentuated and eventually took on a rôle of major importance, so that it actually came to form a part of the religious practice, to dig up obeah.

As I have remarked elsewhere, in Ashanti, the okomfo openly combated the obayifo as a matter of principle, and he had the whole force of Ashanti religious traditions and public sentiment to support him, until he eventually looked down with more or less disdain on the benighted disciple of Sasabonsam. In Jamaica, on the other hand, native religious assemblies were proscribed by law which greatly hampered the okomfo in his sphere of influence, even his title being changed to myal-man, while the obayifo or obeah-man, who had always worked in secret, flourished in his trade. For the very status and restrictions of slave life put his fellows more and more at his mercy and filled them with a growing fear of his spiteful incantations, backed up as they were with active poisonings. Their gods had abandoned them; why not cultivate the favour of the triumphant Sasabonsam, or at least assuage his enmity and placate his vengeance?

It was natural, too, for the okomfo to adapt his practice to the new state of affairs. His hated rival, the obayifo, must be conquered at any price. Personal interests demanded this as strongly as religious zeal. Since public service of the deities was no longer possible, he in turn was forced to work in secret, and it is not surprising that he met fire with fire, incantation with incantation. His religion had aimed primarily at the welfare of the community, even as the object in life of the obayifo was the harm of the individual. Open intercession for tribal success and prosperity necessarily gives way to secret machinations to break the chains of bondage. A fanatical zeal takes hold of the myalist okomfo and he devises the most impressive ritual he can, to arouse the dormant spirits of his fellow slaves.

Thus it came to pass that it was the okomfo and not the obayifo, as is generally assumed, who administered the terrible fetish oath. It was he who mixed the gunpowder with the rum and added grave dirt and human blood to the concoction that was to seal upon the conspirators' lips the awful nature of the plot for liberty, and steel their hearts for the dangerous undertaking. It was he, no less, who devised the mystic powder that was to make their bodies invulnerable, and enable them to meet unscathed the white man's bullets. Finally, it was the okomfo and not the obayifo who, taking advantage of herbal knowledge, induced a state of torpor on subservient tools, that be might seem to raise the dead to life.

Yet, through it all, while he frequently substitutes for his own religious ceremonial the dark and secret rites of his rival practitioner, his aim at least is still within the tribal law, as he works white magic for the welfare of the community, no less than he continues to combat the black magic of his adversary.

It is not surprising, then, that the rôle of the myalist okomfo has been so little understood, and that his most effective work was ascribed by the Whites in Jamaica to the agency of obeah, and that myalism itself should become confused with witchcraft and even regarded by some as an offshoot of obeah.

Even in the days of slavery the Jamaica Planters came to recognize a two-fold menace. Danger to the individual from carefully devised but secretive poisonings, and danger to the peace of the entire colony from a spirit of unrest that was engendered at the assemblies of slaves. And yet these same Planters were entirely blind to the presence of witchcraft among the slaves, and completely unsuspicious of the element of devil-worship that was becoming accentuated.

Legislation forbidding all religious assemblies of slaves and particularly the time-honoured dances with drum accompaniment only tended to increase the secret machinations that confused more and more the field of influence of the okomfo and the obayifo. And if the Planter did at times hear stories of existent obeah, he regarded it with amused toleration as foolish superstition and nothing more, and failed absolutely to associate with it the increasing menace of subservient fear that was effectively supplemented by secret poisonings.

When at length the rebellion of 1760 disclosed the connexion of obeah and poisoning, and there arose a set determination to crush it out at any cost, even then the true condition of affairs was never suspected. Popular opinion, it is true, quickly swung to the opposite extreme and everything was now ascribed to obeah. But the legislators themselves failed to realize that they were not dealing with witchcraft alone but with a recrudescence of the old religious spirit in a new and more dangerous guise, wherein it had actually entered into league for the time being with its arch-enemy, obeah, against the oppressor of both.

As a matter of fact, when the Assembly met to deal with the whole question of the rebellion and its suppression, at first they saw no reason for revising the general principles that had guided them in the past. Thus The Annual Register for the Year 1760, reports: "Regulations made at a sessions of the peace at Jamaica, May 1, 1760, to prevent disturbances for the future amongst the Negroes of that island. That no Negro shall be suffered to go out of his plantation without a white with him, or having a ticket of leave. Every Negro playing at any game whatever, to be whipt through the public streets. Every rum or punch-house keeper suffering it in their houses to forfeit forty shillings. Any proprietor suffering his Negroes to beat a drum, blow a horn, or make any other noise in his plantation, to pay ten pounds, or the overseer of a plantation five pounds, and any civil or military officer has power to enter the plantation and demand the money, or distrain it, etc." And there is not yet any mention of obeah!

Even when the formal Act that aimed at the regulation of the conduct of the slaves for the future was introduced in the Assembly on December 6, 1760, there was still no reference to witchcraft. But the discussion that followed so overwhelmed the assembled legislators that when the Act was passed on December 13th it contained the first specific mention of obeah in a public document. The full text of this Act of 1760 which was never printed as it failed of the Royal Assent and consequently never became a Law of the Colony, may be found in the Public Record Office,[5] London. The preamble runs as follows: "Whereas there has largely been very dangerous Rebellions and Rebellious Conspiracies amongst the Slaves of this Island; and Whereas Suffering slaves to be instructed with Arms and Lodging large Quantities of Arms and Ammunition in Houses improperly guarded may be a means of enabling such Rebellious disposed Slaves to Execute their bloody Intention; and Whereas permitting Slaves to go abroad from their respective places of Abode without Tickets or Suffering them to Assemble from different Plantations or Places to Beat their Drums, Gourds, Boards, Barrells, or other Instruments of Noise, or Blow their Horns in production of the most dangerous Consequences; And Whereas on many Estates and Plantations in this Island there are Slaves of Both Sexes commonly known by the name of obeah-men and obeah-women by whose Influence over the minds of their fellow Slaves through an Established Opinion of their being endued with Strange Preternatural Faculties many and great Dangers have arisen Destructive of the Peace and Welfare of this Island; In Order to prevent for the future such

Rebellions or Rebellious Conspiracies and the fatal Consequences of such Meetings, We Your Majesty's most dutiful and
loyal Subjects, etc."

Coming to the section on obeah, we read: "And in order to
prevent the many Mischiefs that may hereafter arise from the
Wicked Art of Negroes going under the Appellation of obeah-
men and women pretending to have Communication with the
Devil and other Evil Spirits whereby the weak and Superstitious
are deluded into a Belief of their having full Power to Exempt
them whilst under their Protection from any Evils that might
otherwise happen; Be it therefore enacted by the authority
aforesaid that from and after the first Day of January which will
be in the Year of our Lord One thousand Seven hundred and
Sixty one Any Negro or other Slave who shall pretend to any
Supernatural Power and be detected in making use of any
Blood, Feathers, Parrots' Beaks, Dogs' Teeth, Alligators' Teeth,
Broken Bottles, Grave Dirt, Rum, Egg-Shells, or any other
materials related to the practice of Obeah or Witchcraft in
Order to delude and impose on the Minds of others shall upon
Conviction thereof before two Magistrates and three Freehold-
ers suffer Death or Transportation, anything in this Act or any
other Act or any other Law to the Contrary notwithstanding,
etc."

Here it is to be noticed, in the first place, that obeah is
specifically identified with witchcraft, and secondly, that it is
regarded as a form of pseudo-diablerie, since the obeah-men
and women pretend to have communion with the Devil and
other evil spirits precisely as a basis of their claims to preternatural powers. Thus the Ashanti devil, or Sasabonsam, has
definitely become the Jamaica Obboney according to the point
of view adopted by the Jamaica Assembly. Moreover, the work
of the okomfo or myal-man is entirely lost sight of and hereafter
from a legal aspect at least the obayifo is to reign supreme.

True it is that when slavery was coming to a close, the descendants of the old priestly class made one last effort to regain their old prestige, bringing themselves to the notice of the Whites especially by their zeal in digging up obeah. But their identity had been so long submerged in the chaotic superstitions of the plantations that the new activity was not recognized as a recrudescence of the old Ashanti religious practices, but was commonly regarded as merely an offshoot of obeah, and even the title of myal-man given by the Whites to the readjusted okomfo had so evolved that it left absolutely nothing that was suggestive of the ancient Ashanti priesthood.

Edward Long, the first historian to mention obeah by name, joined the Jamaica Assembly shortly after the passage of the Act of 1760, and for the next seven years he assisted at the discussions of the subject as it recurrently came up for consideration. His account, then, may be accepted as a fair portrayal of what was commonly accepted at the time in popular belief regarding obeah.

Thus he writes concerning the slaves: "They firmly believe in the apparition of spectres. Those of deceased friends are duppies; others, of more hostile and tremendous aspect, like our rawhead-and-bloody-bones, are called bugaboos. The most sensible among them fear the supernatural powers of the African obeahmen, or pretended conjurers; often ascribing those mortal effects to magic, which are only the natural operation of some poisonous juice, or preparation, dexterously administered by those villains. But the Creoles imagine, that the virtues of baptism, or making them Christians, render their art wholly ineffectual; and for this reason only, many of them have desired to be baptized, that they might be secured from obeah.

"Not long since, some of these execrable wretches in Jamaica introduced what they called the myal-dance, and established a kind of society, into which they invited all they could. The lure hung out was, that every Negro, initiated into the Myal Society, would be invulnerable by the white man; and although they might in appearance be slain, the obeah-man could, at his pleasure, restore the body to life. The method, by which this trick was carried on, was by a cold infusion of the herb branched calalue; which, after the agitation of dancing, threw the party into a profound sleep. In this state he continued, to all appearance lifeless, no pulse, nor motion of the heart, being perceptible; till on being rubbed with another infusion (as yet unknown to the Whites), the effects of the calalue gradually went off, the body resumed its motions, and the party on whom the experiment had been tried, awoke as from a trance, entirely ignorant of anything that had passed since he left off dancing."

Here again we must remark the confusion of ideas regarding the functions proper to the myal-man as distinct from those which belonged by right to the obeah-man, although in practice no doubt the same individual had by this time frequently assumed to himself the dual rôle.

Writing in 1740, Charles Leslie describes what might well be called a myalistic séance. It is in reality a religious ordeal, on the pattern of those practised in Africa, and not as is so often stated a true example of obeah. It runs as follows: "When anything about a plantation is missing, they have a solemn kind of oath, which the eldest Negro always administers, and which by them is accounted so sacred, that except they have the express command of their master or overseer, they never set about it, and then they go very solemnly to work. They range themselves in that spot of ground which is appropriated for the Negro burying place, and one of them opens a grave. He who acts the priest, takes a little of the earth, and puts into every one of their mouths; they say, that if any has been guilty, their belly swells, and occasions death. I never saw any instance of this but once; and it was certainly a fact that a boy did swell, and acknowledged the theft when he was dying. But I am far from thinking there was any connexion betwixt the cause and the effect, for a thousand accidents might have occasioned it, without accounting for it by that foolish ceremony."

Building his account around the Report of 1789, Robert Renny declared: "Whatever their notions of religion may have been, they, not unlike their European masters, seem to pay little regard to the ceremonies of any system in Jamaica. But they are not on that account, the less superstitious. A belief in obeah, or witchcraft, is almost universal among them. The professors of this occult science, are always Africans, and generally old and crafty. Hoary heads, gravity of aspect, and a skill in herbs, are the chief qualifications for this curious office. The Negroes, both Africans and Creoles (i.e. those born in the island), revere, consult, and fear them."

In the following year, 1808, adopting the viewpoint usually put forward by the missionaries of the time, J. Steward asserted: "There is one good effect which the simple persuasion of his being a Christian produces in the mind of the Negro; it is an effectual antidote against the spells and charms of his native superstition. One Negro who desires to be revenged on another, if he fears a more open and manly attack on his adversary, has usually recourse to obeah. This is considered as a potent and irresistible spell, withering and palsying, by indescribable terrors, and unwonted sensations, the unhappy victim. Like the witches' cauldron in Macbeth, it is the combination of all that is hateful and disgusting; a toad's foot, a lizard's tail, a snake's tooth, the plumage of the carrion crow, or vulture, a broken egg-shell, a piece of wood fashioned into the shape of a coffin, with many other nameless ingredients, compose the fatal mixture. It will of course be conceived that the practice of obeah can have little effect, without a Negro is conscious that it is practised upon him, or thinking so: for as the sole evil lies in the terrors of a perturbed fancy, it is of little consequence whether it is really practised or not, if he only imagines that it is. An obeah-man or woman upon an estate, is therefore a very dangerous person; and the practice of it for evil purposes is made a felony by the law. But numbers may be swept off by its infatuation before the practice is detected; for, strange as it may appear, so much do the Negroes stand in awe of these wretches, so much do they dread their malice and their power, that, though knowing the havoc they have made, and are still making, many of them are afraid to discover them to the whites; and others, perhaps, are in league with them for sinister purposes of mischief and revenge. A Negro under this infatuation can only be cured of his terrors by being made a Christian; refuse him this indulgence, and he soon sinks a martyr to imagined evils. The author knew an instance of a Negro, who, being reduced by the fatal influence of obeah to the lowest state of dejection and debility, from which there were little hopes of his recovery, was surprisingly and rapidly restored to health and to spirits, by being baptized a Christian; so wonderful are the workings of a weak and superstitious imagination."

In the second edition of this work, published fifteen years later, and under the new title of A View of the Past and Present State of the Island of Jamaica, this passage is rewritten and after ascribing to a superstitious imagination the principal efficacy of obeah, it is now stated: "But if the charm fails to take hold of the mind of the proscribed person, another and more certain expedient is resorted to the secretly administering of poison to him. This saves the reputation of the sorcerer, and effects the purpose he had in view. (The Negroes practising obeah are acquainted with some very powerful vegetable poisons, which they use on these occasions.) An obeah-man or woman (for it is practised by both sexes) is a very wicked and dangerous person on a plantation; and the practice of it is made a felony by the law, punishable with death where poison has been administered, and with transportation where only the charm is used."

Clearly, then, at this period, according to the common opinion of the slaves, obeah was essentially a preternatural agency that could accomplish even death. Since they were convinced that Baptism was the only efficient protection, it would seem that the Devil was regarded as the principal agent in its operation. Without entering at present into the question of the soundness of this popular belief, we are safe in describing the obeah of the period as a form of witchcraft in which the ends were attained by means of superstitious fear, supplemented when necessary by the subtle use of poison.

In connexion with this same period, we find The Edinburgh Review for August, 1817, under the caption "Present State of West India Affairs," reviewing Medical and Miscellaneous Observations relative to the West India Islands by John Williamson, M.D., Fellow of the Royal College of Physicians of Edinburgh, and late of Spanish Town, Jamaica. Herein Doctor Williamson is quoted as follows: "On a property of that description, we have rather to fear the lurking and concealed practices of obi, the superstitiously depressing consequences of threats from a Negro of weight and influence in the estate against a Negro not aware of the futility of such pretensions." He has been dealing with a stomach evil, or mal d'estomac, which from the accompanying propensity of what he calls "dirt-eating" is unquestionably the effects of hook-worm, a circumstance which naturally he does not recognize, as the disease itself was not understood until comparatively recently.

The review continues: "The effects of the obi sorcery have been glanced at in one of these passages. Another extract will illustrate its influence, and confirm the position, that there is almost always, if not in every case, an intimate connexion between the stomach-evil and mental suffering. After describing some cases of the complaint, our author goes on to say, 'These cases were much aggravated on account of the obi impressions which had unluckily laid hold of their minds. A particular terror against returning to the mountain, where these superstitious apprehensions were formed, seemed to gain possession of their minds. It is absurd to reason with most Negroes on a subject of that kind; and very often, on grounds we cannot fathom, they will not discover the individuals they have an obi dread of.'"

Another case quoted from Williamson runs as follows: "Agnes was sitting alongside of the Negro doctress, and exulting in the advances she was making to recovery. In that state she was in the evening. On the following morning, she was accosted by an oldish Negro, named Dick, belonging to the estate, who had established his name as a great obi-man. Agnes, not long before, had declined his amorous addresses; on which occasion threats were made by Dick; and she was so much impressed by apprehension from these circumstances, that, on his addressing her, she fainted, and could not be again fully restored to her senses. In course of that evening, she passed fæces insensibly, and used Dick's name often in terror. In a few days she sunk.

"A general outcry of the Negroes succeeded her death against Dick; and such was their violence, that the overseer found it necessary to yield to an inquiry. A party proceeded to his house, to search for obi implements, which Dick and the overseer accompanied. The floor of his house was dug; a small coffin was removed from it, which he said he had placed there to the memory of a friend. This the Negroes denied; and pronounced it to be one of the instruments of his obi practices.

"It is incalculable what mischief is done by such designing, crafty people as Dick, when they establish a superstitious impression on the minds of the Negroes, that they possess powers beyond human. Such persons gratify revenge against their own colour in a destructive manner; and when bent on ruin to their masters, that malignant disposition is gratified by also destroying the Negroes his property. Mineral poison has been sometimes artfully procured; and it is believed that there are vegetable poisons which are less likely to lead to discovery. The agency of neither is often required; for the effect of a threat from an obi-man or woman is sufficient to lead to mental disease, despondency and death.

"The evidence against Dick was undoubted; and the Negroes regarded his stay on the estate with horror. The whole was submitted to the proprietor; and he was transported to some of the Spanish possessions."

Here again we have it clearly set down by a witness whose sceptical regards for the whole process really strengthens the value of his evidence, that the real effective influence for evil on the part of obeah-men consists in the fact that "they establish a superstitious impression on the minds of the Negroes, that they possess powers beyond human."

Another testimony of this same period appears in The Times of London, for December 5, 1818, under the general heading "Colonial Intelligence." Herein we read: "By a recent Act of the house of Assembly (Barbados), an endeavour has been made towards more effectively suppressing the practice of obeah. Our readers are aware, that by this name is designated a kind of necromantic power, which is mostly exercised by the Negroes for the attainment of the worst purposes. By the above Act, however, it is decreed that 'any slave who shall wilfully, maliciously, and unlawfully pretend to any magical and supernatural charm or power, in order to promote the purposes of insurrection or rebellion of the slaves within this island, or to injure and affect the life or health of any other slave; or who wilfully and maliciously shall use or carry on the wicked and unlawful practice of obeah, shall upon conviction thereof, suffer death or transportation as the Court shall think proper. Also, that if any slave wilfully and maliciously, in the practice of obeah, or otherwise, shall mix or prepare, or have in his or her possession, any poison, or any noxious or destructive substance or thing, with an intent to administer to any person (whether the said person be white or black, or a person of colour), or wilfully and maliciously shall administer to, or cause to be administered to, such person any poison, or any noxious or destructive substance or thing whatsoever, although death may not ensue, upon the testimony thereof, every such slave, together with his or her counsellors, aiders, and abettors (being slaves), knowing of and being privy to such evil intentions and offences, shall upon conviction thereof, suffer death, transportation, or such other punishment as the Court shall think proper.'"

All this in principle is but the extension of the Jamaica Act on the subject of obeah to the island of Barbados where conditions were pretty much the same as in the larger Colony.

The past century may be briefly reviewed by a few citations which will show that substantially obeah remains the same but that as time goes on, the obeah-man has been appropriating to himself more and more of the functions and the technique of the myal-man, until the latter as a separate entity has practically ceased to exist.

As stated in Voodoos and Obeahs: Immediately after Jamaican emancipation, and during the trying days of reconstruction of the entire social order, with a readjustment to conditions that were so vastly different from the accepted status of nearly two hundred years when the word of the master usually stood against the world, free rein was given to the religious frenzy that brought again into vogue the myalistic spirit so long repressed. A spirit of exultation naturally drove the slave of yesterday to take advantage of his freedom and sate himself with long-forbidden joys and the outbursts of religious fanaticism became so intermingled with nocturnal saturnalia, that for a time it was difficult to distinguish the one from the other. The old objective of myalism quickly reasserted itself. Now that the shackles had been stricken from their bodies, why not strike the chains from their souls as well? To "dig up obeah" consequently became widespread and persistent.

This gave witchcraft a set-back for a time, or rather made it even more secretive and vindictive.

As a consequence, there was no abatement in the general fear and terror in which it was held by Negroes without exception. And it cannot be surprising if occasionally the practitioner of obeah, for self-protection, assumed the rôle of myalist, and "dug up" perhaps the obeah that he himself had planted. In public, too, he might become a myalist doctor, while in secret he was still the obeah-man. He could apply the healing properties of herbs to counteract the very poisons he had occultly administered. Finally, together with the vile concoction devised at the midnight hour for harm and ruin, he might fashion the protective fetish as a counter-irritant. And the myal-man would naturally be expected to retaliate. Is it entirely improbable that he may have on occasion stooped to unprofessional practices, and with his knowledge of vegetable poisons played the rôle of his rival in herbal lore? In any case, from this time on, we find an ever increasing confusion of obeah and myalism in the accounts that have come down to us.

Doctor R. R. Madden was one of the six stipendiary magistrates who were sent out to Jamaica in October, 1833. Writing from Kingston on September 8, 1834, he describes a case of obeah that had been brought before him at Spanish Town, in which the obeah-man was alleged to have bewitched a child by smoking a particular "bush" to windward of his victim who was overcome by the fumes. In the course of the trial, the obeah-man "confessed that he was a practiser of obeah, that he did it not for gain or vengeance, but solely because the devil put it into his head to be bad." And again: "He had no spite against the father or mother of the child, nor wish to injure them. He saw the child, and he could not resist the instigation of the devil to obeah it, but he hoped he would never do it any more; he would pray to God to put it out of his head to do it." Doctor Madden adds: "Such was the singular statement made to the attorney-general by the prisoner; and the attorney-general informed me, made with an appearance of frankness and truth which gave a favourable impression of its veracity."

Here at least there is clear indication of the obeah-man's belief that he is acting as a tool of the Devil, and it may be safely said that the same point of view is taken by his victims generally.

Reverend Benjamin Luckock declared in 1846: "Obeahism, or obeah, as it is most generally called in the islands, attains its power by a supposed, or pretended, intercourse with spirits, both capable of inflicting and controlling evil." However, he expresses the doubt: "There is some difficulty in understanding whether the belief was given to Obi, or Obeah, as a fancied personage, or to obeahism, as a system founded on the imaginary influence of malignant spirits."

He is face to face with the old difficulty of confusing the craft of obeah with the evil spirit back of it that resulted in the transformation of the Ashanti Sasabonsam into the Jamaica Obboney.

It is not surprising, then, to find Charles Rampini writing in 1873: "Serpent or devil worship is by no means rare in the country districts; and of its heathen rites the obeah-man is invariably the priest."

Reverend R. Thomas Banbury, a native Jamaican, who was Rector of St. Peter's Church, Hope Bay, published in 1894, a pamphlet of fifty pages entitled Jamaica Superstitions; or The Obeah Book. As he tells us in the Preface that this is a curtailment of what he had written thirty-five years before, we may accept it as a fairly accurate exposition of the superstitious beliefs and practices that were current in Jamaica in the latter half of the nineteenth century, at least as regards the country districts with which he was familiar.

Mr. Banbury opens his treatise with the following words: "OBEAHISM. What wicked, immoral, disgusting, and debasing associations are called up in the minds of those who are acquainted with the baneful effects of this superstition in Jamaica at the mere mention of its name. A superstition the most cruel in its intended designs; the most filthy in its practices; the most shameful and degrading in its associations. It has not only directed its baleful influence against popular society in the island at large; but alas! it tends greatly to the pulling down of the Church of Christ. There is hardly any of the people connected with religion whose minds are not to some extent imbued with it--who do not believe that the influence of obeah is capable of exerting some evil effects either on their minds, bodies, or property; and there are very few we have reason to believe, who do not directly practice it. . . . Superstition is the parent of idolatry and all the concomitant evils of this sin. What 'pestiferous Demon' has swept through the land of Africa with 'tainted breath' devouring its inhabitants? It is Superstition."

In connexion with the importation of obeah from Africa, Mr. Banbury makes the amusing observation: "It is stated that the African obeah-man carried his obeah magic with him under the hair of his head when imported. For that reason the heads of the Africans were shaved before being landed, or if that was not done, he swallowed the things by which he worked in Africa, before leaving."

As regards the obeah-man himself, Mr. Banbury declares: "He is the agent incarnate of Satan. The Simon Magus of these good gospel days; the embodiment of all that is wicked, immoral and deceptious. You may easily at times distinguish him by his sinister look, and slouching gait. An obeah-man seldom looks any one in the face. Generally he is a dirty looking fellow with a sore foot. But some few have been known to be decent in their appearance, and well clad. He never goes without a bankra, wallet or bag, in which he carries his 'things.' He is a professional man that is as well paid as the lawyer or doctor, and sometimes better. It is a well-known fact that in cases of lawsuit the obeah-man is retained as well as the lawyer, and at times he not only 'works' at home on the case, but goes into Court with his client for the purpose, it is called, of 'stopping' the mouths of the prosecutor and his witnesses and of influencing the judge and jury. The obeah-man is to be feared in the system of poisoning which he carries on. He is well versed in all the vegetable poisons of the island, and sometimes has them planted in his garden. He is up to the knowledge that vegetable poison is not so easily detected after death as mineral, and therefore prefers to do his diabolical work with that. He takes advantage also of this to poison by the skin as well as by mouth. He is known to make a thin decoction of these poisons and soak the undergarments of people taken to him, which when taken back, and put on by the unsuspecting owner, the poison is absorbed along with the perspiration, and engenders some direful disease in the system. Many have suffered in this way and have not been able to account for their maladies."

Before leaving the subject of obeah and going on to consider myalism, Mr. Banbury makes the rather startling statement: "Whilst treating about obeahism and other superstitions of Jamaica, we do not wish to leave the impression on the minds of our readers that it is only the black people of the country that have faith in them. The majority of the coloured people also come under the category of the superstitious, and even some white people are not exempted. As we have already hinted in setting out, there are but few among the people whose minds are not imbued with a superstitious dread of obeah influences, though they may not enter into the practice of it."

Five years after the appearance of Mr. Banbury's pamphlet, W. p. Livingston declared: "Obeahism runs like a black thread of mischief through the known history of the race. It is the result of two conditions, an ignorant and superstitious receptivity on the one hand, and on the other, sufficient intelligence and cunning to take advantage of this quality. The obeah-man is any Negro who gauges the situation and makes it his business to work on the fears of his fellows. He claims the possession of occult authority, and professes to have the power of taking or saving life, of causing or curing disease, or bringing ruin or creating prosperity, of discovering evildoers or vindicating the innocent. His implements are a few odd scraps, such as cocks' feathers, rags, bones, bits of earth from graves, and so on. The incantations with which he accompanies his operations are merely a mumble of improvised jargon. His real advantage in the days of slavery lay in his knowledge and use of poisonous plants. Poisoning does not now enter into his practice to any extent, but the fear he inspires among the ignorant is intense, and the fact that he has turned his attention to particular persons is often sufficient to deprive them of reason. Obeahism is a superstition at once simple, foolish, and terrible, still vigorous, but in former times as powerful an agent as slavery itself in keeping the nature debased."

Writing of this same period, a missionary who had worked for more than a decade in some of the worst obeah districts of Jamaica, thus critically sums up the situation: "Obeah may be defined in general to be a superstitious belief that certain men and women, known as obeah-men and obeah-women, can exercise certain preternatural power over places, persons and things and produce effects beyond the natural powers of man, by agencies other than divine.

It seems to be a combination of magic and witchcraft. Magic, we are told, is an attempt to work miracles by the use of hidden forces beyond man's control, so it is in obi; it is an attempt to produce by some undetermined, invisible power, effects out of proportion to and beyond the capabilities of the things and activities employed. In witchcraft, we are told. . . . there is involved the idea of a diabolical pact, or at least an appeal to the intervention of the spirits. In the history and make up and practice of obi there is involved the idea of association with the devil. . . . His Satanic majesty is the invisible head of obeah. The visible agent, head and front of obeah is the obeah-man or obeah-woman, more often and more characteristically the obeah-man. Who and what is the obeah-man? In general the obi-man or woman is any man or woman who is supposed to have communication with some invisible agent through which he or she can exert preternatural power over animate and inanimate beings. You have obi-men of all sorts, just as you have professional doctors and quack-doctors. As obeahism is so common among the people and is a form of religion, it comes natural for any individual to practise it as he would practise any religious rite. From this you can easily understand how any rascal who wants to gratify his revenge, avarice or lust, can work upon the superstitious, practise obi and get a following as an obi-man. Hence obi-working is very common."

Again the same writer tells us: "The obi-man's incantation is generally the muttering of strange sounds, often meaningless, the pronouncing of some word or words over the objects to be obeahed, joined with some grotesque actions. It may consist in words or actions alone. The following lines which I find in my notes on obeah, by a Jamaican poet describe an obi-man at work:

"Crouched in a cave I saw thee and thy beard
    White against black, gleamed out; and thy gaunt hand
Mixed lizard skins, rum, parrots' tongues and sand
    Found where the sinking tombstone disappeared.
Sleek galli-wasps looked on thee; grimly peered
    Blood-christened John Crows with a hissed demand
Who art thou? then like ghouls to a dim land
    Fled for they saw thee working and they feared.

"Compare this description of the obi-man making obeah or an obi-charm with that given by Shakespeare in Macbeth of the witches making a charm through which they raised spirits and deceivingly foretold to Macbeth his future; and you will find that they have much in common."

As was stated in Voodoos and Obeahs, during the long years of slavery, myalism might be regarded as dormant. There was no opportunity of its development or branching out. It was preserved secretly and cherished as the fondest tradition of the past. No doubt the hours of amusement allowed to the slaves on their own cultivations preserved in some: degree the myalistic rites, disguised as one of the social dances that were countenanced by the planters.

The native African is essentially religious in his own way and as formal ceremonies were debarred he found an outlet by associating with obeah an element of worship, if not of Accompong, at least of Sasabonsam or Obboney. If he could not venerate the Supreme Being through the minor deities and ancestral spirits, he might at least placate the evil one, and bespeak his influence for purposes of revenge or to coerce his master to grant him something that he sought.

We find obeah thus really becoming a form of devil-worship in the Christian sense, and when at length myalism entered into an alliance with it for the overthrow of the white régime it naturally gained in the popular estimation of the slaves, since its arch-enemy myalism had come to recognize its power. And yet this public esteem was not one of devotion but of unholy fear, which the obeah-man naturally played up to his own advantage.

With Emancipation, myalism made haste to assert itself in an endeavour to regain its pristine ascendance and made open war on obeah, at the expense be it said of the general peace of the community. Its newly found independence led to excesses of every kind and in course of years it became as great an evil as obeah itself. Its old priestly class was dead, for a generation none had come from Africa, and there had been no opportunity of establishing a succession in the craft or of passing along the ritual in practice. The traditions and nothing more could have remained, and it is questionable whether the new leaders had any legitimate claim to the exercise of the rôle that they assumed. It is simple, then, to see that the decay of myalism as a religious force was inevitable. And it would certainly have soon been entirely eliminated had not its spirit and much of its traditional ritual found new scope in the kindred spirit of the emotional revivalism which was fostered for a time by the Methodists and even more so by the Native Baptist Congregations. But this recrudescence of myalism has found its climax with the Bedwardites, so characterized by the peculiar hip-movement that is clearly African, and which shows itself not only in their dances but also in the religious processions, and gives a peculiar lilt to all their hymns.

Here, strictly speaking, myalism disappears, and its very name is dying out except as a mysterious something that has endured in its opposition to the obeah-man who more and more assumes the dual rôle of myalist by day and obeah-man by night, using the title as a safeguard from the law in the prosecution of his real aim in life. As a further consequence, obeah is assuming more and more of a religious aspect and it is now, not undeservedly, classified by many as devil-worship.

In Chambers's Journal for January 11, 1902, there appeared an article entitled "Obeah To-day In The West Indies." The course of the narrative shows that the writer had been living in Jamaica for three years at the time of writing. However, it should be observed that the term obeah as used in this article includes voodoo and all other forms of West Indian witchcraft. Thus it is asserted in accordance with the old theory that an Egyptian origin is to be ascribed to the whole practice: "The name is derived from obi, apparently an evil deity worshipped on the West Coast of Africa by the ancestors of the present West

Indian Negroes before they were shipped off as slaves to the plantations. The Reverend John Radcliffe, a noted Jamaican scholar, has proved the word obi to mean a snake, and to this day the snake is commonly used as a symbol of the baleful rites."

The article continues: "The obeah-man is generally a sinister, terrifying figure-aged, decrepit, often diseased, and half-mad; but with a baleful gleam in his bloodshot eyes, that does not belie his pretended intimacy with the Author of Evil."

In connexion with the prevalence of obeah practices, the author states: "I have known coloured schoolmasters scatter these ridiculous trifles about their schoolrooms with the idea of compelling the Government inspector to give them good reports; and missionaries have told me that members expelled from their Churches for evil living commonly work obeah in order to be restored to the fold. When the minister enters his pulpit, and, opening his bible to give out the text, finds a quaint assortment of cats' claws, feathers, dried leaves, and egg-shells, he is by no means puzzled as to the meaning of it all. He knows it expresses Hezekiah Da Costa's wish to be received back into Church membership without abandoning his career as the village Don Juan."

In the foregoing passage, I fear, the author has drawn unduly on the imagination. If such manifestations have actually taken place in rare, isolated instances, they are so unusual that they should not be cited as if they were regular occurrences. Certainly I have never encountered anything in even the most out-of-the-way sections of the "bush" that could in any way support the story of Hezekiah Da Costa's method of regaining good-standing as a Church member.

In any case, the following passage from the same article is deserving of more attention in keeping with our present study: "In many countries superstitious rites are practised to bring good luck; but that is not the case as a rule with obeah. Its root idea is the worship and propitiation of the Evil One: it is essentially malevolent. A Negro usually goes to the obeah-man to harm his neighbour, not to do any good to himself; and that is why the law regards the matter so seriously. The principal exception to this rule is the not infrequent case of the young Negress who goes for a love-philtre to make some 'high gentleman' marry her. The obeah-man is often called upon to exorcise 'duppies' driven into a man or woman by a brother in the craft. In former days this used to be the exclusive work of the myal-man. It was the old story of 'white' and 'black' magic. One wizard did the mischief, and the other supplied the antidote. Nowadays myalism is complete merged into obeah-ism, and the law punishes both equally."

Claude McKay, a native of Clarendon, who from a little-known Jamaica poet has become one of the more popular writers of Harlem fiction, is in general agreement with all this. Thus he writes: "Obeah is black people's evil God." And again: "Of the thousands of native families, illiterate and literate, in that lovely hot island there were few indeed that did not worship and pay tribute to Obi--the god of Evil that the Africans brought cover with them when they were sold to the New World."

May Robinson, writing in Folk-Lore. A Quarterly Review of Myth, Tradition, Institutions, and Custom, on the subject "Obeah Worship in West Indies" stated in 1893: "The mystery with which the professors of obeah have always surrounded themselves, and the dread Negroes have always had, and still have, of their power, have made it very difficult to find out much about the worship or superstition." However, she observes: "Obeah practices of the present day seem similar to those of a hundred years ago, and information about them has been kindly supplied to me by Mr. Thomas, Inspector Jamaica Constabulary, and gleamed from his interesting pamphlet, Something About Obeah. In addition to the Law of 1760, another Law for the suppression of obeah was passed in 1845, which gave to the executive authorities very comprehensive powers to deal, not only with the obeah-men themselves, but also with those who sought their services."

The present legal aspect of obeah, may be briefly outlined as follows. The Rules and Regulations for the Jamaica Constabulary of 1867 simply enumerates among those that the constable is called on to arrest "every person pretending to be a dealer in obeah or myalism."

The Sub-Officers Guide of Jamaica, published in 1908, is more specific when it defines the implements of obeah as follows: "Grave dirt, pieces of chalk, packs of cards, small mirrors, or bits of large ones, beaks, feet, and bones of fowls or other birds, teeth of dogs and alligators, glass marbles, human hair, sticks of sulphur, camphor, myrrh, asafoetida, frankincense, curious shells, china dolls, wooden images, curiously shaped sticks, and other descriptions of rubbish."

However, the mere possession of the paraphernalia of obeah is no longer sufficient ground for prosecution under the law. This was settled by the following decision of the Supreme Court of Jamaica: "Unlawful possession of implements of Obeah. This is an appeal from a conviction by a Resident Magistrate charging the appellant with being in the unlawful possession of implements of obeah. A person found in possession of such implements is deemed by Section 8 of Law 5 of 1898 to be a person practising obeah until the contrary is proved, but such possession is not in itself a substantive offence, and can only be used as evidence in support of a charge of practising obeah. In the circumstances the appeal must be allowed and the conviction quashed. (R. v. Bulgin (1919), S.C.J.B. Vol. 10, p. 86, A. M. Coll, C. J., Beard, p. J. and Brown, Ag. J.)."

Towards the close of the last century, the Reverend Mr. Banbury was of opinion: "The laws affecting the punishment of this superstition (obeah) in Jamaica are too lenient; otherwise it would not be so rife. The Courts of Justice are apt to laugh at the thing, and treat it as mere nonsense."

But the very opposite view is taken by a recent correspondent in The Daily Gleaner of Kingston, Jamaica. The letter is dated January 15, 1934, and runs as follows:

"OBEAH LAW REPEAL SUGGESTED

The Editor:

Sir,--The time has arrived when the Legislature should eliminate the Obeah Law from our Statute Book.

Jamaica passed that stage long ago. The constant reference in the newspapers to this or that arrest for obeah is a reflexion on our present day civilization and does the country harm.

I will concede that this African cult was brought here from the West Coast by some of the poor slaves, but having no recruits it burnt itself out as some diseases do, decades ago.

I will also concede that there exists some artful poisonings by the so-called 'obeah-men', but the rascals when caught should be charged under a different and more serious act, flogging and imprisonment being the requirements.

The bulk of the rest so charged in our courts is merely receiving money by false pretences or by a trick, and should be also flogged.

I discussed the subject with my friend the Honourable A. G. Nash only a week before he died. He agreed with me and had intended in protection of the fair name of Jamaica to have brought the matter before the Legislative Council.

I am, etc.

A Jamaican."

And yet, on February 26, 1934, The Daily Gleaner, under the headlines: "Obeah and Voodooism. Still Practised in West Indies. Says Judge Bullock." runs as a news item a digest taken from The Brighton Herald of February 5, 1934, which concludes as follows: "The lecturer supplemented his pictorial and geographical details of the British West Indies with some fascinating stories of obeah worship, which with voodooism, is still secretly practised among the native communities." The lecturer, it is noted, was judge Willoughby Bullock, formerly Chief Justice of St. Vincent, British West Indies.

Undoubtedly, the present-day practice of obeah particularly as found in city and town does include a great deal of charlatanism pretty much as is to be found in the spiritual séances in all large American communities, together with an ingraft of superstitions that have been borrowed from the Whites. Even modern books, professedly treating of the mysteries of magic, are greedily assimilated and their formulae are attempted in practice. But my personal observations throughout the "bush" which have aggregated in all about six years, during the past quarter of a century, lead me to conclude that the obeah-man as a rule takes himself very seriously and honestly believes that he can and does exercise supernatural powers, and assuredly the great mass of the populace, whatever their protestations to the contrary may be, live in veritable dread of some nefarious influence of the obeah-man whose enmity must be avoided at any cost.

Further, I am convinced that I have witnessed more than one death where the sole cause was an overpowering fear due to the conviction that obeah was being worked against the sufferer who literally pined away.

What is more, I am driven to the conclusion that just as in the days of slavery, obeah was too long regarded with amused toleration merely as a foolish superstition devoid of real efficient power to do harm, so to-day there is a tendency in Jamaica to shut the eyes to the true nefarious influence of the cult on the entire Negro population of the island, and to regard this practice of the black art as an exuberance of superstition and nothing more. The real menace comes not from the quixotic external practices, professing by a sort of sympathetic magic to control ghosts, to prosper some love affair, or assist in legal disputes and commercial transactions, but from the underlying conviction of the potency of a spiritual force which is nothing more nor less than an assumption that if Properly invoked, his Satanic Majesty will exert an efficient directive force in the affairs of man's daily life. Certainly, if you can persuade anyone who has gone to an obeah-man for a love-philtre to disclose what really went on in the nauseating process and the accompanying incantations, the last doubt will vanish from your mind regarding the diabolic association of the whole practice. In fine, obeah as such, in its purpose and acceptance must be classified as a form of devil worship.

This does not mean that a diabolic influence is actually controlled by the obeah-man. In the ordinary course of events such a supposition, in my opinion, would be repugnant to Divine Providence, although it might be permitted on rare occasions. But the real obeah-man, as far as lies in his power, places his confidence in the Evil One as he formally invokes his assistance, and his intention if not the result classifies his act as one of communication with the Devil. The client, too, approaches the obeah-man with the firm conviction that the evil which he purposes is to be wrought through the machinations of Satan and he forthwith puts himself under an obligation to the arch-fiend, even if what he seeks fails of accomplishment.

As noted in Voodoos and Obeahs, the obeah-man has a wholesome fear of the priest and usually tries to avoid his presence. There is a conviction among his ilk that the priest can exercise a more powerful influence than any obeah-man. This belief is expressed by the aphorism: "French obi, him strongest." The first priest to become well known through the Jamaica "bush" was a Frenchman, and the Catholic Church in consequence came to be known familiarly as the French Church. Hence, "French obi, him strongest" really means that the Catholic Church exercises the strongest obeah. It is also accepted as a fact by the devotees of the obeah cult that the priest can give evidence of his dominant power by "lighting a candle on them." This process is thus described: "Fadder take pin and Fadder take candle, and him stick der pin in der candle; and him light der candle on you. Der candle him burn and him burn and him burn. And you waste and you waste and you waste. And when der flame touch dat pin--you die." So that it is only necessary for a priest to make the playful remark to some black fellow in the "bush," "I think I'll have to light a candle on you," to bring him to his knees with: "O Fadder, don't." On one occasion I was actually approached by the most notorious obeah-man of a "bush" district who in the real spirit of a Simon

Magus professed his desire to become a Catholic precisely in the hopes of acquiring this fictitious power of the lighted candle.

APPLIED MAGIC

DESPITE the fact that obeah is clearly defined as regards its origin in Ashanti witchcraft, and its early develop-ment among the Jamaica slaves, in course of time it has become so confused with voodoo and other superstitious practices that now the word is used as a generic term for any kind of West India witchcraft and by extension it embraces even "a fetish or magic object used in witchcraft."

As a consequence, it is difficult for the average reader to clearly differentiate the real from pseudo-obeah unless he keeps in mind the fundamental principles which were established in the preceding chapter, and which may be briefly summarized as follows.

Obeah, as the continuation of Ashanti witchcraft, is professedly a projection of spiritual power with the harm of an individual as an objective. Practically, its end is attained through fear, supplemented if needs be by secret poisoning. The agent is the servant of the Sasabonsam or Devil who is invoked and relied upon to produce the desired effect. Consequently real obeah must be regarded as a form of Devil-worship.

In daily practice, much that is referred to as obeah is in reality only applied magic which may be called pseudo-obeah, and it is with this that we are now to interest ourselves.

During my researches in the British Museum, I came across a pamphlet of thirty pages entitled The Monchy Murder. The Strangling and Mutilation of a Boy for Purposes of Obeah. It is a sordid story. The boy, Rupert Mapp, twelve years of age, had been enticed away from Bridgetown, Barbados, by Monteul Edmond and brought to St. Lucia. The day after their arrival at the town of Monchy, the lad disappeared. A week later his body was dug up but it was found that the two hands, and the heart had been removed. The missing parts had been found in the possession of an accomplice of Edmond who was forthwith arrested and charged with the crime.

The search of the prisoner's person brought to light a notebook in which had been copied in French a number of formulae and instructions connected with magical practices. One of these was entitled La Main de Gloire and it prescribed: "Take the hand of one who has been hanged, or strangled, dry it in the sun in the dog days, (August, September, October) or if the sun should not be hot enough to dry thoroughly and quickly, dry the hand in an oven. When thoroughly dry, sprinkle the hand with salt and a number of other ingredients (which are stated) and wrap it in a piece of coffin-pall. Then make a taper of virgin wax, anoint it with various fantastic oils and fats. Fix the taper between the fingers of the dried hand. The light of the taper will paralyze completely the faculties both mental and physical of everybody who comes within its influence."

Unquestionably, it was Edmond's purpose to apply this formula in the hopes that he would be able in this way to enter any house that pleased him and to rob it with impunity as the victim would supposedly be rendered utterly incapable either of resisting the intrusion or of remembering later who it was that perpetrated the crime. However, it is a serious mistake to associate such practices with obeah in the true sense of the word.

It was brought out in the course of Edmond's trial at St. Lucia that the formulae which had been found in his possession had been "copied from a work entitled Petit Albert the pretended author of which is claimed to be a monkish occultist of the middle ages." Edmond had spent many years in Haiti where he had formally studied the black art and had gained access to the book from which he had copied his formulae for spells, etc.

The volume ascribed to Petit Albert, written originally in Latin was for a time regarded as a posthumous work of Albertus Magnus either as a whole or in part. However, such a supposition is definitely disproved by a critical edition of the work which appeared in Paris in 1885 under the title Les Secrets Admirables du Grand Albert comprenant son traité des herbes des pierres et de animaux avec son traité des merveilles du monde suivi du Trésor des Merveilleux Secrets du Petit Albert avec Préface et Annotations par Marius Decrespe. Herein Decrespe explicitly discredits the opinions of those who "attribute this dual work either to Albertus Magnus or to a compiler of about the 15th century who based them on an unedited manuscript of Albert the Great supplemented by the works of more modern authors, such as Paracelsus, Cornelius Agrippa, etc." On the following page, Decrespe insists: "What appears much more probable is that Grand Albert as well as Petit Albert are both the work of several individuals whose discoveries have been joined together regardless of order by some poorly instructed and unscrupulous librarian, who produced these disorderly collections at Lyons, towards the end of the 16th century. Actually, there is a tradition, very useful in practice, that when one gives himself to the study of occultism, just as when one experiments in Chemistry, he should have a Laboratory Record wherein he records all experiments with their results."

This suggestion is supported by the fact that La Main de Gloire does not appear in the edition of Petit Albert which I have before me as I write and which was published at Lyons in 1668. It was evidently added to the collection after that date.

Consequently, such abnormalities as the Monchy Murder should not be attributed to the practice of obeah or any other form of Negro witchcraft. It was nothing but cold-blooded murder, instigated, if you will, by medieval superstitions which had become impinged on Haitian voodoo, but even then it was not the product of the Negro in any way beyond the fact that he had borrowed it from the white man.

Another common mistake is to classify as obeah the use of protective charms simply because they are the product of the obeah-man when he is actually working in the capacity of myal-man. We have seen in the case of slave rebellions how general was the misapprehension that the instigator was the obeah-man, when as a matter of fact it was the myal-man who stirred up the trouble and administered the terrible oath of secrecy and distributed powders that were supposed to impart invulnerability against the weapons of the white man. So, too, it has become customary to regard as obeah-practice much that is really myalistic in the amulets imparted to individuals to enable them to overreach the law or to defy their enemies by a charmed life.

Thus we have the example of the notorious outlaw known as Three-fingered Jack from the fact that early in his career he had lost two fingers in an encounter with a Maroon. His depredations, after the scattering of the little group of runaway slaves who gathered around him at the beginning of his career, were actually accomplished single-handed. Moreover, his operations covered so wide an area that it left the impression that he was leading a numerous and well-organized band of desperadoes, and his name became synonymous with terror throughout the country districts, especially as it was generally accepted that his reliance was the machinations of a particularly powerful obeah-man from whom he had received a gruesome amulet which will be described later. As this incident is absolutely unique in the history of Jamaica, we may be pardoned going into some details.

Under date of August 5, 1780, we find the following Newspaper item: "A gang of run-away Negroes of above forty men and about eighteen women, have formed a settlement in the recesses of Four Mile Wood in St. David's; are become very formidable to that neighbourhood, and have rendered travelling, especially to Mulattoes and Negroes, very dangerous; one of the former they have lately killed, belonging to Mr. Duncan Munro of Montrose, and taken a large quantity of linen of his from his slaves on the road: they also have robbed many other persons' servants, and stolen some cattle, and great numbers of sheep, goats, hogs, poultry, etc., particularly a large herd of hogs from Mr. Rial of Tamarind Tree Penn. They are chiefly Congos, and declare they will kill every Mulatto and Creole Negro they can catch. Bristol, alias Three-fingered Jack, is their Captain, and Caesar, who belongs to Rozel estate, is their next officer. This banditti may soon become dangerous to the Public, if a party agreeable to the 40th and 66th Acts in Volume I of the Laws of the Island, or the Maroons, are not sent out against them; which should be applied for, and no doubt it would be ordered."

December 2, 1780, it is announced: "Three-fingered Jack continues his depredations in St. David's; last week he intercepted three Negroes coming to town with loads, and carried them off. A Mulatto of Dr. Allen's with a party, went in pursuit of him and recovered the Negroes, who gave him information where Three-fingered Jack was, and he laid a plan for securing him, but Jack being on his guard, shot the Mulatto through the head and made his escape."

Three weeks later, there is the further item: "We are informed that the wife of Three-fingered Jack has been lately removed from St. David's, to the jail in this town; and that directions have been given some time since, to deliver her and the other Negroes, taken by the Maroons, to be dealt with as the law directs."

Another fortnight, and we find a formal Proclamation that continues through several issues of the Royal Gazette.

By the King.

A PROCLAMATION.

Whereas we have been informed by our House of Assembly of this our Island of Jamaica, that a very desperate gang of Negro Slaves, headed by a Negro Man Slave called and known by the name of

Three-fingered J A C K

hath for many months past committed many Robberies and carried off many Negro and other Slaves on the Windward roads into the woods, and hath also committed several Murders; and that repeated parties have been fitted out and sent against the said Three-fingered Jack, and his gang, who have returned without being able to apprehend the said Negro, or to prevent his making head again: And whereas our House of Assembly hath requested us to give directions for issuing a Proclamation, offering a reward for apprehending the said

Negro called Three-fingered jack, and also a further reward for apprehending each and every Negro Man Slave belonging to the said gang, and delivering him or them to any of the gaolers of this island; We have taken the same into our consideration, have thought fit to issue this our Royal Proclamation; hereby strictly charging and commanding, and we do hereby strictly charge and command all and every our loving subjects within our said island, to pursue and apprehend, or cause to be pursued and apprehended the body of the said Negro man named, Three-fingered Jack, and also of each and every Negro Man Slave belonging to the said gang, and deliver him or them to any Gaolers of this Island. And we do, at the instance of our said House of Assembly offer a reward of one hundred pounds, to be paid to the person or persons who shall so apprehend and take the body of the said Negro called Three-fingered Jack: And we do, at the instance of our said House of Assembly, offer a further reward of five pounds over and above what is allowed by law, for apprehending each and every Negro Man Slave belonging to the said gang, and delivering him or them to any of the gaolers of this island, to be dealt with according to law." Then follow the usual signatures and attestations.

An additional offer of reward on the part of the Assembly immediately follows:

HOUSE OF ASSEMBLY
DECEMBER 29, 1780

Resolved: That over and above the reward of One Hundred pounds offered by his Majesty's Proclamation for the taking or killing the rebellious Negro called Three-fingered Jack, the further reward of Freedom shall be given to any slave that shall take or kill the said Three-fingered Jack; and that the House will make good the value of such slave to the proprietor thereof. And if any one of his accomplices will kill the said Three-fingered

Jack, and bring in his head, and hand wanting the fingers, such accomplice shall be entitled to a Free Pardon, and his Freedom as above, upon due proof being made of their being the head and hand of the said Three-fingered Jack." This is signed in the name of the House by Samuel Howell, Clerk of Assembly.

Within a month, under date of February 3, 1781, the announcement is made: "We have the pleasure to inform the public, of the death of that daring freebooter Three-fingered Jack.--He was surprised on Saturday last, by a Maroon Negro named John Reeder, and six others, near the summit of Mount Libanus, being alone and armed with two muskets and a cutlass.--The party came upon him so suddenly, that he had only time to seize the cutlass, with which he desperately defended himself, refusing all submission, till having received three bullets in his body and covered with wounds, he threw himself about forty feet down a precipice, and was followed by Reeder, who soon overpowered him, and severed his head and arm from the body which were brought to this town on Thursday last. Reeder and another Maroon were wounded in the conflict.--The intrepidity of Reeder in particular, and the behaviour of his associates in general justly entitle them to the reward offered by the public.

As an aftermath of this whole incident, we find in the Postscript to the Royal Gazette of June 9, 1792, the information that a runaway Negro named Dagger, a former comrade of the notorious Three-fingered Jack, and now on trial for his many crimes "has so much confidence in a supernatural agency that he not only defies every effort of justice to bring him to punishment but even threatens the severest revenge in retaliation." And again in the Postscript to the Royal Gazette Of July 7, 1792, we read: "After the trial of Dagger was closed two other Negroes that have been for a considerable time in the practice of obeah and who, from the evidence given, appeared to be thorough adepts . . . were found guilty and also sentenced to be transported."

Concerning Three-fingered Jack himself, the most authentic account which has come down to us is furnished by Doctor Benjamin Moseley who was a resident of Jamaica at the time of his exploits. Fixing the date of the death of Three-fingered Jack as January 27, 1781, Doctor Moseley tells us: "I saw the obi of the famous Negro robber, Three-fingered Jack, the terror of Jamaica in 1780. The Maroons who slew him brought it to me. His obi consisted of the end of a goat's horn, filled with a compound of grave dirt, ashes, the blood of a black cat, and human fat; all mixed into a kind of paste. A cat's foot, a dried toad, a pig's tail, a flip of virginal parchment of kid's skin, with characters marked in blood on it, were also in his obian bag.

"These with a keen sabre, and two guns, like Robinson Crusoe, were all his obi; with which, and his courage in descending into the plains and plundering to supply his wants, and his skill in retreating into difficult fastnesses, among the mountains, commanding the only access to them, where none dared to follow him, he terrified the inhabitants, and set the civil power, and the neighbouring militia of the island at defiance for nearly two years.

"He had neither accomplice, nor associate. There were a few runaway Negroes in the woods near Mount Libanus, the place of his retreat; but he had crossed their foreheads with some of the magic of his horn, and they could not betray him. But he trusted no one. He scorned assistance. He ascended above Spartacus. He robbed alone; fought all his battles alone; and always killed his pursuers.

"By his magic, he was not only the dread of the Negroes, but there were many white people, who believed he was possessed of some supernatural power.

"But even Jack himself was born to die. Allured by the rewards offered by Governor Dalling, in proclamations, dated December 12, 1780 and January 13, 1781; and, by a resolution of the House of Assembly, which followed the first proclamation; two Negroes, named Quashee and Sam (Sam was Captain Davy's son, he who shot a Mr. Thompson, the master of a London ship, at Old Harbour), both of Scot's Hall Maroon Town, with a party of their townsmen, went in search of him. Quashee, before he set out on the expedition, got himself christianed, and changed his name to James Reeder.

"The expedition commenced; and the whole party had been creeping about in the woods, for three weeks, and blockading, as it were, the deepest recesses of the most inaccessible part of the island, where Jack, far remote from all human society, resided,--but in vain.

"Reeder and Sam, tired with this mode of war, resolved on proceeding in search of his retreat; and taking him by storming it, or perishing in the attempt. They took with them a little boy, a proper spirit, and a good shot, and left the rest of the party.

"These three, whom I well knew, had not been long separated from their companions, before their cunning eyes discovered, by impressions among the weeds and bushes, that some person must have lately been that way. They softly followed these impressions, making not the least noise. Presently they discovered smoke. They prepared for war. They came upon Jack before he perceived them. He was roasting plantains, by a little fire on the ground, at the mouth of a cave.

"This was a scene:--not where ordinary actors had a common part to play. Jack's looks were fierce and terrible. He told them he would kill them.

Reeder, instead of shooting Jack, replied that his obi had no power to hurt him; for he was christianed; and that his name was no longer Quashee. Jack knew Reeder; and, as if paralysed, he let his two guns remain on the ground, and took up only his cutlass.

"These two, had a severe engagement several years before, in the woods; in which conflict Jack lost the two fingers, which was the origin of his present name; but Jack then beat Reeder, and almost killed him, with several others who assisted him, and they fled from Jack.

"To do Three-fingered Jack justice, he would now have killed both Reeder and Sam; for, at first, they were frightened at the sight of him, and the dreadful tone of his voice; and well they might: they had besides no retreat, and were to grapple with the bravest, and strongest man in the world. But Jack was cowed; for, he had prophesied, that white obi would get the better of him; and, from experience, he knew the charm would lose none of its strength in the hands of Reeder.

"Without further parley, Jack, with his cutlass in his hand, threw himself down a precipice at the back of the cave. Reeder's gun missed fire. Sam shot him in the shoulder. Reeder, like an English bull-dog, never looked, but, with his cutlass in his hand, plunged headlong down after Jack. The descent was about thirty yards, and almost perpendicular. Both of them had preserved their cutlasses in the fall.

"Here was the stage,--on which two of the stoutest hearts, that were ever hooped with ribs, began their bloody struggle. The little boy, who was ordered to keep back, out of harm's way, now reached the top of the precipice, and during the fight, shot Jack in the belly. Sam was crafty, and coolly took a round-about way to get to the field of action. When he arrived at the foot where it began, Jack and Reeder had closed, and tumbled together down another precipice, on the side of the mountain, in which fall they both lost their weapons. Sam descended after them, though without weapons, they were not idle; and, luckily for Reeder, Jack's wounds were deep and desperate, and he was in great agony. Sam came up just time enough to save Reeder; for, Jack had caught him by the throat, with his giant's grasp. Reeder then was with his right hand almost cut off, and Jack streaming with blood from his shoulder and his belly; both covered with gore and gashes. In this state Sam was umpire; and decided the fate of the battle. He knocked Jack down with a piece of a rock.

"When the lion fell, the two tigers got upon him, and beat his brains out with stones. The little boy soon found his way to them. He had a cutlass, with which they cut off Jack's head, and three-fingered hand, and took them in triumph to Morant Bay. There they put their trophies into a pail of rum; and followed by a vast concourse of Negroes, now no longer afraid of Jack's obi, blowing their shells and horns, and firing guns in their rude method, they carried them to Kingston, and Spanish Town; and claimed the rewards offered by the King's Proclamation, and the House of Assembly."

William Burdett, also a contemporary in Jamaica, thus described the obeah-man who bestowed the gruesome amulet on Three-fingered Jack, whom he calls Manson in his narrative: "Amalkir, the obeah-practitioner, dwelt in a loathsome cave, far removed from the inquiring eye of the suspicious whites, in the Blue Mountains; he was old and shrivelled; a disorder had contracted all his nerves, and he could hardly crawl. His cave was the dwelling-place, or refuge of robbers; he encouraged them in their depredations; and gave them obi, that they might fearlessly rush where danger stood. This obi was supposed to make them invulnerable to the attacks of the white man, and they placed implicit belief in its virtue." As might be expected, he thus played the part of myalist as well as that of obeah-man.

A far less reliable narrative is entitled: The Wonderful Life and Adventures of Three-Fingered Jack, the Terror of Jamaica! "Giving an Account of his persevering Courage and gallant Heroism, in revenging the Cause of his Injured Parents; with an account of His desperate Conflict with Quashee! Who, after many attempts, at last overcomes him and takes his Head and Hand to Jamaica, (sic) and receives a large Reward for destroying him." This little book, published in London in 1829, is a melodramatic piece of fiction of no historical value whatever. Its mission is to stir up a morbid sentimentality for the slave. In some respects it is a forerunner of Uncle Tom's Cabin but devoid of the latter's literary merit. It is crude withal, and evidently the work of one who knows little or nothing about Jamaica. On page 7, Jack is made the offspring of Makro and Amri, "a beautiful slave, the property of Mr. Moreton, of Maroons Town." Actually Maroon Town was reserved for the Maroons and there could have been no white man established there on a plantation with slaves. Then, too, there are no Savannahs around Maroon Town as described on page 17. Again page 18 places the plantation near enough to Mount Libanus for a night journey there to the cave of Bashra, the obi-woman, who is represented as slinging the obi-horn around Jack's neck as she starts him on his way of revenge. On page 25, "Quashee, a brave black of Scot's Hall, Maroon Town, on the promise of that liberty which was so dear to him, resolved to try the effect of an expedition." But, being a Maroon, he was already free. Finally on page 26, when Amri is to be burned at the stake, "a priest, in Christian mercy, implored rest for her soul," despite the fact that at the date of the supposed incident there were no priests in Jamaica, unless the Anglican Rectors are meant and they were never referred to under this title. And yet caricatures of this sort find their way at times into presumably historical descriptions of obeah in Jamaica.

There is preserved in the Jamaica Institute of Kingston a Scrap Book that contains many interesting items, usually, however, without disclosing the source of the clippings. Thus we find on page 10, a couple of tracts that were used as evidence by the Hon. D. G. Gideon in the Legislative Council when discussing the Obeah Bill, on March 17, 1898. We have here the confession of an obeah-man named Daniel Hart, a native of Long District, Portland, who is dying to all appearances under the curse of another obeah-man of stronger power than his own. He acknowledges that in his own practice of obeah his fees varied from a few shillings up to six pounds for a single "job." His efforts had been directed to all sorts of ends--mainly to kill people, to drive them mad, to exact revenge for jilted lovers, to make goods sell better in the market, etc.

He frequently uses in his confession the terms: "I play hell"; "I play fire"; "Like rolling calf"; as regards different people. He declares that he often sent john-crows, i.e. buzzards, as ministers of his evil power, but that the main instruments were obeah-pots and vials which he planted at the places where his influence was to work. He sent other men who killed for him. He put duppies on people and they went mad. He openly confesses to the gross immorality of his personal actions.

One passage of this confession runs as follows: "On Monday evening this wicked obeah-man cry out: I am going to die and cannot wait until the 10th of this month for I am only skin and bones. I wanted Portland people to come and see how flies eat my skin. To-day is my ripping day. I will call names, and who want mad, can mad. Me da Bungo man and make it plain ABC, that you can know friend from enemy. I play hell with people, but the devil is riding me down to hell." It might be remarked that "Bungo" is probably a corruption of the Ashanti bunkam, to be supereminent.

On page 55 of the Jamaica Institute Scrap Book, are three printed tracts. The first of these describes the death and confession of a notorious obeah-woman who had been known as "Old Mother Austin." She died on June 25, 1892, after having lived and practised her art at Llandewey in St. David's. She called herself "Fire Rush" and makes the terrible avowal that she has killed twenty-five babies, seven women and thirteen men in the district. She claims to have employed two "Old Higes" and "when dey gash der fire in dem eyes, it shine as lightning." "Any way I send, death must come," is her boast. By means of a "peace-cup and spoon" she says that she dropped off all the fingers and toes of a woman who had stolen from her, possibly she had communicated leprosy to her victim by mixing the saliva of a leper in what she calls the "Peace-cup." On her death bed she cried out: "Fire, O! Fire, O!, Fire."

The second tract consists of the disclosures contained in the obeah-book of a dead obeah-man named John Nugent who had hidden the book in a cave-hole. He professes to have killed a man for cutting a bunch of plantain off his father's plantation; to have killed another man for a fee of twenty-five pounds; to have put a frog in a woman's womb and made her carry it for two years; to have received eighteen pounds and ten shillings for cutting the nose and teeth of a woman; to have killed her husband for another woman who gave him her body in payment; to have charged fifteen pounds for killing another man, but as three pounds were not paid he let the man off, "but the ghost still blow on him and he don't get over as yet."

The third tract purports to be the confession of "Old George Elleth," a native of Hampton Road in Porus. His father and his grandfather had been famous obeah-men before him. It is his claim to have killed 241 persons and to have "put 655 persons to suffer." According to his testimony, "Suck River is a little Hell below"; "Kendall, that dreadful place, the people run to me day and night, I was working for that place twenty years; in that district I play hell"; "Watson Gate at the cross road of evil deeds, the people around are like bitter weeds, there are nine obeah-men in that place, no young man can make a rise there." He asserts that people went to church and "call God's name in vain" and then on the way back call to him for obeah.

Another tract on page 56 of the Scrap Book declares how Richard Daly consults about killing an old man for his money. The obeah-man sends him to fill a bottle from an old stagnant pool. The old man dies. Daly further confesses before his death to several other murders, and to a friend who comes to offer prayers at his death-bed, he says: "Go to hell," and drives him out. He declares that he sees a gulf and asks for his mule to ride across.

Page 57 of this same Scrap Book contains still another tract which tells how Peter was a vicious obeah-man with a very loose and obscene tongue. He is said to have killed many people and to have been killed himself by the overflow from a cup of poison which he had been preparing for another.

These cases from the Scrap Book are for the most part workings of real obeah, in marked contrast with the examples of recent occurrences to be mentioned shortly. Daniel Hart, in striving "to make goods sell better in the market," does display a myalistic tendency, but even he is habitually true to form in his obeah-practice. The objective is almost invariably harmful or vindictive.

As a general rule such cases as are brought to trial under the Obeah Law, which does not distinguish between obeah and myalism, are usually instances of applied magic, and that too of the "white" variety.

It would be a difficult matter to prosecute for real obeah. Even a clear case with serious consequences would have to rely almost entirely on circumstantial evidence. No one would dare take the witness-stand against an obeah-man charged with grave misconduct. Sooner or later he would have to pay the penalty for incurring the enmity of the servant of the Devil.

In his real professional practice, the obeah-man to-day is as secretive as ever. He has a wholesome respect for British Colonial administration of the law. He will take his chances removing duppies, helping in market or Court and even further the interests of lovers--all of which is merely applied magic.--It is simply a gamble with him. If caught, he pays the price, and returns to his trade and adds a little to his next fees to recoup his losses or as a balm for his injured feelings. But when it comes to real obeah, he will take good care to assure himself of inviolable secrecy as he will never risk having a capital offence proved against him. Hence it is that most of the cases that are aired in Court must be regarded only as applied magic, and usually of a most amateurish type, as a means of livelihood, and characterized in great part by imposition and pretence.

One has only to pick up a newspaper file in Jamaica of any period at all, to realize the enduring prevalence of such practices. Thus on the occasion of my last visit to Jamaica in the Summer of 1931, I noted down the following cases as reported in The Daily Gleaner of Kingston, and I do not imagine that I was so observant that none escaped my notice.

June 10, 1931:--"Obeahman Given 3 Months Hard Labour in Whithorn R. M. Court". Charles Slater pleaded guilty "to a charge of practising obeah in the St. Leonard's District of Westmoreland on Wednesday the 20th May, 1931."

June 23, 1931:--"Ganja and Obeah Case at Spanish-Town To-day." George Sykes of Bog Walk is charged with having ganja in his possession and also with having implements for practising obeah.

July 8, 1931:--"Three Men Sentenced to 3 Months Each for Practising Obeah." Case at Chapelton, July 2nd.

July 11, 1931:--"Obeahman Sentenced to Prison for 6 Months." In the Kingston R. M. Court (on July 9th) James Thomas.

August 4,1931--"Worked Black Art: 70-yr. Old

Man Fined £15. Joseph Reid Found Guilty of Charge in Whithorn R. M. Court."

August 8, 1931:--"Charged at Richmond for Practising Obeah." Thomas Steward accused of working Obeah at "Big Gut" on Monday, 27th July.

August 28, 1931:--"Obeahman Fined £25 in Linstead Court." Robert Watson of Bog Walk.

August 31, 1931:--"Jamaican Obeahman in British Honduras to Be Deported Home. Alexander Brown Practised Deception on Countrymen And Sent to Serve Sentence. 7 Yrs. Hard Labour. Case Heard by Acting Chief Justice and Jamaican Jury in Colony." Sentenced in Belize to seven years' imprisonment in British Honduras, at the expiration of which he was to be deported to Jamaica.

Since then I have watched the papers from Jamaica that have reached me from time to time, and the regular recurrence of similar items are to be noticed. Thus The Daily Gleaner for January 11, 1933 gives considerable display to one such case: "Claims to Be Spiritualist, Fined £10 on Obeah Charge. Mrs. Beatrice Hanson Brought Before R. M. For Kingston Yesterday. The Defence Set Up. Magistrate's Decision. Defendant Is Given Time to Pay The Fine." The defence was made by Mrs. Hanson that she was a certified Spiritualist. "She was a clairvoyant medium, which meant one could hear something without seeing the object before him or her. It meant also auto-suggestion. She was taught by a pupil of Sir Conan Doyle. She acted on the principle of 'mind over matter.'" His Honour Mr. Bertram B. Burrowes, the presiding Magistrate, in giving the decision in the case, replied "that whatever obeah was originally, what he knew was that it was well defined in the Jamaica Laws. In that case, the particular section which struck him was that which was defined as follows: 'Any person who pretends to use occult powers or means to gain.'" He claimed that since "she said she used clairvoyancy, which meant to see clearly, her ability to see certain things, admitted the offence. He had found that what she did came within the meaning of the Law, and he found her guilty of the offence."

The following further examples are all taken from The Daily Gleaner.

September 1, 1933:--Costs Woman £26 17/ to Take 'Ghosts' Off Man. Spirit of 'Coolie' Variety, 'Was Keeping Back A Husband From Doing Business.'" In the Kingston Police Court, Ambrosene Allen was convicted of imposing on Ada Bogle. "The process of ghost-ridding included drinking some rum neat, giving an alleged and invisible ghost some to drink, anointing the face with oils, sundry blowing of powders, lighting of candles, etc."

November 10, 1933:--"Held on Charge of Practising Obeah." Clifford Johnson is arraigned before the Kingston R. M. Court, accused of having "told a woman that another member of the gentler sex had set a 'ghost' on her to take away her lover who would soon transfer his affections, Johnson, it is further alleged, told the woman that he could help her to stave off the 'evil spirit' which was going to torture her and would eventually cause her death."

November 24, 1933:--Here appears the same heading "Held on Charge of Practising Obeah." But this time it is Vitelleus Brown who is before the Resident Magistrate of Kingston. He has attributed a swollen knee to obeah by saying that some one "had set hand" on the victim whom he offers to cure for the sum of three pounds.

November 25, 1933:--"Man Charged with Practising Obeah." Alexander Brown had been approached by a man and woman who claimed to be sick. After examining them, he "informed the woman that a ghost was on her and that it was a policeman who had put the evil spirit on her. He demanded, it is further stated, a fee of three pounds to 'take off the duppy.'"

December 4, 1933:--"Arrested on Charge of Practising Obeah: Alleged Consultant." At Bog Walk it is alleged that Henry Francis "was caught red handed to-day practising obeah."

December 6, 1933:--"Mysterious Slips of Paper Found on Men Held by Police. 'I Breathe Upon Thee The Drops Of Blood I Took From Thy Soul' Etc. They Say." These mysterious slips of paper it is recorded have been "found by the police in the pockets of at least three men arrested in recent times. It is evident that some Charmer is at work distributing these bits of manuscript to afford protection to his clients." Now James Adolphus Turner is caught as a thief and on his person is found a slip bearing this inscription: "I, James Adolphus Turner breathe upon thee the drops of blood I took from thy Soul; the first out of thine heart; the second out of thy liver; and the third out of thy vital powers. And with this I deprive thee of the strength of thy manliness. Amen."

December 9, 1933:--"No Deception Practised by Faith Healer." Florence Sur, a faith healer, was arraigned for practising medicine, and acquitted by the Resident Magistrate who implies in his decision that she might be successfully prosecuted under the Obeah Law.

December 14, 1933:--Here we find three distinct cases of obeah in different parts of the island. "2 Held on Charge of Practising Obeah" introduces a case at Llandewey against Timothy Jackson, alias Stanley Reynolds, who has proposed to a woman that "he would so 'fix' her, that she would not fall out with her employer." "Held on Charge Under Obeah Law" regards Henrietta Wiles of Kingston where she offers to restore to a client a lost-job. But the principal case of the day bears the headlines: "Six Months for Obeahman: Case Tried at Spanish Tn. Man Who Pretended To Be Able To Keep Away Ghosts From A Woman." David Simon of Thompson Pen district is convicted of contracting to remove the duppies who are supposed to be annoying Ada Bogle, her "house was being stoned, the windows scratched, and the doors pushed by ghosts." It was to be his task to "drive away the ghosts."

December 15, 1933:--"To Serve 6 Months for Practising Obeah." This is the trial of Timothy Jackson, at Llandewey, referred to yesterday.

December 17, 1933:--Two separate cases.

"Arrested on Charge of Practising Obeah" refers to Sophie Wallace who has offered to remove a ghost from Maud Wilson, which it is asserted has been put on her by the wife of the "friend" who accompanies her. "Woman Given Six Months for Working Obeah" relates how Viola Phillips for a consideration undertook to give help in a Court case.

December 2 1, 1933:--"12 Months Hard and 12 Lashes with 'Cat' for Obeah Worker." Michael Ferguson, in the Half-Way Tree Court House is convicted of another "Get-Back-job" imposture with the usual implications of the removal of ghosts or duppies which have been "set."

January 5, 1934:--"Faces Court on Obeah Charge." Ivan O. Baker of Berryvale district, is before the R. M. Court at May Pen on a charge of practising obeah.

January 9, 1934:--"Mechanic Fined £12 10/ on Charge of Practising Obeah. 'Used His Brains To Exploit On Ignorant People.'" George Washington Pitt who was convicted of practising obeah had boasted: "He could cure, he could kill, and he could give jobs."

January 12, 1934:--"Obeah Charge Fails." Henrietta Wiles who was referred to on December 14th when brought to trial was acquitted.

January 13, 1934:--"Held on Charge of Practising Obeah." Oscar McFarlane is always having trouble with his motor car and professes to believe that "someone had done something to 'keep him down.'" And accordingly Agatha Connell, the defendant, "told McFarlane that she would be able to 'fix him up.'" Her attempt to do so leads to her arrest.

January 30, 1934:--This time three cases are reported. "Four Months Term for Hanover Obeahman." At Lucea, Ebernezer Clarke is convicted of imposing on Newton Brown, a shoemaker at Mount Pleasant, who reports having been informed by Clarke that "Duppy is on me and on my shop." He is to receive a "dealing stick" that is to be kept in his shop "to keep away the duppy." "Six Months for Man Who Practised the Black Art." In the Sandy Bay R. M. Court, Leonard Weakley, of Cold Spring is convicted. What is of particular interest here is that the following books were found in his house: "The Sixth and Seventh Books of Moses; The Albertus Magnus or the White and Black Arts for Men and Beasts; The Great Book of Black Magic; The Book of Magical Art Hindoo Magic and Indian Occultism"; a fact that would indicate that we are not here dealing with obeah in any sense of the word but a practice of magic similar to that found in St. Lucia in the case of the Monchy Murder.

Meanwhile "One Conviction in Obeah Case Is Quashed" regards the appeal from the conviction of Viola Phillips which was recorded under date of December 17, 1933. The Appeal prevailed on the ground that the evidence on which the conviction had been secured was insufficient. In connexion with this case it would be well to notice an argument advanced by

Mr. N. W. Manley, K.C., in behalf of the appellant, to the effect "that it was necessary, in order to constitute obeah, not merely that a person should do something utterly foolish and futile on a pretence that it would accomplish something, but that they should definitely use occult means or pretend to supernatural powers. The use of the word 'pretend' was, he supposed, that the framers of the statute did not believe that there was any such thing. Obeah was connected with a pretence to invoke occult or supernatural powers. It bore, he supposed, some resemblance to what used to be considered witchcraft or necromancy. Necromancy was a branch of occult power, but in his submission many cases that might be considered a mere obtaining of money by false pretences were being treated as obeah. If the powers one professed were considered to arise from oneself and not from any supernatural thing one was not practising obeah. There was no representation that the process was supernatural."

Mr. Manley would have been interested in the discussion on witchcraft which took place at the recent Congrès International des Sciences Anthropologiques et Ethnologiques in London. Frank Hulme Melland, speaking from an experience of more than a quarter of a century in Northern Rhodesia where he had held many positions as Native Commissioner and Magistrate, called attention to the fact that the law relating to witchcraft in British African colonies and dependencies started with the fundamental idea that witchcraft being an "impossibility" was non-existent, and despite this basic assumption, enactment after enactment was promulgated against "what does not exist" to the endless confusion of the native mind. It was Mr. Melland's contention regarding witchcraft in general: "It is necessary to study this subject from the point of view of those who live in fear of witchcraft, because only in this way can we hope effectively to eradicate the belief and the fear which it engenders. Even if witchcraft be nonexistent the belief in it is real. Moreover, while African primitive religions are local, centred in the home-district, witchcraft, in native eyes, is universal, and its terrors follow the native when away from his home, deprived of such help as he feels his ancestral spirits might afford him, which affords exceptional opportunities for the 'quack' witchdoctor. Our present official attitude and our law seem to the African unjustified and unjust, incomprehensible and unreasonable. This must necessarily detrimentally affect relations between governors and governed and, apart from the legal aspect, it is not in accordance with the equitable idea that laws should be in the interests and by the consent of the governed. Africans feel that they must have some protection against this power of evil. We do not provide it, and we therefore drive them to have recourse to the men whom we prescribe as criminals: the witchdoctors." By witchdoctor here is meant not the sorcerer but his official antagonist, what we technically understand to be the myal-man as distinct from the obeah-man.

According to Mr. Melland: "Penal legislation in witchcraft matters is ethically unsound and politically has proved demonstrably harmful. In effect we have said to the African: 'You are a foolish people, and we know better.' It is rather smug, and has proved singularly ineffective. Practically the whole population believes that every one can be, and at any moment may be, bewitched." After citing a typical case, he added: "Many who used to believe that this sort of thing was dying out now admit they were wrong."

Professor L. S. B. Leakey of Cambridge University who represented Kenya in the discussion was equally outspoken, and outlined his observations in the Official Program as follows: "Wherever the white man goes in Africa he finds himself sooner or later up against some aspect of witchcraft, and whether he is missionary or Government official or trader he cannot avoid giving expression to his views on the subject. The reactions of the African native to the various European attitudes to witchcraft are full of interest, and can teach us a lot, and the best way to find out what the African thinks about the white man's attitude is to listen to conversations between Africans upon the subject. This I have often had opportunity to do. What has always struck me most is that the African considers us to be the most illogical people living, and I must say he is not unreasonable in thinking so, for when the statements and actions of white men concerning witchcraft are looked at from the black man's point of view, nothing could be more absurd and illogical. To the African the European (a) on the one hand himself practises witchcraft in many forms; (b) attacks witch-craft where he finds it being practised by black men; (c) says it is wrong for Africans to punish members of their community whom they find practising black magic; (d) refuses to punish people who are accused of having killed people by witchcraft, on the ground that this is not possible and therefore cannot have been done; (e) denies the existence or possibility of doing things by means of witchcraft, and yet does them himself; (f) not only attacks black man's witchcraft, but also tries to prevent Africans from using white man's witchcraft. In short, to the African the attitude of white men to witchcraft is incompre-hensible, illogical and selfish, besides being unutterably foolish."

According to Doctor Leakey, the native's statement of mind is summed up in the statement: "They tell us that there is no need to be frightened and yet they use their own magic all the time." The clinical thermometer, the taking of blood tests and fingerprints, gramophones, wireless and the camera are all regarded by the native as white man's magic, and it is the general conclusion of the Africans that the whites are seeking a monopoly of magic for themselves.

Among educated Jamaicans, I fear, there is also just a little lack of appreciation regarding the real attitude of the "bush" towards witchcraft. The law may assume the impossibility of the fact and stress the pretense at supernatural power, as constituting the offence, as Mr. Manley states. But it is the conviction of the practitioners of obeah that the obeah-man can and does control a super-human influence that may destroy life itself without any physical contacts, and further that this projection of power does not arise, as Mr. Manley suggests, from the obeah-man himself. For the obeah-man is merely an agent of the Evil One who really produces the effect desired in virtue of the incantation of the devotee and the acceptance of the client, both of whom are placing themselves in communication with him with full reliance on his co-operation. The obeah. man only directs the necessary power or force which ultimately comes from the Author of Evil.

After this lengthy digression, let us return to the files of The Daily Gleaner.

February 1, 1934:--"Held on Charge of Practising Medicine as Well as Obeah." This regards Robert Giscombe in Kingston.

February 5, 1934:--"Convicted in May Pen Court on Charge of Practising Obeah." Ivanhoe Baker had sold a ring to Ada Bogle to keep a ghost off her. More will be said shortly about this type of ring, but it should be remarked that in this case again we find mention of a book entitled, 6th. and 7th. Books of Moses with other works on Astrology and Personal Magnetism.

February 6, 1934:--"Held on Obeah Charge, Annotto Bay." Alexander Decton is accused of offering for seven pounds, two shillings, to remove an obnoxious party. He "would either kill or run him away from the property." This savours of real obeah.

February 15, 1934:--"Held by Police on Obeah Charge." Peter Robinson is accused of offering to protect a woman from her enemies.

March 2, 1934:--"Alleged Revivalist and Healer Before Court on 2 Charges. Annie Harvey And Her Husband Charged With Practising Obeah And Medicine For Gain." In this case the Island Chemist is called in to give evidence regarding the forty articles exhibited.

March 16, 1934:--"Alexander Brown to Serve 12 Months for Practising Obeah. Acting R. M. for City Says He Proposes to Deal Severely with Those Found Guilty."--"Alexander Brown entered a plea of guilty to an information charging him with practising obeah." In passing sentence, His Honour said: "Brown your solicitor has made a very eloquent plea for you, but I cannot lose sight of the fact that there is far too much belief in obeah in this country, and this has been the cause of its insistent practise by you and others like you. So far as I am concerned, I intend to treat anyone found guilty by me with the utmost severity. In spite of all that has been urged on your behalf by Mr. Wynter I cannot be lenient with you, and so you will have to go and serve a term of twelve months with hard labour and you will also receive twelve lashes of the cat-o-nine."

March 31, 1934:--"Man and Wife Are Convicted on Charge of Working Obeah." This is the sequel of the case of Annie Harvey and her husband mentioned on March 2, 1934.

April 6, 1934:--"Obeah Case Dismissed by Kingston R. M. Accomplice Testifies How Peter

Robinson Said He Could Assist Her. 'Ghost Set on Her' Position Of Bed Changed To Confuse Spirit: Cuttings of Nails, Hair And Garments." The account states: "The ground for Robinson's dismissal, before the prosecution closed, was no doubt that the person chiefly concerned in the matter, a woman named Operline Dwyer, was admittedly an accomplice whose testimony was. not corroborated, but in vital issues, contradicted by a man, Phillibert Dunkley, who set up the police to lay a trap for Robinson." In the course of the examination His Honour asked a witness: "Then you believe in obeah?" which immediately caused laughter only to draw from His Honour the remark: "And so do 70 or 80 per cent of those laughing at the back of the Court." Which goes to confirm the wide-spread belief in the superstition.

April 9, 1934:--"Father and Daughter Held as Obeah Workers in the Metropolis." James Lee and his daughter Olive are accused of having told a client "that another woman had taken away her 'gentleman' and was trying to injure her. The woman said that she would like to get back the 'gentleman' and to prevent the other woman from injuring her. The defendants agreed to do the 'job' and it is alleged bargained with her."

One of the features in many of these cases is that the practitioner of obeah is reported as "speaking in an unknown tongue," which is supposedly a regular characteristic of the practice. It should further be remarked how the great majority of the citations refer to legal proceedings in Kingston or the principal towns of the island. There are comparatively few trials for what is going on in the "bush."

One of the latest institutions of applied magic is known as the obi-ring, to which reference was made in the case of Ivanhoe Baker as cited in The Daily Gleaner of February 5, 1934. I can find no mention of it in any book to which I have had access which leads me to the conclusion that it is of comparatively recent origin. During my own stay on Jamaica I was never able to trace the ring itself, but since my return a captured obi-ring was sent to me. In appearance it is an ordinary signet ring made of brass, or at best cheaply plated, such as usually sells for a few shillings. On the inside a hole has been drilled and this serves as a receptacle for a little charm that looks like the head of a very tiny rivet, in which the "medicine" is contained.

In the particular case connected with the ring sent to me, a woman had been ailing for some time when she was approached by an obeah-man who offered to cure her by means of this ring which was to cost one pound. The terms were accepted and the patient rapidly recovered her health. However, circumstances in the case lead me to believe that the same obeah-man had already administered poison with the connivance of the woman's cook and the receptacle in the ring contained the antidote which was absorbed through the skin and counteracted against the poison. In this supposition the ring should be called not an obi-ring but a myal-ring. But as has been said so often, the two functions are now included in the practice of the obeah-man.

POPULAR BELIEF IN GHOSTS

SR HENRY HESKETH JOUDOU BELL, who recently retired as Governor of Mauritius, spent many years in the British Colonial Service in the West Indies, where he began his career in 1882.

Writing of his experiences in Granada and describing Quashie's "love for and unshaken belief in the uncanny" with consequent "profound faith in the existence of" ghosts, or as they are called in the West Indies, "jumbies" or duppies, Sir Hesketh relates the following experience of his own.

"I rented for some time a place rejoicing in the name of 'Paradise.' It was in rather a lonely situation and had no near neighbours. On account of the reputation the house bore, namely, of being haunted by troops of jumbies, it was with the greatest difficulty that I could induce a groom to sleep in the place, and only succeeded in getting one to stay by allowing him to sleep on the mat outside my bedroom door.

"I certainly used to hear, during the night, all sorts of peculiar noises and gruesome sounds, but the house, being an old one, was infested by rats, and to the gambols of these gentry I ascribed the uncanny noises.

"The groom, however, emphatically denied the culpability of the rats, and insisted on blaming the ghosts for the noise. Over and over he would tell me that he would have to leave the work, as 'De jumbies does trouble me too much,' and frequently, in the middle of the night, I would wake up with a start, hearing the boy yelling out to me. 'What on earth is the matter, you----?' I would call out in exasperation, only to receive every time the same answer about the jumbies. 'Just listen, sah, dey lighting matches all round the house.' I certainly could hear sounds as of matches being drawn, but that was all, and the other sounds could be put down to the hats that infested the place.

"One night, however, I was really horribly alarmed, and experienced a good share of the feelings engendered by reading some of Edgar Poe's ghastly tales. I was quite alone in the house and had given the boy leave to sleep out for the night. I went to bed as usual and was awakened after a few hours' sleep by some sound or other. The wind was pretty high, and whistled mournfully through the trees. I had not had a pleasant dream, and awakened with a feeling of uneasiness, while my thoughts reverted to unpleasant ideas and some gruesome tales I had read the day before.

"The mournful cry of an owl resounded from time to time, and it seemed to me the rats and bats seemed unusually restive and ghostlike. Heavens! what was that rustling sound just outside beneath the window? It sounded like a footfall. There it is again! Gracious! I'd swear that was the clank of iron, it sounded like fetters! A cold perspiration broke over me, my hair was quite damp. I held my breath to catch the slightest sound. Again I heard the clank of the chain, now close beneath the window. All the blood-curdling stories of fettered ghosts I had ever read flew through my brain. The moon shed fitful rays from behind a cloud and enabled me to distinguish objects. Again the clank and a rustle.

"Do all I could, I could not tear my eyes away from the window, and every second I expected and dreaded to see a cold, white face with gleaming eyes pressed against the window pane. I could stand it no longer, and don't know what I was about to do, when an awful sound broke the ghostly stillness of the night. 'Hee Haw! Hee Haw!' 'Twas the other donkey loose outside. Never had I thought there was such enchantment in a donkey's bray, never so sweet a sound had I ever heard, nor one so full of comforting melody. Once more I was at peace, and, calling myself some inelegant names, I turned on my other side and slept till morning."

No doubt, many a ghost-story in Jamaica may be as easily explained away by the incredulous visitor to the island, but certainly neither he nor anyone else will be able to shake the superstitious belief of the "bush" in the active agency of spiritual entities that exerts a really extraordinary influence on the daily life of practically every Negro whether he is in the West Indies or elsewhere.

Unquestionably, many a hair-raising experience is wrought with terrors that have their sole foundation in hysteria or imaginative fear as a consequence of an attack of nerves, and one must be careful about the uncritical acceptance of every story told, particularly if it is of the hear-say variety.

On the other hand, it has been my experience, that the seasoned missionary is naturally so sceptical on these matters that his tendency is to sift all evidence and try to find a normal explanation for everything and as a general rule his quest is not in vain.

Thus the very next district to my own was at one time in charge of a missionary who suddenly found that his alarm-clock had developed a strange propensity. He would leave it on the table and at his return find it on the floor under the table. Sometimes he was awakened at night by the clock's insistence on returning to the floor. Circumstances precluded all possibility of the perpetration of a practical joke--he was alone in the house. Finally, one day in broad daylight, while in an adjoining room, he heard the clock crash to the floor from the table. This started a serious investigation. The clock was an old one and would run only when placed on its back. After due experiment and long observation, it was found that the unwinding of the main-spring caused the key at the back to revolve, and as the clock was resting on it, a slow but perceptible movement was noticeable which made it gradually edge off the table. Thus another perfectly good ghost story was spoiled.

Later the same missionary was able to trace a troublesome knocking that had disturbed a household at all hours of the night, to an inoffensive dog which in the customary fashion of easing the annoyance of fleas had caused the mysterious disturbance.

These instances are cited merely as illustration of the usual calm and determined attitude of those who are habituated to the "bush" and who necessarily cannot afford to let their nerves run away with them. They instinctively seek to find a normal explanation for the phenomena that would otherwise destroy their peace of mind.

What, then, am I to think of the accounts that have reached me from seasoned missionaries and other equally reliable wit-nesses, giving me such personal experiences as have defied their every effort at explanation by natural causes? Several such signed statements are before me on my desk. The writers generously give me permission to use the facts but naturally ask to be spared undue publicity. I can appreciate their feeling as it has taken me a quarter of a century to find enough courage to state openly my own views and experiences. Personally I know each witness and can vouch for his sincerity and soundness of judgment. Let me outline a few cases. Some of these incidents are of comparatively recent occurrence, others happened as much as thirty years ago or more. I have gathered them as I could pick them up. But in every case I have obtained the account in writing and over the narrator's signature.

Here we have an incident in Kingston. A man is annoyed by his dead brother who "appeared to him several times over his bed and at eleven o'clock in the morning, looking just as he did when he was in the coffin, but no words were uttered." Two ordinary blessings of the house have no effect. The apparition continues on unchecked. A special blessing is employed and the spectre comes no more. To all appearances, the harassed man is sane and normal. If it is only a delusion, it has so taken hold of the unfortunate that he is certainly convinced of its reality.

Also in Kingston we have a distracted woman and her children who are almost driven mad by the repeated apparition of a man in their house who disappears as soon as accosted. The account continues: "Upon going to the house and questioning the woman, what struck me as sincere and genuine was that the woman and especially the son of about ten years were really terrified, so much so that I was concerned for the boy lest he become deranged by fear. There was no fooling about his story, and no contradictions in it. I made him tell me the details, and show me the places where he stood and where the man was, in the repeated apparitions. I blessed the house and warned the mother to keep the boy's mind off the whole affair. They were bothered once or twice again and then the trouble disappeared. At least the people were sincere in their fear. There was no request for money or material aid. Certainly the little boy was living in an agony of terror. The mother was a very nervous person and I suspected her for a while of terrorizing the boy.

But I found out that to them, at least, it was real. Who can say, whether it was so or not?"

Out in Westmoreland we encounter the conviction that unless a child of four is "properly" buried, the ghost will come back and haunt the home.

Up in the Dry Harbour Mountains, an unbaptized boy is "troubled with spirits" and his father seeks the help of the priest who writes: "I started out with the boy's father and tramped through the mountains until I wondered whether a white man had ever penetrated into that part of Jamaica before. After a long climb, we at last reached the hut. Much to my amazement I found the sick boy sitting on a high home-made bed. He looked far stronger and more healthy than myself with apparently nothing wrong with him. When I questioned him, he gave me the same story as his father had given me, that he was troubled with spirits. As he lived so far away from civilization, I gave him what instruction was necessary and baptized him. A few days later I heard that the boy had died almost immediately after my departure."

Now we have the example of an unfortunate leper who "during his sickness used to be taken up and thrown around the room by some unknown spirit."

From another part of the island this comes to us: "A woman sent for me to come and bless her house for the reason that she and her daughter were annoyed by evil spirits. I went and first questioned her on the nature of the molestation. Her first complaint was that the malignant spirits 'rattled the shutters.' 'But that could be the wind,' I suggested. 'But den dey trow stones in der window.' 'Some boys plaguing you.' She was visibly annoyed at my difficulty to be convinced. 'Fader, I gwine tell you der whole trute.

My daughter and me in bed and dey empty der pitcher of water ober us.'"

Here is a somewhat longer account in the very words of the narrator. "The following is the story told me by a black boy at X. He was lodged by a woman who owns and lives in a haunted house. His bed was placed across the floor in front of the door leading to the woman's bedroom. Though he slept there for some time, he saw something only once, but he often heard footsteps walking up and down the front steps. He swears to the truth of these footsteps and also to the following. One night he awoke and saw a woman standing above him. She stood there for a time while he looked at her. She said never a word and finally turned and went out. He gathered the impression that she wanted to get into the bedroom but his presence had stopped her.

"The next day I spoke with the woman who owns the house. She says that she used to see ghosts when she was a little girl but was never afraid because they never harmed her, but just appeared to her. That stopped and she had never any more experiences with the supposedly preternatural until eight years ago, she is now about forty-five years old.

"She had bought a house and was living there alone. One night as she entered her home, something took her by the arm and led her into the house and then departed. She gathered it was a person. This was her first experience. From that time to this day, she has been constantly frightened by noises of various kinds and of a haunting character but mainly by footsteps climbing the stairs. This is always at night, never in the daytime.

Among others which she did not have time to tell me, these were her special experiences.

"One night she woke up and heard footsteps coming to her door, in through the door and across to a washstand which stood in the way to her bed. She sat up, the ghost splashed in her wash basin and then flicked her face with water. She screamed and the ghost departed. She touched the drops of water on her face and wiped them off.

"Another night, she had a woman sleep with her to whom she told nothing of the haunted character of the house. The woman in the morning, in great fright, told her the same thing had happened to her, the flicking of the water, and refused to sleep in the house with her again.

"Still another night, and this has happened a number of times, she woke up from sleep, although not roused by noises. She turned over on her side and screamed with fright, for she had turned over on an, other body. It disappeared and she went to sleep again. Sometimes she is awakened by a suffocating feeling and finds something pressing down on her shoulders and body and enveloping her.

"Another night footsteps came across the floor; she sat up in bed; the ghost approached and gave her a terrific blow in the abdomen. Since that time she has suffered from a fiery internal fever which no doctor on the island seems to be able to cure although she has seen many of them.

"Whenever she screams, the ghost departs. She cannot see the ghost but only hears it and feels it.

Asked if she knew any obeah-man, she said that she didn't, but if she did, she would go to him if he could help her.

"Apparently the ghost is afraid of men. For, when she has a boy sleeping in the house she is not disturbed. But when a woman is with her the ghost bothers her as usual.

"I believe there is something in her story. She was so certain of the details, and there are a number of people who support her testimony. She vowed several times that she was telling the truth and is tortured by the ghost and she wants to sell a house on which she has spent money and energy in making it comfortable for herself."

Whatever may be thought concerning the physical actuality of these various incidents, even if the credibility of the witnesses should be called into question by some, this much is certain, that to those unfortunates who went through the experiences they were of terrifying reality; and no amount of explanation or argument to the contrary would shake their belief that they were victims of some spiritual force, call it duppy, shadow or any other name you please.

This does not mean that they regard the agent, whatever it may be, as in any way diabolical. Far from it. According to "bush" ideas concerning the human composite of body and soul, there are qualities in the spiritual element of man that enables it under particular circumstances to produce certain extrinsic phenomena and to exercise a powerful influence for good or evil as regards others, occasionally here in life but especially after death when it is freed from the trammels of the body. In other words, the operations of duppy and shadow are not to be regarded in themselves as supernatural but purely natural since there is no intervention of a spiritual force outside themselves, except perhaps as happens in the case of the obeah-man, when he undertakes the control and use of these natural forces of the human soul. And even then, it is really a supernatural use of a natural force that is understood by the "bush" psychology.

Be that as it may, whether we regard them as psychic phenomena or merely as popular superstitions, two elements are to be carefully distinguished in Jamaica, the duppy and the shadow. It was once commonly the belief that the obeah-man could catch the shadows of living people and imprison them in a silk-cotton tree, with the consequence that the victim of the lost shadow pined away and died unless the myal-man undid the mischief by releasing the shadow and returning it to its owner. So, too, while the obeah-man might "set duppies" on people for their endless annoyance, the myal-man could free them from their spectral tormenters. To differentiate properly these two elements, the shadow and the duppy, we must go back to the Ashanti from whom they were originally brought to Jamaica in the days of slavery.

Captain Rattray tells us: "The Ashanti use a number of names translated into English by the words soul or spirit or ghost." He then goes on to define the various terms employed. Thus he writes: Saman is "a ghost, an apparition, a spectre; this term is never applied to a living person or to anything inherent in a living person. It is objective and is the form which the dead are sometimes seen to take, when visible on earth, and in it they go about in the asaman or samandow (the place of ghosts); samanpow is the 'thicket of ghosts'; samanfo, the ghosts, i.e. spirits of ancestors. The word has no connexion whatever with any kind of soul." Elsewhere Captain Rattray asserts: "A saman is in the form and shape of the mortal body and has all its senses, or some at any rate, and feels hunger and thirst." It is further explained by the same author that according to Ashanti belief, when a man dies, his spirit or saman immediately appears before the Supreme Being, or as some think, before a subordinate deity, and ascertains whether it is to go to the spirit world below or haunt the earth for a time, if not permanently. He adds: "Such a spirit then becomes 'a wait-about, wait-about spirit . . . . . . It does not seem," he says, "to have much power for harm, and is shy generally, and confines itself to frightening people. The saman, whose stay on earth has been only ordained to last until his destiny has been fulfilled, eventually disappears to the world where all spirits live." It is also observed that "food is constantly placed aside" for the saman, and that when they are visible to the human eye they are "reported generally as being white or dressed in white." This is the Jamaica duppy in every detail.

The Reverend R. Thomas Banbury describing Jamaica of his day, expressed the opinion: "The word duppy appears to be a corruption of doorpeep, something peeping through the keyhole." Personally I am absolutely opposed to this derivation of the word duppy, but as far as I can determine it is the only one that has been suggested in Jamaica. Doctor Werner, writing to me, ascribed the origin to Dupe, "ghost" in the "Bube" language of the southern and eastern parts of the island of Fernando Poo. But while the cultural influence of the Ashanti in Jamaica is paramount, there is no indication of influence from the Fernando Poo group of slaves. Since, then, Ashanti terminology has so dominated everything Jamaican, it is but reasonable to turn to the Ashanti again when seeking further elucidation of Jamaican problems. As a matter of fact we find in Ashanti the word dupon signifying "the broad and large part of the root of certain trees above ground, projecting like a buttress from the low part of the trunk," and it gives reference to the odum, or silk-cotton tree. Now it is precisely among these buttressed roots of the silk-cotton tree that the duppies in Jamaica are supposed to reside, and I cannot help feeling that either the word duppy is derived from dupon, or possibly the latter has acquired its name from the duppies who frequent the roots.

Mr. Banbury further states: "Duppies are ghosts which are supposed to appear to persons in this country termed foyeyed or gifted with second sight. It is commonly believed that departed souls return to earth, haunt their habitations, or remain near where their bodies are buried. These eat and drink like living beings and are displeased when the inmates of houses leave nothing for them in the house at nights. For this reason the superstitious are known to let food remain on the table for the duppies." He further observes: "The duppies generally appear in their grave clothes."

While the duppies are primarily spiritual entities, they unquestionably include a material element in their composition. On occasions of deaths in the neighbourhood, especially if by violence, good care is taken at night to plug up every crack and crevice in the hovels, "to keep the duppies out." In fact, when about a hundred unfortunates were drowned at Montego Bay during the hurricane of 1912, it was almost impossible to find a messenger to go on an errand that would keep him out after dark, the general excuse being, "Too many det (dead) round, sah!" Moreover, while Mr. Banbury maintained: "Duppies are believed to act the part of guardian angels to their friends and relatives," I certainly never met any Jamaican who was not averse to meeting the duppies of even those who had been nearest and dearest to him in life.

Father Emerick writes: "The usual meaning of the word duppy, when not taken in connexion with other superstitions, is the same as that of our word ghost. The Jamaica duppies, like our ghosts, retain an interest in the persons and the world they left behind, and seek intercommunication with them. But their interest is seldom, if ever, otherwise than selfish, or malicious, or vindictive. To be able to see and converse with duppies you must be a 'foyeyed,' that is a four-eyed, gifted with a second sight, by which you can see what is going on in the spirit world. For the foyeyed to see duppies it is not necessary for them, like the mediums in our modern spiritualism, to shut themselves up in a spirit cabinet or pass into a hypnotic sleep of any kind; they simply cannot help seeing the spirits when they are around. Like our ghosts, duppies amuse themselves by haunting houses, frightening people by slamming doors, upsetting chairs, drawing bed curtains, etc. They have a special attraction for untenanted houses and lonesome places. Haunted houses are common in the country and to be found even in the city."

Father Emerick goes on to relate the following personal experience. "One of the city duppy houses was a large two-storey house. When I was sent to Jamaica in 1895, to help Reverend Patrick Kelly, he was in the throes of resurrecting a school in this same building. Father Kelly and myself lived in this building, sleeping there during the night. This building was said to be haunted by the soul of a wealthy leper who died in it. Whether it was due to the dead leper or some other kind of a duppy, we had some curious duppy experiences. One night we were both disturbed by someone apparently coming to our door. About an hour or so after I had grabbed quickly the knob of my door to keep out the mysterious intruder, I heard Father Kelly calling out lustily from beyond a vacant room between us, asking me if I had come to his door."

Later the same author tells us: "But the Jamaica duppies do not limit their operations to haunting houses, but, like the fairies they like to wander about. On this account, according to duppy belief, you must not speak to unknown persons you meet in the road at night. You might make a mistake and address a duppy and be knocked by it." And again: "These duppy knockers not only knock people but they have a peculiar way of knocking in and about houses and making it very uncomfortable for those living in them. There was scarcely a district where these knocking duppies were not busy bothering some house."

The Jamaica duppy, then, for all practical purposes, may be regarded as substantially the same as our ghost, both as to its nature and its method of manifestation and annoyance.

As already mentioned, according to Ashanti acceptation, the "wait-about, wait-about spirit" is doomed to haunt the earth permanently. The name for such a spirit is osaman-twentwen which is explained by Christaller as "a departed spirit that is not admitted to the asaman, on account of his wickedness in his life-time, but must hover about behind the dwellings." Twen literally means "to wait" and the reduplicated form is an adverb signifying nimbly or cleverly.

In the Jamaica "bush" there is a similar belief that in the case of notoriously wicked individuals, their ghosts of duppies go about ordinarily in the form of a calf, with a piece of chain attached to the neck, as a warning of the consequences of evil-doing. These creatures are known popularly as "Rollen Calves," and they are thus described by Mr. Banbury.

"1 now advert to a curious superstition that is still rife in Jamaica that is, the belief in what are called Rollen Calves. These are a set of animals, or rather as it is believed, evil spirits in the shape of animals, which travel at nights, and are often seen by the people. There is hardly any of them but who will tell you that they have met with Rollen Calves in the dark. These creatures of transmigrated souls are seen in a variety of forms, like cats, dogs, hogs, goats, horses, bulls, etc., and are said to be most dangerous and inveterate when met in the feline form and of a black or brindled colour. A bit of chain is generally attached to their necks, which they carry with them from the infernal regions. People affirm that they often hear the rattle of the rollen calf's chain about their yard at nights, and listened to his battle with the dogs, who are its bitter enemies. They fly at it with precipitation and compel it to retreat when they encounter it. They are supposed to take up their abode in the daytime at the roots of cotton trees, bamboos, and in caves, as duppies do. But at such a time are not visible except to the foyeyed, or those that can see spirits.

"These creatures are also believed to be sometimes under an obeah spell, when they will attack people in the night, and obstinately dispute the path with them. They possess the extraordinary power of suddenly growing from the size of a cat or dog to that of a horse, or bull. The only way of getting rid of the infernal monster on such occasions, is to flog him with the left hand. He is exceedingly afraid of a tarred whip. Waggon men and others who affirm that they have encountered the roaring calf, declare that they have heard him cry out when flogged 'Me dead two time, oh,' (I am twice dead.) They are very fond of molasses, and for that reason are often seen at crop time about sugar estates at nights, seeking to satiate themselves with this article. For the same cause they have been known to follow the sugar wains, in the night, conveying sugar to the wharf. They are said to be fond of cattle, this occasions the breaking of the 'cow pen', the rollen calf getting in among the cattle, and causing terror."

In passing, Mr. Banbury illustrates his account with the following anecdote. "A man who is a member of the Church of a certain denomination, an educated and upright man, one whom I believe would not tell a lie, informed me that he was travelling late one night, the moon was shining brightly--when he came upon a very large black creature lying at full length across the road. No dog, he said, could have been so large. He made a lick at it with his stick in terror. The stick flew out of his hand, and he never saw where the beast went. He got home, and took in with fever and was ill for some time-no doubt from the fright. Of course, he set it down to have been one of these fabulous creatures of the night. His terrified imagination transformed what was most likely a large black dog into a Rollen Calf."

That Mr. Banbury regards the whole belief with absolute scepticism, is clearly evidenced. "I remember," he says, "one night riding on a mule very late, and dozing going along, when the mule made a leap on a sudden up a steep bank, from the road, and began to snort at a great rate working his ears backwards and forwards. Nor with all my efforts would he go down again. I was determined to find out the cause of his fright, I alighted, went down into the road, and saw a very curious-looking animal lying in the middle of the way, doubled up. I could not make out what it was at all. It had long woolly hair of a whitish colour. I gave it a sharp lick with my supple-jack, and up it sprang. I then saw by the light of the moon that it was a young ass. After going on a little further, I came upon the mother feeding. If there was ever a close resemblance to a Rollen Calf, that was one; and any superstitious person, without taking the trouble to examine it, would have set it down to be one. These circumstances in point prove most conclusively that 'Mr. Rollen' is nothing more than one of our domestic animals seen in the night; or an animal that is not generally met with, as was before hinted."

Mr. Banbury suggests that the word rollen does not signify rolling but roaring. Once again I must disagree with him. Never did I find any indication of such an interpretation in any part of the "bush." I am rather inclined to think that we have here one of the rare examples where rolling is used in the sense of wandering or roaming.

As regards the superstition itself, this belief in the Rollen Calf is rapidly dying out in Jamaica. The "bush" still talks about it, but in an incredulous sort of a way with an air of amused toleration. At least, that is the conclusion I drew from personal contacts in various parts of the island.

Entirely distinct from the saman or duppy or ghost, is the Ashanti sasa which according to Captain Rattray "is the invisible spiritual power of a person or an animal, which disturbs the mind of the living, or works a spell or mischief upon them, so that they suffer in various ways. Persons who are always taking life have to be particularly careful to guard against sasa influence, and it is among them that its action is mainly seen, e.g. among executioners, hunters, butchers, and as a later development--among sawyers--who cut down the great forest trees. The remorse that might drive the murderer in this country to confession or to suicide, the Ashanti would explain at once as the operation of the sasa of the murdered man upon his murderer. I have mentioned occasionally in the preceding pages of steps taken to avoid the vengeance of the sasa. The sasa is essentially the bad, revengeful, and hurtful element in a spirit; it is that part which at all costs must be 'laid' or rendered innocuous. The funeral rites . . . are really, I believe, the placating, appeasing, and the final speeding of a soul which may contain this very dangerous element in its composition."

This is substantially the shadow of Jamaica. However, as in the case of the duppy, we find a material element connected with the shadow in the general acceptation of the "bush." Further it should be noted in passing that at a Jamaica funeral, as will be seen later, at times the sasa or shadow is "laid" with as elaborate a ceremonial as happens among the Ashanti.

In connexion with what is known as the Apo Custom, an annual festival among the Ashanti, there is a lampooning liberty which is thus described to Captain Rattray "by the old high-priest of the god Ta Kese at Tekiman."--"You know that every one has a sunsum (soul) that may get hurt or knocked about or become sick, and so make the body ill. Very often, although there may be other causes, e.g. witchcraft, ill health is caused by the evil and the hate that another has in his head against you. Again, you too may have hatred in your head against another, because of something that person has done to you, and that, too, causes your sunsum to fret and become sick. Our forebears knew this to be the case, and so they ordained a time, once every year, when every man and woman, free man and slave, should have freedom to speak out just what was in their head, to tell their neighbours just what they thought of them and their actions, and not only their neighbours, but also the king or chief. When a man has spoken freely thus, he will feel his sunsum cool and quieted, and the sunsum of the other person against whom he has now freely spoken will be quieted also. The King of Ashanti may have killed your children, and you hate him. This had made him ill, and you ill, too; when you are allowed to say before his face what you think, you both benefit. That was why the King of Ashanti in ancient times, when he fell ill, would send for the Queen of Nkoranza to insult him, even though the time for the ceremony had not come round. It made him live longer and did him good."

1 sometimes wonder if this ceremony may not have given rise to the practice still in vogue in Jamaica of "throwing words at the moon?" You may tell the moon the most insulting things about a party within his hearing without being liable for libel, as you would be if you addressed the same words to your victim or to another person. Thus you in turn may be called "a tief" or "a

liar fee true," every word reaching you and those who are standing about, and yet if you ask the vilifier what he is saying, the answer will be: "Not you, sah, Him moon talk." It certainly "cools the sunsum" of the speaker who goes away contented and satisfied, though it must be confessed it has a far different effect on the object of the remarks. I speak from experience.

At all events, with the Ashanti it is believed that malignity towards another can physically affect the object of one's hatred, inducing sickness and even death. It is this spiritual power of the soul, or as Captain Rattray called it, "the bad, revengeful and hurtful element in a spirit," that is known as the Ashanti sasa or Jamaica shadow. This is its normal or natural function, independent of any supernatural co-operation. It is, however, believed that it is within the scope of obeah-practice to dissociate from living man this sasa or shadow, which accordingly must have some entity of its own independent of the sunsum or soul. Furthermore, unless the victim of this obeah interference succeeds in regaining his lost shadow through the instrumentality of the myal-man, he is doomed to waste away with fatal results.

On the other hand, when a man comes to die in the ordinary course of events, his sasa or shadow tends to demand an independent existence of its own to the annoyance of those who remain in life, unless it is captured and "properly laid" at the funeral, as will be seen in the next chapter.

Accordingly, Mr. Banbury tells us that depriving persons of their shadows is also called in Jamaica "setting the deaths on them," and he explains: "It is believed that after the shadow of any one is taken, he is never healthy; and if it be not caught, he must pine away until he dies. The shadow when taken is carried and nailed to the cotton-tree." This of course, would be the work of an obeah-man.

It now becomes the task of the myal-man to try and restore the shadow to the person from whom it had been taken.

After the great myalistic revival that followed on the emancipation of the slaves the catching of shadows became almost as important as the digging up of obeah, on the part of the myal-man who according to Mr. Banbury, "declared that the world was to be at an end: Christ was coming, and God had sent them to pull all the obeahs, and catch the shadows that were spell-bound at the cotton-trees. In preparation for that event they affected to be very strict in their conduct. They would neither drink nor smoke. Persons who were known to be notorious for bad lives were excluded from their society. At {Two pages (167 and 168) missing in book--jbh.} been properly laid at the funeral, is ordinarily ascribed to the duppies. This is probably due to the fact that, as in many parts of Africa, it is not well to speak of the dead, especially under the malevolent aspect, and so duppies in general are blamed for everything and there is then no need of any reference to a particular shadow, which otherwise hearing itself named, might feel called upon to make its presence felt to the utter annoyance of the invoker.

Still another Ashanti term is the sunsum which is thus described by Captain Rattray: "It is a man's sunsum that may wander about in sleep. 'It may encounter other sunsum and get knocked about, when you will feel unwell, or killed, when you will sicken and die.' Perhaps the sunsum is the volatile part of the whole 'kra'" i.e. the human soul. It was only on very rare occasions that I came across any indications of vestiges of belief in this dream-soul during all the time I was in Jamaica. Possibly there are still some who secretly place credence in the theory that his dreams are actual experiences of a portion of his soul far afield during the hours of sleep. But, I feel quite sure that even the most ignorant in the "bush" have become too sophisticated to openly admit such a belief.

Another superstition, now rapidly dying out in Jamaica, is that regarding "Ole Hige," a sort of vampire that haunts the hovels of the Blacks or is seen at times gliding along the roads at night in a fiery glow. For many years I was convinced that this was nothing more than an ingraft on Negro superstition due to contacts with the whites, as "Ole Hige". really means Old Hag and when she assumes her rôle as vampire, in good European witch fashion, she doffs her skin before setting out on her mission. In this connexion, we even find recorded the time-honoured story of the husband who suspected the nefarious practice of his wife and feigning sleep until her departure rubbed pepper and salt inside the temporarily discarded skin. The usual discomfiture of the witch followed in natural course. What was my surprise, then, to find Christaller in connexion with the Ashanti stating under the term Obayifo, meaning witch, hag; wizard, sorcerer: "The natives describe a wizard or witch as a man or woman who stands in some agreement with the devil. At night, when all are asleep, he (or she) rises or rather leaves his (her) body, as a snake casts its slough, and goes out emitting flames from his eyes, nose, mouth, ears, armpits; he may walk with his head on the ground and his feet up; he catches and eats animals, or kills men either by drinking their blood or by catching their soul, which he boils and eats, whereupon the person dies; or he bites them that they become full of sores."

Concerning the Jamaica belief in "Ole Hige" in his day, we are informed by Mr. Banbury: "This is another most curious creature of the imagination which was much believed in times of old and greatly dreaded; and the notion respecting the fabulous being of blood has not quite died out. It delights in human blood, especially that of new-born infants. In days gone by the "Old Suck," as she was also designated on account of her imagined propensity, was to be seen enveloped in a flame of fire, wending her way late at nights through the 'nigger houses,' or along the high road, bent on robbing some poor innocent of its newly circulating blood of life. For this reason infants just born were guarded with the utmost care from the voracious creature of blood. This has given rise to the foolish notion, still generally practised amongst the people throughout the island, of keeping up the ninth night after the birth of an infant. This night is thought the most critical, as on it the old hag uses her utmost endeavour to get at the babe. It is the night previous to 'coming out of room' after child and mother are confined for some days. On this night a constant watch is kept up by the anxious mother, the midwife, and her friends. If the infant comes off safe this night there is no more fear. The hag would not after that molest it. Knives and forks, and sometimes the bible are placed at the head of the infant to scare away the 'blow-fire'. The doors are marked all over with chalk. This has the effect of keeping the old hag all night counting until it be too late to enter. Sometimes mustard seeds are scattered before them which have the same effect. Her approach is suspected by an irresistible drowsiness and the flickering of the light. If those who are watching should give way to this feeling and fall asleep, woe to the unfortunate infant. The hag enters and sucks it. As soon as this is done the child cries, the people wake up in a fright, the babe takes in immediately with the locked-jaw and refuses the breast. The little one is now considered doomed. The locked-jaw was always believed an invariable sign of the suck of an old hag, and in times of slavery a great majority of infants died of it, no doubt from the bad treatment of the mothers near up to the time of delivery by their owners, and from exposure of the infants after birth. There were mothers also, who on account of the rigour of slavery, no doubt used means to get off their babes, rather than that they should have been subjected to the same hardships as themselves. The strangest thing in connexion with this superstition is, that it was believed to be the living that acted the part of the 'old hige.' Women who were addicted to it had the power of divesting themselves of their skins, and with their raw bodies issued out at nights, in quest of blood. People have affirmed that they have seen the 'ole hige' going along in the night as swift as lightning, with blazes of fire issuing out of her armpits."

Strictly speaking, therefore, ole hige should have been dealt with in the previous chapter on witchcraft, for she is a witch pure and simple. And so she would have been, were it not for the fact that the little residue of the superstition that still remains in the "bush" is, by common consent, usually associated with duppies in general, probably for the same reason as in the case of shadows already referred to, that no one wants to attract ole hige's attention by naming her.

Mr. Banbury further speaks of the Jamaica "Rubba Mumma" or River Mother which is known in Haiti as Mère de l'eau, and in Surinam as Water Mama. Thus he says: "This superstition most likely took its rise from the story of the mermaid or water nymph of England; she is believed to inhabit every fountain-head of an inexhaustible and considerable stream of water in Jamaica. For this reason the sources of such streams were worshipped, and sacrifices offered to the 'Rubba Missis.' It is a well-known fact that the slaves on water-works used to persuade their overseers or masters, to sacrifice an ox at the fountain-head of the water turning the mill in times of much drought, in order to propitiate the mistress of the river, that she may cause rain and give an adequate supply of water to turn the mill. It is said a bullock was yearly killed on some of the sugar estates at such places for this purpose."

One's first impulse would be to agree with Mr. Banbury and find here nothing more than a European nymph transplanted to a West Indian setting. But maturer consideration leads me to think that this is rather a residue of the old Ashanti myth about the divine origin of water, as well as a reflexion of what constitutes the very basis of Ashanti theological beliefs, as Captain Rattray calls it, namely, the accepted relation of every important body of water in Ashanti to the Supreme Being as "a son of God." For, as we are told, "Waters in Ashanti, some in a greater, others in a lesser degree, are all looked upon as containing the power or spirit of the Divine Creator, and thus as being a great life-giving force. 'As a woman gives birth to a child, so may water to a god,' once said a priest to me."

Among Jamaica Proverbs concerning duppies in general, the following may be mentioned in passing: In the Jamaica Alphabet we have: "D is for duppy, him yeye shine like fire," which would rather seem to have reference to Ole Hige than to the ordinary run of duppies.

"Man don dead, no call him duppy," showing that a duppy is an after death manifestation. This is clearly a use of duppy in its strictest sense.

"Duppy say: 'day fe you, night fe me,'" meaning "Every man to his taste," and implying the activity of the duppy by night.

"Ebery cave-hole hab him own duppy," that is, "Everyone has his own trouble," but indicating the association of duppies with the darkness of the caves.

"Duppy know who fe frighten," signifying "People will only injure those who they know cannot retaliate." Doctor Martha

Warren Beckwith, President of the American Folk-Lore Society, paraphrases this as "The devil knows whom to frighten," and defines a duppy as a ghost or an evil spirit of any kind. This, of course, is the most extended use possible for the word duppy, but there are times in Jamaica when it is so used.

The present chapter has been concerned with the "bush" ideas in Jamaica on ghosts and kindred spirits. Its purpose has been to analyse and differentiate these beliefs as beliefs, and nothing more. There is no question here of determining the underlying facts, if any.

The average Englishman or American in Jamaica, as elsewhere, would scorn to admit any belief whatever in ghosts. And yet, if put to it, either at home or abroad, how many of them would be ready to go alone into a cemetery at midnight without bolstering up their courage by whistling? They may not believe in ghosts, but they are at least a little nervous, to say the least.

So, too, I am convinced that while educated Jamaicans generally are apt to protest loudly against this foolish superstition concerning duppies, yet in their heart of hearts, after dark they have a wholesome respect for the reputed habitat of Mr. Duppy, if not a positive dread of meeting him.

Certainly, in the "bush," duppies are accepted as fearsome realities. Even were we able to prove dogmatically that such an entity could not possibly exist, we would make little impression on the minds of the masses of the simple children of Nature among the Jamaica hills. For, as the Ashanti say: "If the spirit world possesses nothing else, it has at least the power of its name."

FUNERAL CUSTOMS

ONE of my fondest memories of Jamaica, and carrying me back to the closing days of the year 1906, has already been told in Whisperings of the Caribbean.

As you leave Falmouth, travelling east, and abandon the shore road, the ascent leads you up through the Trelawney Mountains, and if you are fortunate enough not to lose your way, you may come to a peaceful spot, far from the busy turmoil of the world, that is not inaptly named Refuge.

To the north, the undulating country, studded with palms and other tropical trees, with here and there areas of sugar cane and bananas, stretches far away to the purple Caribbean.

The little mission church with its red roof and simple bell cupola has been built upon a gently rising knoll, the whitewashed walls forming a pleasing contrast with the green of the surrounding shrubbery.

God's acre has found its place around the church, and even as we arrive, the bell in the cupola begins to toll. With mournful, resonant note, it breaks the peaceful silence of the hour to speak the prayerful remembrance for the passing of a soul. Up from the valley, a funeral procession is finding its tortuous way. Old John Ferreira is dead. Marse Marny he was always called in fond affection by the children of the "bush."

Only a few short months ago, a visiting missionary had written back to the States concerning this dear old man: "Old John

Ferreira, who lives near the church is a Portuguese, seventy years old, who came to Jamaica in 1857, and has been in this one spot ever since. In spite of his years, he is still a good strong specimen of a man and his solid piety is refreshing when one meets it in such uncongenial surroundings. Somehow or other I could not help thinking of Saint Alphonsus Rodriguez as I looked at him; whether it was his simplicity and earnestness combined with real old-world holiness, or the fact that he is a widower unaffectedly devoted to God, or perhaps the union of the two things in him, I can't tell; but such was the impression left on me. Looking up at the heavens this evening, after the usual night prayers and catechism instruction by the priest in the church, his eyes fell on the constellation of Orion. Whereupon turning to me and pointing to the line in it of three upper stars which was almost parallel to the horizon, he said: 'In my country we call those three Marys and the other three near them, we call the three Kings. And those two stars close by which shine together so as to seem almost to be one star, we call St. Lucy.' As he spoke, I could imagine the peace sanctified by religion which is afforded in a truly Catholic country, a peace, which in this case, this Madeira peasant had not lost with departure from the scenes of his faraway childhood."

So wrote the Reverend Patrick F. X. Mulry, S.J., under date of April 2, 1906. What he did not write, however, was the fact that for half a century good Marse Marny had endeared himself to the trustful children of the "bush" by his kindly words and endless little acts of charity. Thus he had become in course of time, in the esteem of all, not merely a generous benefactor but a gentle and truly sympathetic friend. So, at his death, there was on every side deep and heartfelt mourning. Throughout the "bush" each one regarded it as a personal loss, and at the funeral the entire countryside assembled to pay the last respects to one whom they felt as near to them as if he had belonged to the very household.

Like a cry of universal lamentation their wails swept up the hill. Even the crippled and the aged had gathered in groups along the path that the funeral was to follow. Little children, frightened at they knew not what, cast themselves prone and buried their kinky little heads in Nana's skirts, weeping through sympathy for the tears that coursed unchecked down the furrowed visage of the disconsolate old woman. And the aged Nana herself sat there in a huddled heap, with chin between her hands as with unseeing eyes she gazed off towards the distant Caribbean.

When the funeral cortège reached the foot of the hill, as if on a preconcerted signal, the groups of blacks spread out and formed two lines along the way. In every hand was held a tree-branch from the nearby shrubbery, and as the body was carried by, in solemn unison the branches waved, while the touching anthem of that multitude, with many sobs and lamentations passed down the breeze, "Goodbye, Marse Marny; Good-bye Marse Marny; Goodbye, Marse Marny." Then as the last rites were finished and the grave was filled, these children of the "bush" in mute affection placed the branches on the little mound and wandered disconsolate back through the fields to the sheltered nooks and hollows where in their humble homes for many a day they moaned the loss of their well-loved Marse Marny.

Many a funeral have I since attended in the "bush" but never have I seen this ceremony repeated anywhere. It was a spontaneous outburst of love and gratitude on the part of the simple and devoted people and it stirred me deeply as it brought home to me a fuller realization of the true spirit of the "bush."

There is the firm conviction that death is not the end of all things. Despite what the private life may be, whether members of a Church or not, all cling tenaciously to the hope of the life to come, and purport a reform in the not too distant future. But for the present, "Can't do better," and that is all there is about it. The carping visitor makes note of figures on one violation of the moral code, forgetting all the time that much of the seeming wrong in the Isle of Springs may be perhaps in the sight of God what theologians call material and not formal sin. Moreover, if one type of wrong-doing does stare you in the face, Jamaica is remarkably free from other and greater evils that are so rife to-day in the white man's country.

Herbert G. DeLisser, who knows his Jamaica so well, with good reason asserts: "Tropical man is not all vile. He is like man in almost every part of the world, a composition of good and bad, angelic and bestial, false and true. He has his virtues as well as his shortcomings, and we must take him as we find him and not expect perfection."

The advent of the automobile has wrought great changes in Jamaica, bringing the Metropolis closer to every section of the "bush." New roads have opened up entire sections that were previously inaccessible to any except the sure of foot among men and beasts. As a consequence, old-time customs are rapidly dying out and even funerals in the "bush" have lost within the last decade or two many practices that could be traced not merely to the days of slavery but back to their origins in distant Africa.

M. Malte-Brun, speaking of the West African Negroes, stated in 1827: "In their funerals, which are attended with much howling and singing, a very singular piece of superstition prevails. The bearers of the body ask the deceased, if he has been poisoned or enchanted, and pretend to receive a reply by a motion of the coffin, which is no doubt produced by one of their boldest jugglers. The person whom the deceased accuses of having killed him by enchantment is at once condemned to be sold as a slave."

In December, 1855, the United States Sloop-of-War Jamestown, then flag-ship of the African Squadron, visited the Gold Coast, and the Chaplain of the Ship, the Reverend Charles W. Thomas, thus describes a wake at Elmina. "In our walk through the town, we entered a house in which there was a corpse, a wife of the tenant. The chief mourners, who were slaves, were painted all over in white mud, literally whitewashed, and the remaining wives of the landlord were seated on the dirt floor of the room entertaining the company. Near the deceased, and on the mat on which she lay, was a plate of boiled rice and fowl, and a bottle containing a little rum. These, they said, afforded her nourishment on her journey, and were very acceptable. Two old hags sat at the feet of the corpse, beating time on pieces of iron hoop, and to this music two women were dancing in a space near the bed . . . 'Why,' I asked through the interpreter, 'do you dance and laugh on such an occasion?' They replied, 'Because she is gone to a better place.' I felt very much like acquiescing in the conclusion, for a worse place than Elmina I can hardly imagine. But how strongly, deeply fixed in human nature, thought I, is the conviction of another state of existence. There are but few tribes, if any, in Africa, and none out of it, more debased and ignorant than this people, yet here, though vaguely, and without shadow of reason, is held and cherished one of the foundation truths of all religion."

Captain Rattray in his description of Ashanti funerals, goes into considerable detail. After the body has been washed, dressed and laid out, food is prepared "for the journey upon which the deceased is supposed to have started. This food generally consists of a fowl, eggs and mashed plantains or yams and water, which are placed beside the body."

"A 'wake' is now kept up, night and day, until the body is buried. The whole time is spent in firing guns, drumming, dancing and singing."

"Grief and sorrow are very real where the clan (blood) relations are concerned, for the tears demanded by social custom are none the less a token of genuine grief. For others, not clansmen and women, such occasions are perhaps not so tragic, and on this account these rites may seem to the uninstructed to be somewhat heartless shows, as mirth and jollity are not altogether absent."

Captain Rattray observes in passing: "The simple faith of the mourners that all that was said was heard by the dead was very touching." I could not help noticing that the same was true at the funeral of Marse Marny in Jamaica.

"The offerings of food are arranged on low tables before the corpse, who is informed, as water is poured on the ground before it: 'Here is water, wash your hands and eat.'"

"The body is generally buried on the third day. In olden times the actual interment took place at night, but daytime burials are now not uncommon."

When the funeral is ready to start, a hole is knocked in the wall of the house, and the body is removed through this "improvised doorway, which later is closed up, in order to cheat the ghost if it wished to return to the house."

As the body is about to be placed on the ground outside the house, the ceremony of the triple lowering and raising is performed in deference to Asase Ya, the earth goddess, as was mentioned in our opening chapter.

In connexion with the Ashanti Proverb: "The corpse which is coming to knock against (some one) cares nothing for cries of sorrow," Captain Rattray explains: "The custom of 'carrying the corpse' when the cause of death is supposed to be witchcraft is briefly as follows. An open stretcher is made of palm branches, and on this the corpse is laid, being surrounded by leaves . . . The stretcher is then placed on the heads of two men, who carry it out into the street. The whole people assemble. The chief, or head man of the village, advances cutlass in hand, and addresses the corpse saying, 'If I were the one who killed you by magic, advance on me and knock me.' And so on each in turn comes up till the guilty one's turn comes, when the corpse will urge the carriers forward to butt against him with the litter. A person so accused can appeal for a change of carriers."

In a later volume, Captain Rattray returns to the subject, and tells us: "The custom of 'carrying the corpse' is well known; it is even still sometimes put in practice. The rite consists in imploring the spirit of the dead man or woman to assist the living in pointing out the 'bayifo (witch) who, by his or her black magic, has compassed the death. This the dead person does by causing those who are 'carrying the body' to push or knock against the guilty party."

Captain Rattray then gives in detail the court record of a case that was tried before him in his capacity of magistrate, and observes: "The evidence which was given to the court on this occasion was remarkable. It seemed to point to the fact that the persons concerned, who appeared to have had every motive not to incriminate the accused, were not entirely free agents. In this modern example, typical of hundreds of such cases that once decimated whole villages, the tradition of centuries was so firmly instilled in the mind of the accused, that he seemed to have forgotten that he had only to appeal to the nearest European court to find redress."

Briefly the case was this. A woman, when dying, had declared that her death was caused by someone at D. Her relatives accordingly decided to make the test of "carrying the body" despite the fact that such a process was forbidden by British Colonial Law. The body was tied in a cloth and two men carried it. Asked to show who killed her, the body forced the carriers to a certain house and knocked up against a man whom we may call A. In accordance with his right, A demanded a change in carriers and suggested his own two sons for the purpose. This was granted. But again the body came to his house and knocked him. That night he went to the "bush" and shot himself.

We need not repeat the story as told by the two first carriers who might easily have been guided by personal hostility towards A. But the evidence of his own sons is a different matter. The first son testified: "I carried the corpse at the head, my brother carried the feet; we carried the body from our yard on our heads into the street. When we got outside my father questioned the corpse . . . When my father spoke thus to the body, my whole body shook and I felt weak and as if a great weight was upon me. The body pulled me backwards and then suddenly pushed forward . . . My father tried a second and a third time." Asked by the Court, "Did you want to make the corpse rush at your father?", he replied: "He is my father and I could not want to do that . . . I knew I was going to knock my father, but I could not help myself, my whole body became weak."

Captain Rattray adds: "The evidence of the second son who had carried at the feet, and had been taken out of court whilst the previous witness was giving his evidence, was somewhat similar to the above. He also said: 'I did try to stand firm on one place but could not help going forward. I knew if the body knocked my father, he would be killed. I could not prevent it. I tried to, but could not.'"

We may now return to the general description of the Ashanti funeral as described by Captain Rattray.

"Before the grave is dug, a libation is poured on the spot with the words:

> "Goddess of Earth, receive this wine and drink;
> Your grandchild so-and-so has died.
> We beg of you that we may here dig a hole."

"All the food that had been exposed in front of the body is collected . . . and taken with the body to the burying ground."
"Wine is poured on the grave, with the words: 'So-and-so, here is wine from your family, do not cause any of us who have carried you to fare ill.' All drink some of the wine. They then return home; when they arrive at the village, one of the clansmen brings water and all wash, not only their hands and feet, but the hoes or other tools used at the grave side. Dancing, drinking, and singing continue until sheer exhaustion sends every one home."

On the sixth day "the ghost departs for the land of spirits." On the eighth day there is further dancing, etc. as the funeral accounts are gone into and a final settlement is made. Other celebrations take place on the fifteenth, fortieth, eightieth days as well as on the anniversary.

If one is astonished at all this dancing and drinking at a funeral, we must keep in mind that Captain Rattray calls our attention to the fact: "Dancing in Africa invariably has a religious significance. It forms an indispensable accompaniment of all funeral rites."

We are further informed by J. B. Danquah in connexion with Akan funerals: "Nobody sings for a half-hour without drink. Both at home and at the burial grove drink is being blindly served."

Now let us see how much of the funeral ceremonial was continued by the descendants of the Ashanti in Jamaica during the days of slavery.

One of the earliest accounts that has come down to us is that of Charles Leslie which was published in 1740. Of the funerals of the slaves, he writes: "When one is carried out to his grave, he is attended with a vast multitude, who conduct his corpse in something of a ludicrous manner. They sing all the way, and they who bear it on their shoulders, make a feint of stopping at every door they pass, pretending, that if the deceased person had received any injury, the corpse moves towards that house, and that they can't avoid letting it fall to the ground, when before the door. When they come to the grave, which is generally made in some savannah or plain, they lay down the coffin, or whatever the body happens to be wrapt up in; and if he be one whose circumstances could allow it, or if he be generally beloved, the Negroes sacrifice a hog, in honour of him; which they contribute to the expenses of, among themselves. The manner of the sacrifice is this. The nearest relation kills it, the entrails are buried, the four quarters are divided, and a kind of soup made, which is brought in a calabash or gourd, and, after waving it three times, it is set down; then the body is put in the ground; all the while they are covering it with earth, the attendants scream out in a terrible manner, which is not the effect of grief, but of joy; they beat on their wooden drums, and the women with their rattles make a hideous noise. After the grave is filled up, they place the soup which they had prepared at the head, and a bottle of rum at the feet. In the meantime cool drink (which is made of the Lignum Vitae bark, or whatever else they can afford) is distributed amongst those who are present; one half of the hog is burnt while they are drinking, and the other is left to any person who pleases to take it; they return to town, or the plantation, singing after their manner, and so the ceremony ends."

When slavery was at its height in Jamaica, during the second half of the eighteenth century, the following account of slave customs was rendered by Edward Long: "Every funeral is a kind of festival; at which the greater part of the company assume an air of joy and unconcern; and, together with their singing, dancing, and musical instruments, conspire to drown all sense of affliction in the minds of the real mourners. The burthen of this merry dirge is filled with encomiums on the deceased, with hopes and wishes for his happiness in his new state. Sometimes the coffin-bearers, especially if they carry it on their heads, pretend that the corpse will not proceed to the grave, notwithstanding the exertion of their utmost strength to urge it forwards. They then move to different huts, till they come to one, the owner of which, they know, has done some injury to, or been much disliked by, the deceased in his lifetime. Here they express some words of indignation on behalf of the dead man; then knock at the coffin, and try to soothe and pacify the corpse; at length, after much persuasion, it begins to grow more passive, and suffers them to carry it on, without further struggle, to the place of repose. At other times, the corpse takes a sudden and obstinate aversion to be supported on the head, preferring the arms; nor does it peaceably give up the dispute, until the bearers think proper to comply with its humour. The

156

corpse being interred, the grave is but slightly overspread with earth. Some scratch up the loose mould, with their backs turned to the grave, and cast it behind them between their legs, after the manner of cats which have just exonerated. 'This, they say, is done, to prevent the deceased person from following them home. When the deceased is a married woman, the husband lets his beard remain unshaved, and appears rather negligent in his attire, for the space of a month; at the expiration of which, a fowl is dressed at his house, with some messes of good broth, and he proceeds, accompanied by his friends, to the grave. Then begins a song, purporting, that the deceased is now in the enjoyment of complete felicity; and that they are assembled to rejoice at her state of bliss, and perform the last offices of duty and friendship. They then lay a considerable heap of earth over the grave, which is called covering it, and the meeting concludes with eating their collation, drinking, dancing, and vociferation. After this ceremony is over, the widow, or widower, is at liberty to take another spouse immediately; and the term of mourning is at an end."

The Reverend William James Gardner in describing the manners and customs prevalent in Jamaica prior to the anti-slave struggle which began in 1782, has this to say on our subject: "The funeral ceremonies bare some resemblance to Irish wakes. A feast was provided, at which there was singing, drumming, and dancing. When at length it was time to carry the coffin to the grave, it was borne more frequently on the heads than on the shoulders of the bearers. After a little progress had been made a sudden stop was almost sure to take place: the corpse, it was said, was obstinate, and would not go on; something was surely the matter. Presently the cause would be explained. Perhaps, just by, a man lived who had been at variance with the dead: he must be visited and soundly scolded, and then the departed spirit would rest. Quietude seemed to come much quicker if the accused person was liberal in his offers of rum.

"Occasionally the corpse was displeased with the mode of conveyance, and this had to be changed. When at length the grave was reached and the coffin was lowered, cooked food, in which no salt had been put, was placed upon it; and in covering up the grave the attendants often turned their backs to it and threw the earth in from between their legs. This was an infallible way of preventing the spirit of the departed from returning with them to their homes. Sometimes the spirit was caught with many ceremonies in a box provided for that purpose, and then the box was carefully buried. The surviving widow of the departed was expected to go more careless in dress than usual for some few weeks; but when tired of the single state she cooked a fowl, and carried it, with the broth, to the grave, accompanied by friends who either sympathized with her or perhaps merely wished to spend a pleasant evening. A song was sung expressive of confidence in the happiness of the departed, fresh earth was piled upon the grave, some of the viands were cast upon it, and the rest eaten. More singing, and also dancing followed, and the party, returning home, left the bereaved one to select another companion. No propitiatory offerings could, however, keep the departed from occasionally breaking bounds. Hence every Negro trembled at the mention of duppies; these are the ghosts of northern climes. Even now, among the ignorant, when a corpse is prepared for the grave, dressed, as is not unusual, in a full suit of clothes, the pockets are often cut away, lest the duppy should fill them with stones and annoy the living on his return. For nine days the room in which death took place was undisturbed, and a light left burning at night; nor were little conveniences to which the departed was accustomed, as water to bathe the feet, etc., omitted. Food was often prepared, and if a bold-hearted but hungry member of the household consumed it in secret, the appetite of the duppy became the occasion of remark."

Later, when he comes to consider the manners and customs of the period immediately preceding the emancipation of the slaves, at the beginning of the nineteenth century, Mr. Gardner states regarding the funerals of the slaves: "Some changes had taken place in the mode of conducting them as compared with those related in a former chapter on manners and customs. When a person of any kind of importance died, preparations were made for a wake. If the family were not able to bear the expense, plates enveloped in black crape were sent round from house to house, and the gifts of those kindly disposed collected. It was thought something extremely mean not to contribute for such a purpose. All who chose to come to the wake were freely welcomed. It was a grand time for gossip, feasting, and too often drunkenness. Similar customs to those described under the former period prevailed.

"The ceremony of catching the shadow of the dead person was usually gone through with many strange antics; and when this wonderful feat was declared to have been accomplished, the shadow was put into a small coffin and carefully buried. After this there was no fear of the duppy, or ghost, giving any trouble.

"Still the dead man could not, as a rule, go quietly to his last resting-place, unless all outstanding matters were adjusted. The friends or relations who bore the coffin often received some hint, the nature of which was best known to themselves, and then placing their ears to the coffin, they professed to interpret the utterances of the departed, who it seems had not yet lost the gift of speech. Slanders spoken against him, or injuries not yet redressed, were now publicly proclaimed. More frequently the corpse was declared to proclaim the name of its debtors: the creditors were invariably forgotten. Woe to the man who owed anything to the estate of the departed. No matter what superhuman efforts the bearers seemed to make, the corpse was obstinate, and would not go past the residence of the delinquent. A living dun is usually a very inconvenient visitor, but what can a man do with a dead one? A coffin before one's door, which no power on earth can lift until the debt is paid, is perhaps one of the most unpleasant modes of enforcing payment that can be well imagined, and, as a rule, it was most successful. Yet it sometimes turned out that the corpse was not honest, that the alleged debt had been paid; and then it was wonderful how light the coffin of the claimant became, and how rapidly the bearers proceeded on their way.

"In 1831, night funerals were prohibited by law: owners permitting them were liable to a penalty of fifty pounds, and slaves attending them to a whipping of thirty-nine lashes. In the early part of the century they were very frequent. The scene presented on these occasions was wild in the extreme, though rarely witnessed by white people, and only then by stealth. One or more Negroes played upon the goomba, and another, at intervals, blew a horn made of a conch shell; another took the solo part of a recitative of a wild funeral wail, usually having reference to the return of the departed to Africa; while a party, sitting in a circle, gave the chorus. These melancholy dirges were often protracted through the night, the coffin not being laid in the grave till the morning star arose. Food, consisting of pork, yam, rum, etc., was placed in the coffin, for the use of the departed in his long journey across the blue water to the fatherland. In later years it became common to use more expedition at the grave, and when the funeral was over, and a few dirges sung, to return to the house and spend the night in feasting, often accompanied with dancing."

However absurd many of these practices appear to us to-day, it must be kept in mind that they were all part of a complicated system of religious beliefs and that there was never any question of witchcraft in the whole process.

According to the animistic view of the Ashanti, in all animal and vegetable life there was a spiritual element that might conserve man's spirit after death just as the material part had been assimilated in the ordinary process of digestion during life. By an extension of this idea, it was thought that the departed spirit of man could draw sustenance from the food at the grave, as no substantial change, it was believed, had been effected in the process of cooking.

Until the interference of the white man put a stop to it, the funeral rites of the Ashanti kings had been elaborate in the extreme. What has been commonly regarded as a "blood-lust" with its seemingly indiscriminate slaughter of victims, was in reality a natural consequence of the accepted doctrine concerning the hereafter. "It was incumbent on those left on earth to see that the king entered the spirit-world with a retinue befitting his high position. Such killings thus became a last pious homage and service to the dead," as we are told by Captain Rattray.

In this way, some of the late king's wives were strangled so that they might attend "their husband on the journey upon which he had set out."

With a like intent, animals were sacrificed at funerals so that their spirits might accompany the departed. According to Ashanti belief even "trees and plants in general have their own particular souls which survive after 'death,'" and it is this "spiritual" element which sustains the soul of man on its way to the land of ghosts.

Mr. Gardner then was in error when he facetiously stated: "Food was often prepared, and if a bold-hearted but hungry member of the household consumed it in secret, the appetite of the duppy became the occasion of remark." In the first place no living mortal could have been driven by the acutest hunger to appropriate to himself any portion of such food. He would have been haunted by the shadow of the deceased to his dying day. Secondly, any diminution of the material bulk of the food would have immediately aroused suspicion, as it was only the supposed spiritual element in the food that was available for the spiritual element in man which had departed this life, and the material element of the body was no longer able to assimilate the material element in the food. They were both dead, and subject alike to decay as their souls had left them.

During the century that has elapsed since the abolition of slavery, it is surprising how many of the old funeral customs have come down to us, at least in a modified form.

The outbreak of myalistic emotionalism which followed close on emancipation, generally yielded to an urgent desire on the part of the former slaves to identify themselves with some Church or other, and they hastened to "join" one or other of the established congregations. But if this were denied to them by reason of their mode of life, at least they "followed" or cast in their lot with one of the newly improvised native groups where ethical standards might not be so exacting.

But then, there were many who were still attracted to the old myalistic influences that were rapidly developing into modern revivalism. Even to-day, one easily distinguishes from all other religious groups in Jamaica these high-strung, emotional fanatics who are recognized by the peculiar tempo of their songs no less than by the grotesque hip movement that characterizes their sliding gait, as clothed in white and in single file, they parade the streets before they have aroused their spirits to the proper pitch of excitement in preparation for the "sarvice" which is to follow.

In the "bush," of course, all this preliminary excitation is unnecessary. There they simply live the life of their myalistic tendencies. As you meet them on the road you are apt to question their sanity, and if you watch them while they work, there is a peculiar exhilaration that shows itself in the glint of the eye and the nervous tension of their utterances. For such as these, it is an easy transition to the spiritual excesses of their formal assemblies. And it is in this myalistic exuberance of spirit that has come in direct descent from the proponents of old Ashanti belief and practice, that, naturally enough, the funeral customs of bygone days have been more or less preserved down to the present in Jamaica.

Out from these revivalistic centres in turn has spread a recrudescence of ancient funeral customs that has never failed to find adopters among the superstitious in the "bush" as a consequence of the persistent belief in duppies and shadows. Churches have done their utmost to stamp out what to them must needs appear as survivals of paganism. Church members openly condemn the practice in others, although I fear some of them may secretly participate in the "laying of a shadow." But among the great mass of those who professedly "follow you church but don' join yet," there is not the slightest qualm of conscience about taking part in any modern wake in the Jamaica "bush" no matter what superstitious practices may be introduced.

Professor Martha Warren Beckwith of Vassar College recently made a critical study of the present conditions in Jamaica. As a result of four visits to the island between 1919 and 1924, she has come to some very definite conclusions. In her delightful little book, Black Roadways, with its sub-title, A Study of Jamaica Folk Life, she opens the chapter on "The Burial of the Dead" with the following words: "All the acts connected with the burial of the dead are based upon a belief in the contaminating power of death and particularly in the continued animation of the dead and his power to return and disturb the living, unless precautions are taken to inter him properly. Hence fear keeps alive to-day much of the folklore which surrounds the rites for the dead. To prepare the body, two men wash it, 'working one on each side from the head down to the feet and both keeping together.' . . . Care must be taken to cut out or sew up the pockets in a man's suit, lest the ghost come back with its pockets full of stones and harm the living. All buttons must be cut off and the clothes sewed or pinned together. After dressing the corpse, two or more persons take it up and lay it back three times before placing it in the coffin." This last is dearly a variant of the custom still in, vogue in Jamaica of raising and lowering the coffin three times which has already been explained.

"To prevent the dead from returning to haunt the family or to, harm some member of it, no member of the family must neglect to bid the dead farewell, and friends flock to the house to perform the same office." But, "Tears must not fall upon the body or the ghost will return to the mourner."

Doctor Beckwith continues: "It is believed that the dead will return and 'ride' (as in a nightmare) one who has done him harm. 'No black man dies a natural death,' says an old resident of the island, and all the evidence to be gathered from the people themselves corroborates this statement. The Jamaica Negro is, firmly convinced that every death which occurs before the allotted span of life is completed is due not to natural causes but to the work of an evil spirit sent by some enemy. When the suspicion of foul play is strong, the family suggest to the corpse the names of this one and that one who may have injured him, and concealing a sharp knife, a razor, or a shilling in his clothing, will say, 'Go do your work!' Or they will wrap up a bit of broom-weed in a white cloth and say, 'Go sweep the yard clean!' a saying which is meant to include the whole household of the murderer in the ghastly vengeance."

"The body must be carried out feet first 'just as a man walks,' and by the front door; 'if you take him out the back way you will never keep him out of the house.'"

"A very old belief refers to the habit of collecting bad debts on the way to the grave, the coffin by its weight or by striking against something on the way indicating where these debts lie . . . If the murderer helps bear the coffin it will be impossible to move it. The same thing happens if the bearers attempt to take it for burial to a place where it does not wish to be laid. Wilfrid knew of a case in which a Manchester man did not want to be buried at his own place but at his sister's, and it took some hours to reach the grave."

"When a dead man's ghost has come back to 'ride' the living and it is desirable to 'plant him' so that he cannot again return, certain expedients are used to 'keep the ghost down,' the most common of which is to plant 'pidgeon peas' on the grave, for as the roots grow downward this will prevent the ghost from taking the opposite direction. At the west end of the island they boil the peas because, as the peas cannot shoot out of the ground, so the ghost must remain in the ground: the peas 'keep him down.' In Manderville it is the cut-eye bean that is used to plant down the ghost . . . Other precautions are taken at the house to guard against the return of the spirit to his old home. As soon as the body is taken out of the house, the room must be thoroughly swept, an observance called 'sweeping out the dead.' The water in which the body was bathed, which has been placed under the bed while the body was in the room, must be carried and emptied with all refuse into the grave; some say it must be thrown after the coffin as it leaves the house. Any looking-glass in the room should be covered in order that the reflexion of no living person may be cast upon it, else the person will pine away. Some say that water and a light must be left in the room for nine nights and the room left unchanged, but the water must be carefully emptied each morning. Others say on no account leave any water in the room. Some place water and even food at the grave. After the proper interval, it is well to rearrange the room, putting the head of the bed in a different position, whitewashing the walls, and even changing the position of the door, so that when the ghost returns, it will think it has come to the wrong house."

"The Jamaica Negroes believe that for nine nights after death the ghost rises out of the grave and returns to its familiar haunts . . . Others say that he 'rises on the third day after burial and returns to the house, which he finally leaves on the ninth night,' or that he rises in three days and 'will go about and take the shadow of all things he possessed during life.' 'After a person has been dead three days,' says another, 'it is believed that a cloud of smoke will rise out of the grave which becomes the duppy.' The idea of the three days' interval is evidently derived from Christian teaching, that of the 'nine nights' is not so clear. During this period every relative and friend gathers at the house of the dead to entertain the ghost, welcome his return, and speed him back to the grave. The idea seems to be that should the ghost mark one absentee he might later harm the recreant member. All 'nine nights' are celebrated to some extent in the eastern end of the island, the ninth night is that demanding principal vigilance. In the west the 'big wake' is held the day after the burial and is sometimes repeated for three days, the ninth night being the occasion merely of a 'big singing.' This festival of the wake or 'set-up' seems to have grown out of the burial ceremony at the grave, as it is described by old writers."

"'To please the dead' is the object of the wake among the more intelligent who still keep up the practice, but many no doubt feel that the ghost would never rest easy in his grave unless certain traditional rites were performed . . . The manner of the wake differs in various localities. Instead of. the African dances there are Moody and Sankey hymns--not church hymns, because the English church frowns upon the wake on account of the licence to which the all-night revel is likely to lead, and reproves its members for attending such occasions. 'Roll, Jordan, Roll' and 'Clash the Cymbals' are good wake hymns. In a well conducted wake, these religious exercises will last until twelve o'clock. After this comes the supper, which takes the place of the African feast."

"In leaving a wake a person should never announce his intention, lest the dead hear him and follow him home; he should merely touch on the sleeve those who are to accompany him. Martial dancing at the grave, as described by Edwards and Phillippo, is to-day represented by the games with which the men and boys exercise themselves during the latter part of the night . . . It is evident that in all these observances the ghost of the dead is supposed to be present and to be pleased and appeased by the honour done him. In some wake customs there. seems to be an explicit effort to cheat the ghost and send him back to the grave from which he came. If he finds the district merry he will think he has made a mistake, or if he finds himself regarded as dead he will himself accept the community verdict."

Herbert G. DeLisser, whose facile pen has drawn such charming sketches of the lights and shadows of his beloved Jamaica, combines a living realism in his descriptions with a sympathetic appreciation of the particular purpose or spirit usually underlying what the indiscriminating stranger might regard as sordid or banal. We may be pardoned, then, in quoting at some length from a graphic account of a "Ninth Night" celebration that came under his own observation.

Writing in October, 1912, Mr. DeLisser tells us: "I was living in Kingston when, one night, about five years ago, I was startled by hearing a long-drawn-out shriek. It fell away to silence, then rose again and again, a series of piercing sounds that stabbed through the darkness and waxed and waned with monotonous regularity. In a minute or two I was out in the street and endeavouring to locate the direction from which the sounds were coming; the only other living beings to be seen were two boys, whose peculiar attitude attracted my attention. They were kneeling with their heads held close to the ground, and listening intently. 'What is the matter?' I asked them. 'Nine-night, sah,' they replied laconically.

"'Where?'

"They bent their heads still nearer to the ground, were silent for a moment, then pointed positively in a north-eastern direction. . . .

"I handed the elder of the two youths a shilling: could I go to this 'ninth night'? He looked at me doubtfully, but agreed. 'I will teck y'u, sah,' he said; 'but a nine-night is a funny ting. Y'u must be sarrawful until it come to be about two o'clock; for if y'u laugh before dat time dere is some man dat will teck stick an' lick y'u. Yu can't meck fun as y'u like.' . . .

"As we walked on they explained to me that all that it was necessary to do at a 'ninth night' was to enter boldly, take a seat if one were vacant, look 'sarrawful', and, for the rest, behave as every one else did. It was also prudent for a stranger to sit near the gate, for many persons had been known to experience a desire to escape hurriedly from the scene of a too enthusiastic 'ninth night.' We walked for about a quarter of a mile, the sound of the incessant singing guiding us, and then I found myself in one of the poorest and most wretched of the slum-suburbs of Kingston. Inhabited by a heterogeneous population whose means of existence has been a problem to those who interest themselves in the condition of the Jamaica poor, it combines the characteristics of a village and a slum. . . .

"As we entered the village the singing, which had ceased for a moment or two, burst forth again with increased violence, and the air was filled with sound. I heard the words,--

> Know that the Lord is God alone,
> He hath created and can destroy,

thundered out by the sonorous voices of the men, and sent to pierce the darkness and the sky above by the shrill ear-splitting crescendo of the women. My guides paused before an open gate; this was the place we were seeking.

"Let me describe the scene exactly as I saw it. A great booth of dirty white canvas, and under this booth a crowd of persons of all ages and of both sexes. This was what first caught and held one's attention. The crowd was assembled in the centre of a large yard, and at some distance from the gate; and above the booth towered a giant tree. There must have been at least a hundred persons huddled under the frail canvas covering, some sitting on chairs and benches, others squatting on blocks of wood. In the midst of them was a table, on which were drinking-glasses and mugs and Bibles and hymn-books; and I noticed a smaller table covered with a white cloth, at the head of which sat a coal-black elderly man, who apparently presided over the proceedings.

"On either side of the booth, and along the whole length of the yard, ran a range of rooms, not more than nine feet in height from floor to roof. At the thresholds of some of these rooms sat women and children, and on nails driven into the poles which supported the booth a few storm-lanterns hung. Kerosene lamps placed on the tables gave forth a brilliant light. The heat was intense, for it was August. Everything stood out distinctly: the sable faces shining with perspiration, the glistening white teeth, the swaying bodies of the hymn-intoxicated people. There was something weird and wild and garish about that midnight gathering of men and women shouting under the calm star-lighted sky, vociferating that the Lord is God alone, while the rest of the city was hushed in the silence of sleep.

"I entered the place with some hesitation, and as I did so all eyes were turned upon me, though the singing did not cease. One man rose and courteously offered me a chair a little apart from the singers; some of the younger women stared and giggled; a few withered dames glared at me suspiciously. Remembering my young guide had said that the religious men present would probably resent anything on my part which smacked of levity or contempt, I looked at the old women with so serious a countenance that they probably decided that I appreciated the importance of the function. While the singing continued I had time to glance curiously round.

"One of the little rooms which I faced stood with its door and windows wide open, and from where I sat I could easily see into it. A large iron bed, covered with a clean white spread, was conspicuous; the rest of the furniture consisted of two small tables; evidently the chairs belonging to the room were being utilized in the yard. The room I observed, and it looked as though it had been garnished for some particular purpose. Seeing me gaze into it, one of my guides came over to me with the explanation, 'In there, sah, the woman dead.' Afterwards I discovered what he meant, and what the meaning of this peculiar 'ninth night' function was.

"Nine days after some one had died in that room, a woman whose children and relatives and friends were now, on the ninth night since her decease, holding a ceremony for the purpose of taking a last leave of her spirit. It is believed by the peasant people of the West Indies that if this leave-taking should be neglected, the wraith of the dead person would constantly hover near her last earthly residence, and be a source of discomfort and even serious danger to its living occupants. The custom, of course, was brought over from West Africa, where, even to-day, it may be witnessed in all its pristine elaboration. On the West Coast, eight days after the death of a husband, the widow proceeds to the seashore, attended by a great concourse of howling people, beating drums and blowing shells. The noise is made for the purpose of scaring away the ghost; arrived at the sea, the woman plunges into the water, throws away the clothes she has been wearing since the death of her husband, puts on a new garment, and returns home. During the interval food and drink have been placed in the but for the use of the dead one, and be is spoken of just as if he were alive. But when the ceremony of ghost-laying has taken place, it is assumed that, if no hitch has occurred in the proceedings, the ghost will have been deprived of all power of working harm to the widow or her next husband. In the West Indies the 'ninth night' ceremony is held not only for men, but for women and children as well. Very rarely a night passes in any large West Indian town but you will hear the sound of vociferous singing, which indicates either a wake or a 'ninth night.' And at some time or other during the proceedings the singers will loudly proclaim that the Lord is God alone, that being the one item which seems never to be omitted.

"On this night of which I write, the hymns were given out verse by verse, so that all should have a chance to sing. The man at the head of the smaller table reads with stentorian voice, and with a sublime disregard of all the rules of pronunciation. He pauses as he ends a verse, then leads the singing, the assembled guests valiantly following in his wake. Jealous of his authority, one or two old women suggest that he is 'taking a note too high,' and endeavour to create a diversion by singing the hymn in an entirely different key. But jealousy does not prevail over vested authority; consequently the hymn, in spite of occasional cacophony, goes on to the last word.

"Another hymn followed, and another; then the leader suggested that 'p'rhaps one of de sisters would like to offer a word of pr'yer.' There was nothing that the sisters would have liked better. Prayer came naturally and fluently from their lips; they embraced the whole world in their supplications, and so vehemently protested their belief that what they asked for would be granted, that they led at least one of their listeners to suspect that they had serious misgivings on that score.

"The singing and praying had been going on from about ten o'clock, and now it was nearly one. I began to hear murmurs. I detected a note of discontent. One man, in a loud whisper, expressed the opinion that though spiritual food was admirable in its way, something more material was required if one was competently to go through with the business of the night. Another guest remarked to a relative of the deceased, 'See here, I come to sing for y'u to-night, an' look how y'u treat me!' The tone was reproachful, the suggestion being that reward sweetens labour, and that the man who sings ought to be strengthened with food and drink for the singing.

"Suddenly I heard a shout-'Fry fish and bread advance!' It came from one of the guests who had so far forgotten personal dignity in his hunger that he had undertaken to solicit refreshments publicly and without shame. The appeal was not ignored. The hymn-book fell from the leader's hands, and a movement on the outskirts of the crowd caused every one to glance with a look of expectance in that direction. Satisfaction was visibly expressed on the faces of most of the people when three or four women were seen approaching with trays, for every one then realised that the religious part of the 'ninth night' was at an end, and that the time for feasting and speech-making and rejoicing had come.

"Small sprats fried in cotton-seed oil, large slices of bread, fritters made of a mixture of flour and picked salt fish and pepper, coloured anatto and fried in oil; bananas and oranges; cups of coffee sweetened with cocoa-nut milk, were handed round. Then there was rum for the men, and a little ginger-wine for the older women, some of whom murmured gently that St. Paul had strongly advised the taking of a little wine for the stomach's sake; and in the midst of a buzz of conversation the feasting began. . . ."

After going into detail regarding this more jovial part of the function, Mr. DeLisser concludes: "Tales are told, games played, wrestling matches between adventurous youths and ardent damsels take place. The 'ninth night' becomes a picnic under the morning stars.

"More refreshments are handed round, the laughter is now as loud as the singing was before. Clearly the period of mourning is over.

"And then the skies begin to lighten and the shrill crowing of a thousand cocks is heard. The air becomes fresh, and the stars grow pale. And soon it is 'good-bye' and 'good-bye,' and yet again 'good-bye.' All the mourners are going home; most of them will have to be at their work an hour or two hence. As they depart, I notice that the dead woman's sister goes into the clean unoccupied room, and, taking up a covered jar pours the water it contains into the yard.

"'Well,' she remarks, 'we done wid Cecilia now,' and those who hear her heartily agree. Thus good bye is said to Cecilia also, and the hope is that she will never return to earth to frighten her friends and relatives.

"And why should Cecilia return, since her life, at best, must have been a hard one."

When the World War broke out in 1914, I had charge of the missions at the western end of Jamaica with headquarters at Montego Bay. The Bugler in the Salvation Army Corps there was a young English lad of sterling, upright character, who had won the respect and friendship of all. When he died he was honestly mourned by the community at large without regard to creed or colour. The day of the funeral business shops were generally closed, and every civic honour was paid to his memory, while the town band escorted the procession to the cemetery. Being a church funeral, everything was conducted with decorum on the way to the grave. But as soon as the service there was finished, the whole order of the procession was changed, as the black population took charge of the band to conduct it back to town.

A lively tune was called for, and the response was the stirring strains of Tipperary, then the marching song of every recruiting party and departing contingent in Jamaica.

Lines were quickly formed, with joined arms and tossing heads, men, women and children, prancing and dancing, in mob formation they came pouring back to town, seemingly desirous that they might keep right on not to Montego Bay but all the way to Tipperary.

As I looked down from a little eminence and watched the singing, dancing throng as it jostled by, I realized what I have often repeated since, that there was no disrespect for the dead intended, nor was any given. It was merely a light-hearted people turning back from sorrow to the ordinary cares of life which they habitually meet with laughter and song.

One really has to live close to the "bush" to hope to understand its spirit and its creed. Many a time, drawn by the witchery of a tropical evening, I have stood out under the stars, and listened to the gentle rustle of the palm fronds, at peace with all the world, when from a distance came the pulsing throbs of that peculiar syncopation of myal dance or revival gathering, to forcibly remind one of witch-bound Africa. Or, again, I have been aroused at the most unearthly hours of the night, by wake or ninth night in the neighbourhood, and forced to rise from bed and sally forth and watch proceedings from afar.

There is invariably a leader with a "selfish voice," that is one who physically and vocally can carry the refrain above the contending claims of rival vocalizers. The self-composed but determined leader proceeds to "raise a hymn." In solemn recitative he repeats a couplet, then sets the note by starting off in strident tones. The entire assembly at once joins in. The couplet finished, the leader recites another line or two, and so they continue through the night until the dawn of day. No matter if the words are known by heart or taken from some popular hymn, this recitative must never be omitted. No end of effort is expended on each and every hymn, and as a necessary consequence rum and refreshments are freely served to all throughout the night. Then at the funeral itself, it was still no uncommon thing to see a black fellow turn his back upon the passing corpse so that the duppy would not recognize him and perhaps later return to annoy him. Moreover, even during my days in Jamaica, the "catching of the shadow" at a "bush" funeral was far from being a thing of the past.

As stated in Voodoos and Obeahs, I have more than once watched the process from a short distance, near enough, in fact, to be able to hear all that was said, and to watch carefully most that was done, as the actors, for such I must call them, scrambled and grasped at empty nothingness, with such realism of pretence, that I found myself actually rubbing my eyes, almost convinced against myself that there must be an elusive something that escaped my vision.

When sufficient rum had been imbibed, and the singing had keyed up the assembly to the proper pitch, someone would excitedly cry out: "See 'im yere!" Immediately two or three or even more rival hunters would start after that shadow at one and the same time. From outside where I stood, it looked as if a general scramble had started in the hovel and I could see forms falling over one another and hear the imprecations and exclamations. After a time, one more "forward" than the rest would claim to have caught the prey, only to be greeted with cries of scorn: "'Im get away! See 'im dah!" Whereupon the scuffle would start anew.

Eventually, when all of them were breathless, dripping with perspiration, their clothes soiled or at times actually torn, and eyes almost popping out of their heads with excitement, while a general condition of hysteria had taken possession of the entire gathering, the fact would be accomplished by some belligerent individual, who would clasp- his hands and let out a veritable scream of defiance: "Me got 'im! Me got 'im!" with such vehemence that he would literally shout down all protests to the contrary, with perhaps just a little hint of possible physical violence that might follow as a support to the power of his vociferation. Then a box or at times a small coffin would be produced and with much ado, not perhaps without a final effort to escape, the poor shadow would be securely fastened in and properly "laid" to be buried later at the funeral.

I have further listened to two disputants on the following morning, while the rum fumes were still assertive, almost coming to blows as to which one of them had actually accomplished the feat of catching the shadow, and yet when I questioned them individually a few days later, despite the fact that I knew them intimately, both of them in perfect scorn, asserted, almost in the same identical words: "Me no belieb in shadow, sah! 'Im all nonsense, sah!"

I could never quite make up my mind whether it was all a self-conscious display of dramatic power, or merely a passing delusion in consequence of the generous potions of rum that had been imbibed. In either case, the entire séance was based on a generally accepted superstition and the participants were utterly reticent about the whole matter when dealing with the white man who questioned them about their having taken part in it.

Some years ago I wrote the following paragraph: "The present day 'bush' funeral is often characterized by many of the old-time superstitions and practices. The Jamaican peasant is a born actor, and the earnestness with which the shadow is duly chased and finally caught makes the onlooker fancy that his dusky friend is really seeing things and surely what he eventually grasps in his hand must be more than an airy nothing. On the way to the grave, too, the wrestling with the coffin, to drag it past some hovel or other, frequently passes beyond description. The carriers, dripping with perspiration from the effort they are apparently making, struggle heroically to urge the burden forward. They even plead with it and 'argify.' Finding the task, however, beyond their combined effort, they lay the coffin down and pull and strain to no avail, while a perfect pandemonium breaks out in the assembled throng that clusters around ready with advice and suggestions of every kind. Finally, the chief spirit in the farce kneels down, and puts his ear against the coffin. His faculty of hearing must be extraordinary, for despite the din and noise, he receives full instructions from the late lamented. The owner of the hovel off the path, who perhaps is standing in his doorway taking in the scene has done the dead man wrong. The entire multitude, abandoning the coffin in the road, troops up to give the unfortunate aggrievor of the dead an unpleasant outpouring of vituperation and abuse, until the price of rum is forth-coming, whereupon all throng back again to the road, pick up the coffin and continue on their way without more ado."

Now with increased experience and study, I find myself in doubt how far I should revise my former judgment in the matter. How much of it is acting? How much of it is self-delusion? How much is hallucination? How much is a reality?

Certainly, I do not believe in ghosts in the ordinary acceptation of the word. Scriptural apparitions of spirits is an entirely different matter. But the Ashanti did believe in ghosts and their funeral customs like their other rites of passage, which really consisted in spirit control, formed an integral part in their system of religion. The Ashanti slaves in turn imposed this religious complex with its placating of spirits on the slave population of Jamaica so that it passed through the stage of myalism to its present form, revivalism.

Moreover, the revivalist to-day, as his prototype in Ashanti of old, in all these funeral customs as well as in his other emotional outbreaks, regards what he is doing as distinctively a religious ceremony. It is the only form of religion to which he wholeheartedly subscribes. He does believe in a Supreme Being, but his principal concern is with the subordinate entities, call them what we will, which play such a major part in his daily life, just as they have done in the case of the Ashanti from time immemorial. Consequently, in principle, revivalism differs little from the ancient Ashanti paganism and is necessarily antagonistic to every form of Christianity.

Furthermore, while duppies and shadows are to the revivalist mere natural phenomena of the human soul, their presumed control by the obeah-man brings them from the natural to the supernatural order where through their association with obeah they become tools of witchcraft and accordingly their manipulation must be included as part of the obeah-man's trade under the aegis of the Devil.

Would it be surprising, then, if on rare occasions, his Satanic Majesty made some external manifestation of the influence that he is exercising on the spiritual life of his devotees? If any man surrenders himself, either explicitly or even implicitly, to an evil control, he must expect to pay the price, and find that control at times exacting subserviency. Thus, in the material order, for example, the victim of drink who had allowed the habit to gradually assert the mastery over him, may lose in time all self-restraint and reach the stage where physically he can no longer resist, until he actually becomes the slave of drink. So, in the spiritual order, may not an unfortunate so surrender himself to the service of the Devil, that he becomes docile to every urge and suggestion of the Evil One? Absolutely he has the power to resist, but he does not choose to exercise his prerogative.

I do not say that all the uncanny knockings of the coffin or the reported annoyances of duppy and shadow are the work of the Devil. Far from it. I still contend that they are in great part delusions or human manipulations. But I cannot help feeling that at least on rare occasions there is something more than human ingenuity back of individual cases. Possibly even then the Devil may not physically direct the séance but what is to prevent his spiritual control over these minions who have gradually yielded to him the mastery over their actions? Such a course of influence would only tend to strengthen them and their brother-revivalists in their self-contained religion and its antagonism to Christianity in any form.

This may explain the fact that in Jamaica the habitual practice of the weird and bizarre is becoming more and more restricted to the revivalists in the "bush" as centres of activity.

Church members of every denomination regularly conduct their wakes in a decorous manner. Still even here occasionally time-honoured superstitions will creep in despite all the clergymen can do or say.

As a general rule, however, the church member professes to despise all this "nonsense" as he calls it, even if he deigns to admit that it does go on at all. And this, although he may be only a "follower" since he has not yet been able to "join." To him, the all-important point is, to have a minister of religion officiate at the funeral of his dear one. Of course, the rum and other refreshments must be provided first of all, and if he cannot afford the price himself, a plate decorated with a piece of crape is still sent round the neighbourhood.

This essential attended to, he approaches the minister of his choice, whom he hopes to cajole into giving as much as possible for nothing, taking care, however, to make a modest beginning in his request, which is apt to run something after this fashion, as I have recorded elsewhere from an actual experience.

"Parson, please, me beg y'u one hole, sah!"' This means, in every-day parlance, that the petitioner wants a free grave, or hole, as they call it, which usually costs a few shillings. The request granted, the wily suppliant takes courage and begins afresh. "Parson, please, me beg y'u one heading, sah!" In other words, he asks that the minister of the Gospel should come free of charge to the hovel where the funeral is to start, and lead the procession to the cemetery. For this added splendor and pomp, the ordinary charge is about double the price of the grave, or hole. This granted, too, the self-appointed Committee of Claims now comes to the real purpose of his quest. "Parson, please, me beg y'u one churching, sah!" He asks nothing less, than that the Reverend Gentleman should not only conduct a service at the house, but that he should then lead the procession to the church, where a more prolonged and elaborate ceremony may be held, with all the singing of hymns that patience will permit, and possibly too a little panegyric on the departed-one's real or fancied virtues, and then again lead the procession to the cemetery. For such a ceremony, it is customary to charge a really substantial fee.

To be perfectly honest, I never had the heart to refuse such an appeal, although I knew full well that in all probability the price was already in hand, and that its holder hoped to conserve it for the "necessary" expenses of the funeral.

POLTERGEIST

IT WAS about three years ago that Lord Olivier, a former Governor of Jamaica, wrote to me: "The occasional outburst of this 'poltergeist' phenomenon in Jamaica is remarkable. I investigated with some care the evidence as to one case which occurred when I was in Jamaica and there have been very full reports in the local Press of another recent occurrence which seems to have been carefully investigated without detecting any possibility of corporeal agency."

The later incident to which reference is made occurred at Roehampton, a little settlement in a remote mountain district of St. James Parish. I was visiting Jamaica at the time and while I was not able to investigate the case personally for want of time, I afterwards collected from The Daily Gleaner of Kingston, whatever had been published on the subject.

The first notice appeared in the issue of June 6, 1931, and ran as follows. "Ghost Mystery for the Spiritualists. Unseen Hands Throw At Girl All Kinds Of Missiles. From Which There Is No Escape: She Says She Is Controlled By Spirit: Hammer Tossed From Her Hand High In Air. Sensation at Roehampton. (From our Correspondent) Mount Horeb, June 2.--Happenings of a mysterious nature are reported to be taking place in the teacher's cottage at Roehampton, occupied by Miss Johnson, the teacher in charge of the school there.

"Miss Johnson lives with a girl about fourteen years old, named Muriel McDonald. About three weeks ago, it is said that some peculiar signs were seen, and heard, but after Saturday things reached a climax, so that the lady had been forced to leave the cottage and seek shelter elsewhere.

"It is, said, and by people of respectability whose words can be credited, and who have visited and seen for themselves, that stones are thrown into the house

BY UNSEEN HANDS

and hit the floor. In many cases a stone appears on the floor, and all of a sudden is lifted, hits the ceiling and rebounds with great force. In addition to stones, books, jars, powder-boxes, pans, and other vessels perform similar feats.

"Strange to say, wherever the little girl is, the stone-flinging is more prevalent, but she shows no signs of fear. At times she is hit--and hard too--but in spite of that goes around the house, and as she goes the missiles follow her.

"Miss Johnson is never hit although the stones and other articles drop near to her. The girl states that she SEES A 'SPIRIT' and whenever she wants to make a report it waves to her to keep silent. On Sunday the girl took up a hammer to give to someone, and all of a sudden it was lifted out of her hands, and taken up a considerable height to fall near to her. In house and kitchen there must be a number of persons surrounding her to protect her. People who have witnessed these mysterious acts, claim that they are the result of some 'spirit' working, as watch has been set, but no one has been seen doing these things.

" On Saturday and Sunday night, people kept 'wake' with Miss Johnson, so as to give her a chance to sleep, and the girl too, but even during sleep, sacks are lifted and stones are flung. As before stated, Miss Johnson has had to leave the cottage, and many are trying to solve this mystery."

On June 12, we find this continuation of the story, in The Daily Gleaner: "Mysterious Happenings at Roehampton. Siege Of 'Spirits' Of Teacher's Cottage Has Become Worse And No Solution. Work of Unseen Hand. Eye-witnesses Tell Of Alarming State Of Affairs--What Girl Victim Says. (From our Correspondent) Mount Horeb, June 8.--Each day the mysterious happenings at the teacher's cottage at Roehampton occupied by Miss C. E. Johnson, the headmistress of the school there, become more puzzling and serious. There has been no cessation of what was already reported in Saturday's issue of The Gleaner and up to this there seems no other solution of the mystery than that a 'spirit' is responsible for all that is happening. Day by day scores of people flock to this haunted house and each one who visits becomes an eye-witness of the events, and the experts no longer doubting the authenticity of the rumours but puzzled by this question: 'What is responsible for all this?'

THREE WORST DAYS

"Saturday, Sunday and Monday were the worst days of a bad lot. People congregated in the house on Sunday in exceedingly large numbers and as many knelt on their knees to pray, stones, bottles, bricks and gravel were hurled at them, so that in this case prayer did not frighten the 'unwelcome visitors.' Eye-witnesses state that they have seen lamps lifted off tables and fall to the ground. On the first occasion they are uninjured but if taken up by someone and replaced, they soon fall with a greater force and shatter in a hundred pieces.

"One part of the house made of Spanish wall, is now broken down by the Spirit, and the stones and marl are used to throw on the occupants of the house, whether they be Miss Johnson,

Muriel McDonald or any visitor. One boy, Martel Hurlock, declared that he took up a special stone dropped in the house, wrote his name on it, and flung it away. In a comparatively short time, the same stone came back into the house hitting the ceiling with lightning velocity and falling to the ground. He took up the stone, flung it away a second time and again it returned. Others present at the time confirm this declaration.

"One Gerald Birch declared he

GOT A SEVERE BLOW

on his hand, when he went to the house to see for himself. These are some of the happenings as told by eye-witnesses.

A lamp was seen to go through a very small hole, and when taken up and fitted to the hole, it could not pass through again.

A stone of about half a pound weight was thrown through a pane of glass and the glass was not smashed.

One Astley Lewis took off his shoes in the house and soon after one disappeared, was seen to 'fly' at a terrific speed and hit a girl at his side.

Stones drop into the house coming to all appearances through the roof of the house.

SUBJECT INTERVIEWED

"Muriel McDonald, the girl who is the target of the 'spirit' was seen and interviewed by our correspondent. She is a young girl, just left school and of a fair complexion. This is what she said:

"'I can see a spirit. When I was living at Maforta saw one. I see all the time in and around house a tall man dressed in white and wherever I go on the premises he follows me. I see no sign, but as soon as I return to Miss Johnson's place, the stone-flinging begins. One day last week I saw him cringing at Miss Johnson's back-door. I flung a stone at him and set the dog after him. He ran into the bushes but returned later on in the afternoon. Another day I climbed a breadfruit tree and I saw him standing at the foot of the tree. He beckoned to me to come down. When I did come down, he waved his hand as if sending me away. Another day I saw him standing at the latrine door to block my entrance inside. I have never seen him fling a stone, but I know it is he.'

HIT MANY TIMES

"Continuing she said: 'I am many times hit with all kinds of missiles. I was hit on the elbow of my right hand with a stone which inflicted a wound (wound seen). He oftentimes knocks my tea out of my hand, throws marl onto my head, pinches me and hits me otherwise. He took out of my hand a piece of breadfruit one morning. He took a pint bottle and hit me over my forehead, and took the lamp out of my hand on various occasions. At nights on entering my room I feel a bit afraid but otherwise I am all right. I love Miss Johnson and I do not mean to leave her.'

"Our correspondent did not see Miss Johnson as she had left from Saturday and has not yet returned.

"The girl cannot be left alone when on the premises. Outside the house stones are thrown at her, inside the kitchen, bricks, and in the house, lamps, bed key, socks, bottles and shoes are thrown. What will eventually happen is left to be seen, and the position of Miss Johnson is certainly not an enviable one."

The next report appears in The Daily Gleaner for June 18, 1931 as follows. "The 'Stone-throwing Ghost' of Mount Horeb (sic). What Is The Truth Of The Mysterious Happenings In District In St. James? Pictures of Scene. Hunting and Persecution of Girl, Muriel McDonald, And Miss Johnson.

"What Is the Truth of the ghostly happenings at the little village of Mount Horeb in St. James?

"Is the girl, Muriel McDonald, the subject of some cunning and malicious human persecution? Or are the thrown stones, the moving objects which follow her wherever she goes, propelled by some agency beyond our ken, beyond the borderland of this world?

"Such questions must inevitably arise in the mind on reading the accounts we have published of the recent ghostly happenings at the house of Miss Johnson, where Muriel McDonald lives, at Mount Horeb.

"To-day we publish photographs, specially taken for this paper, of the haunted house, and the two girls, Miss Johnson and Muriel McDonald, the subjects of the ghostly persecution.

MAIN HAPPENINGS:

"Briefly, the main happenings consist in the hurling of stones on the house by unseen agency; stones and objects such as lamps, books, etc., in the house rising of their own accord and hitting the ceilings and floors of rooms, and also hitting persons in the house.

"The happenings centre around Muriel McDonald, a fourteen years old girl, sturdy, unimaginative, and of good and gentle disposition, who lives in the house with Miss Johnson, teacher in charge of the school in the district.

"The occurrences only take place when Muriel is about; she is the chief target of the missiles, and has many times been struck and hurt by them.

WHAT MURIEL SAYS:

"Here is what the haunted girl herself says about it all." Then follow verbatim the statement as it appeared in The Gleaner of June 12th. The account continues.

EYE-WITNESSES' STORIES:

"Literally hundreds of people have visited the scene and here are some eye-witnesses' stories of what is happening, as told to our own correspondent." And then follow further quotations from the correspondent's report in The Gleaner of June 12th. The account closes as follows.

WHAT IS THE TRUTH?

"This is not the first time similar happenings have occurred in the island--indeed, these hauntings, of which stone-throwing is the principal feature, are fairly frequent here.

"What is the truth of it all?

"Shall we ever find out?"

A few observations are here called for. In the first place, with the exception of the photographs, this article adds little of real value to what has already appeared in the communications from the Mount Horeb local correspondent of The Daily Gleaner. In fact in two places without reference of other credit being given, it copies verbatim from the report that had appeared in the issue of June 12th. Further it attributes the whole incident to Mount Horeb the residence of the correspondent in place of Roehampton which is located about five miles distant. Hence we may safely conclude that the article was actually drawn up in the office of The Daily Gleaner from data already furnished by the Mount Horeb correspondent. Consequently it adds no new value to the evidence already given beyond the apparent acceptance of the facts as true on the part of newspaper staff.

Secondly, the general style as well as the slip regarding the locality of the happenings which is repeated, would indicate that the writer of the article was also the author of the Editorial which appeared in The Gleaner two days later, and which will shortly be reproduced.

Thirdly, it should also be noticed that in the present incident as told, physical harm was suffered by Muriel McDonald when hit by stones, which goes counter to the general principle assumed regarding Jamaica poltergeist, that even when struck by large stones, one suffers no injury.

Fourthly, and this is of real value, we have the clear statement towards the close of the article that poltergeist phenomena in Jamaica are not infrequent, or as it is expressed, "these hauntings, of which stone-throwing is the principal feature, are fairly frequent here."

The Editorial to which reference had already been made appeared in The Gleaner of June 20, 1931, as follows.

THE GHOST OF MOUNT HOREB

"The attitude of mind of the public, and we are speaking now of the educated public, towards the strange occurrences at Mount Horeb is, in general, one of amused, but, none the less, slightly uneasy scepticism.

"This seems to us rather a pity; it seems to us the attitude of the savage, the fool, or the child, who laughs at whatever he cannot understand. An attitude of attentive, scientific interest would be much more what we should expect from the intelligent section of this community-for it is the only attitude which can possibly result in anything helpful to the solution of the problem.

"For it is a problem, and a very serious one.

"Either these occurrences are the result of a malicious and criminal persecution of a highly ingenious nature, or they are manifestations of forces outside our understanding and control.

"Either hypothesis seems to us to call for serious inquiry and attention, rather than an affected and perhaps fearful, disregard. We should like to see the authorities take the matter in hand seriously and make a full and official published report on the occurrences themselves, rather than leaving what seems to us a series of most significant phenomena entirely uninvestigated."

1 heard at the time that the writer of this Editorial had to stand the playful chaffing of his friends for having disclosed his honest opinion too freely for his own peace or comfort. Accordingly, I was not surprised to find another Editorial appearing on July 6, 1931, and almost apologizing for having regarded the incident

as possibly of preternatural origin. This second Editorial, in part, runs as follows.

THESE STRANGE THINGS

"The recent extraordinary happenings at the residence of a certain teacher in the country may perhaps have caused some people to scoff, but others . . . would like to see these things entirely investigated, and in the meantime prudently suspend their judgment . . . A good deal more is known to-day about abnormal psychology than was the case forty years ago.

"Perhaps the outstanding achievement has been to demonstrate the fact that it is unwarrantable to jump to a supernatural or miraculous interpretation of something that we fail here and now to understand. Weights are lifted by unseen hands; objects rise to the ceiling, apparently of their own accord; stones mysteriously are thrown. Such things, it is alleged, have happened in Jamaica during the past few weeks, and there are other well attested cases of occult phenomena. A Catholic priest, who died during the influenza epidemic of 1918, once told us that on a certain occasion a woman was, in his presence, apparently thrown on the ground and soundly belaboured; she bore on her body marks of the beating she had received from some agency which, though invisible, seemed well able to exercise a good deal of physical violence. This incident happened in one of the country parishes; similar things have taken place in Haiti and in other countries-in fact, according to those who claim to have witnessed them, they are taking place all the time. What is the explanation? Ghosts? 'Duppies'? Devils? Or, in the case mentioned, was it merely an epileptic fit, the effect of the 'blows' being due to auto-suggestion, just as a hypnotized person can be made to get drunk on water, if told that it is rum or whiskey? We do not think that in such cases one should fly to the supernatural for an explanation; this is not to deny the existence of another world, but is really in accord with the normal scientific way of interpreting phenomena. That certain things do not appear to fit into the picture of nature that man has constructed for himself proves that the picture is either faulty or incomplete; and the only way to overcome this defect is to study the facts patiently. This of course implies that fact must be distinguished from imagination; not everything that a witness believes to have occurred, actually did occur. In other words, the ordinary laws of evidence are the only safe guide in interpreting such matters. Our personal impression is that a good deal of the occult phenomena in Jamaica as in other lands will one day be satisfactorily explained in terms of abnormal psychology."

Before commenting on the editorial, let me close the case of the happenings at Roehampton from the historical standpoint. I recently wrote to the Editor of The Daily Gleaner asking him to let me know if any official investigation was ever held and what was the upshot of the whole incident. In the absence of the Editor, his assistant kindly answered: "With regard to the Muriel McDonald incident, I am informed that the girl was persuaded to leave her residence and on her leaving the stone throwing ceased. No official investigation was held. It seemed to have been one of the usual cases of playing on the superstitious fears of the occupants of a dwelling."

In the investigation of phenomena of any kind, the editorial writer in The Gleaner is correct in assuming that ordinarily supernatural agencies are not to be ascribed as long as there is any possibility of a natural explanation. Not merely the exigencies of science but common sense itself demands such a mode of procedure. On the other hand, it is equally unscientific as it is directly opposed to sound common sense to start out with the supposition that the supernatural is absolutely impossible and that therefore there must be a natural explanation for every phenomenon. For on some occasion it may be possible to prove that the effect transcends any possible natural cause and that consequently some supernatural influence must be postulated. So, too, it happens now and then that while we may not definitely say that some particular phenomenon is supernatural, on the other hand we cannot possibly say that it is purely natural.

Nevertheless, we must be slow, especially in individual cases, to invoke supernatural agencies as explanatory causes without real need and sound proof. As regards the happenings at Roehampton, for example, too much credence is not to be placed in the exactness of the newspaper correspondent, especially as the account was written five miles from the scene of the phenomena and seemingly on mere hear-say evidence. Nowhere do we find any indication of the necessary investigation and sifting of testimony, nor does the writer offer a single word of evidence based on personal observation, despite the fact that the correspondent does interview the apparent victim, Muriel McDonald. Neither does the newspaper staff give indication of being on the spot at any time, except for the photographs when both the dwelling and the two occupants in separate poses are all in a state of peace and calm, and which might easily have been acquired by mail.

That many strange things did happen at Roehampton, we may safely admit. But we are left absolutely in the dark as regards the part trickery or imagination might have played in the reports which did not suffer in the telling as they travelled the five miles from Roehampton to Mount Horeb, to say nothing of the possible finishing flourishes that might earn a few extra half-pennies for the correspondent who knew what would please the reading public.

So, too, with the many other examples of poltergeist which "are fairly frequent," in Jamaica, as The Gleaner remarked. With the exception of the case officially investigated by Lord Olivier while he was Governor in Jamaica, I know of no instance that was authoritatively examined, nor have I at hand the particulars of the single verified incident. Usually one must rely for information on the more or less incoherent testimony of a wrought-up, hysterical group of witnesses who even in their normal state are over-inclined to see the supernatural in every event that varies ever so little from the customary norm of experience. I do not on that account ascribe all examples of poltergeist in Jamaica to hallucination or hysteria. Far from it. On more than one occasion I have had the suspicion if not the conviction; that some unnatural force was asserting itself, although I would be reluctant in any individual case to say definitely that we were dealing directly with the supernatural.

As related in Voodoos and Obeahs, shortly before I left Jamaica in 1917, I was on the outskirts of a notorious obeah district. It was up in the mountains that are located in the corner of St. Mary's Parish near where it joins St. Catherine's. A non-Catholic came to me and asked me to go with him and bless his house. For, he said, his children were starving, as they could not eat. According to his story, someone had put obi on them and when they tried to eat, the food would fly up and hit them in the face, and they could not get it into their mouths. Naturally I gave little credence to the story but I mounted my horse and followed the poor fellow who was certainly deeply distressed. On reaching his house I found the entire village in a state of panicky hysteria. A large group was gathered about the house and men, women and children were in perfect agreement in their testimony of what had happened, and all supported what the man had told me. It all gave such a diabolic impression that I did not feel justified in provoking the Evil One to an exhibition merely to satisfy my curiosity, so I blessed the house and took my departure without actually witnessing the display myself.

The word poltergeist means, of course, a noise ghost, but I have always felt that it is more suitably rendered as a "rough-house" ghost, on account of the general disorder it usually stirs up, especially in its Jamaica manifestation. Thus many of the examples of phenomena quoted in the previous chapters strictly speaking should be classified under poltergeist manifestations.

The Ashanti commonly associated with the suman or fetish the mmoatia or little people. These strange creatures are sometimes referred to as being "exceeding swift and used by devils and wizards as messengers," or again as "the speedy messengers of the gods who can go and come like the wind." They may aptly be termed imps or fairies according as they are in the service of Sasabonsam and his abayifo on the one hand, or of the abosom, or minor deities on the other.

These interesting creatures are thus described by Captain Rattray: "The most characteristic feature of these Ashanti 'Little folk'--the word mmoatia probably means 'the little animals'--is their feet, which point backwards. They are said to be about a foot in stature, and to be of three distinct varieties: black, red, and white, and they converse by means of whistling. The black fairies are more or less innocuous, but the white and the red mmoatia are up to all kinds of mischief, such as stealing housewives' palm-wine and the food left over from the previous day."

Of these same little folk, A. W. Cardinall writes: "All over the hinterland and in the forest zone the belief in the existence of dwarfs, elves, pixie-folk--call them what you will--is to be found.

These are sometimes visible, but more usually not. They are shaped like human beings and have all the attributes of man. They are pre-eminently mischief-workers, and are said to 'throw stones at one as one passes through the "bush."' That expression I have never fathomed. It is implicitly believed in. Moreover, these little men are blamed frequently for unexpected births; they 'change' children; they make them crazy or deformed. In Ashanti they are called mmoatia, in the Northern Protectorate they are chichiriga; or dialect varieties of that term."

In Jamaica, these little folk with their stone-throwing propensity and all, are included in the generic term of duppies, but I have never heard any reference to their characteristic of having their feet pointing backwards.

While stone-throwing is not an invariable element in poltergeist, it is of such common occurrence that in the Jamaica "bush" it is seldom wanting. Popular opinion has come to ascribe certain general propensities to the missiles of the duppies which may be thus enunciated. The stones may come from any possible direction or from various directions at one and the same time. Or, again they may seem to come from nowhere at all-simply materializing out of nothing. The source of supply may be a tree at some distance, where careful examination shows that there is no human being in the tree or along the line of fire. Stones may come through the roof without leaving any break or hole. They may pass through the window-pane without shattering the glass. They may come into a room and without striking any object turn at a right angle or even partially retrace their course in order to reach a particular individual who seemingly is the object of the bombardment, and who can find no nook or corner where the stones cannot reach him. In short these duppy-flung stones are apt to do everything that a well-behaved stone is supposed not to do, and above all even when weighing several ounces and after a flight through the air of a hundred feet or more, and squarely hitting some individual about the head, absolutely no wound or mark is left in consequence.

A favourite story, met with throughout the "bush," tells of the writing of one's name upon a stone that has just forced its presence on you, then as you throw it out into the most impossible places, to test the reality of his Duppyship, it invariably comes back to you with or without the compliments of Mr. Duppy. This is only one of the many "bush" tales that are current about these pestiferous stone-throwers.

Needless to say, there are many cases reported that are clearly the effect of a nervous imagination. The first rainy season that I was in the "bush," I was living in a substantial house with a stone foundation. Land crabs that had been flooded out of their burrows became a perfect pest. Some took refuge in the underpinning of the house and scrambled along the timbers with their heavy shells knocking in such a way that they produced as perfect an imitation of duppy-rappings on the floor as any high-strung nervous system could desire or rather dread. Then some venturesome fellow would find his way up on the roof of corrugated zinc, with subsequent scratching of slipping claws and continuous knocking of the awkward body, so that, even when you knew the cause, there could be no rest until you dislodged the crab and brought him back to earth. To the uninitiated such sounds as these might easily give rise to gruesome stories of duppy-haunted houses.

Naturally, too, there are cases of out-and-out imposition due to malicious mischief when human hands have cast stones upon the roof or into houses. But when all has been said and every allowance made for human ingenuity, I am forced to admit that

I have on occasions failed completely in my endeavour to find a natural explanation of some of these phenomena.

That examples of poltergeist in the West Indies are not restricted to Jamaica is evidenced by the testimony of Sir Hesketh Bell, and we cannot better close the present chapter than by giving at length the following incident which was related to him by a French priest in Grenada, where Sir Hesketh served in the Colonial Treasury Department in 1883.

"I was once in charge of a large and rather populous country district in Trinidad, and while there a remarkable event occurred which, being still unexplained, has quite shaken my ideas respecting the many stories of mystery one hears so often and laughs at. A friend of mine had bought a large but almost abandoned sugar estate, and the original dwelling-house having fallen to ruins, he was obliged to run up a small temporary wooden building until he could set about erecting a permanent dwelling. This little house was only composed of two good sized rooms, divided by a small wooden partition, and having no ceiling but the roof above them. The whole house was perhaps about thirty feet long by fourteen broad. It had been built and occupied by the planter and a brother of his for some weeks, when one evening I met them rushing towards me with the wonderful assertion that stones were falling in their house, and that they could not explain how. They were in a state of great agitation, and by degrees I extracted from them that they had been sitting in the veranda while the sun was setting, and had remained there until it had become quite dark. One of them was just about to go inside to light a lamp, when the noise of something heavy falling on the floor of the inner room startled him. A moment after came another crash. Hastily lighting the lamp, he opened the door and advanced into the room; on the floor he perceived a couple of good sized stones lying near him. Thinking himself the victim of some trick, he looked towards the window, which, however, was firmly secured. At that instant he heard another crash in the room he had just left. Hastily returning to it, he found on the floor another stone--Bang! Crash! again in the bedroom! Thoroughly alarmed, he rushed outside and called his brother, who, before he had time to speak, asked what he was kicking up all the row for! From outside they could hear distinctly the continual falling of the stones, and, unable to bear it any longer, they had rushed out to beg me to come and see the wonderful and terrifying occurrence.

"Calling a couple of men, we returned all together to the little wooden house, and as we approached we could distinctly hear the crash of falling stones. It was only with great trouble that I could induce my two black fellows to accompany us, so great was their terror of this supernatural business. Taking the lantern in my hand, I entered the porch, and instantly, as the light penetrated the house, the noise ceased. Entering the outer room, we found the floor covered with flinty stones of various sizes, some weighing a couple of ounces, others as many pounds. The windows were all closed, and I was perfectly dumfounded. We were all inside examining the stones when a sudden gust of wind blew out the lantern. Instantly the stones began to descend on all sides. We were glued to the spot with terror, and could hear the stones falling quite close to us on all sides; sometimes I could feel them whistling down quite close to my head, but, marvellous to relate, not one of us was as much as touched. Regaining courage, I managed to relight the lantern, and instantly the miraculous shower stopped. I was at my wit's end to account for the phenomenon; the stones lay in heaps all round the spot on which we were standing, but as soon as the lantern was alight, all became as still as the grave.

"Carefully placing our light in a sheltered corner, we began gathering up the stones and piled them together in a heap outside. Finding all still again, we resolved to pass the remainder of the night there, sleeping on the floor as best we could.

"Everything remained perfectly quiet for a couple of hours, and most of us were soon sound asleep. Being nearest the lantern, and curious to determine the nature of this phenomenon, I plucked up courage and blew out the light. Instantly, as before, the stones began to fall on all sides, and finding that no one had received the slightest hurt, we all began to regain courage and speculate on the causes of this wonderful phenomenon. Every time the lantern was relighted, the shower immediately stopped, only to recommence every time the light was put out. This continued all through the night, and ceased on the first appearance of dawn. The roof was in no way injured, and the mystery was perfectly inexplicable. The amount of stones gathered up in the house formed a large heap outside, and were not of the same nature as those lying about the place.

"Nothing remarkable happened during the day, but the news of this miraculous shower becoming known in the district, crowds of people came from all sides to see the stones, and hundreds begged to be allowed to pass the night in the house, hoping to witness the phenomenon for themselves, in case it was repeated. A few of our friends, and especially those who pooh-poohed the thing and openly expressed their conviction that the whole business was a hoax, were allowed to pass the night in the wonderful house. They were not disappointed, for as soon as complete darkness came on, the stones once more began to descend. The shower, however, was not so continual as on the previous night, but was witnessed by some fourteen or fifteen people. The next morning, on gathering up the stones, we found that the heap collected on the previous day was intact, and that the stones falling during the second night were fresh ones, obtained-Heaven knows where.

"As might be expected, the news of these wonders was very soon spread all over the island, and the place was crowded from morning till night. The mysterious shower, however, never occurred again, and the place returned to its normal condition. Neither the reason, cause, nor effect of these miraculous showers has ever been explained, and the whole thing remains a mystery to this day. That the thing happened, I will solemnly vouch for, but that is all I know about it, and I suppose a mystery it will ever remain."

CONCLUSIONS

IN JAMAICA, from time to time, we hear of cases of table-rapping, planchette-writing, ouija board, and other manifestations, pretty much as they are reported over the rest of the world, except that the circles in which they are held are restricted to a narrow group which has never really popularized the practices.

In passing, let me cite an instance, just as it was reported by eye-witnesses, that would appear to indicate diabolic control, if we can place any reliance at all in human testimony. At a séance held in one of the northern Parishes, I was told, the medium or control called up the Devil who forthwith inquired what he could do for her. "Play to me," was the request. "What shall I play?" asked the Devil. "Home, Sweet Home," was the answer. Immediately, the table around which the séance was being conducted, rose in the air, passed unsupported across the room, and turning edgewise before a piano that was open, with its corner it struck the keys and played the desired tune. This accomplished, the table returned to its former place in the midst of the circle attending the séance. The following evening, the same witnesses reported, that the control again called up the Devil and this time asked what she could do for him. "Sing to me," came the request. "What shall I sing?" asked the control. And the answer came, clear and distinct, "The wail of the damned in hell."

But this and similar phenomena are so clearly ingrafts of recent introduction from abroad, that they can scarcely be regarded as phenomena of Jamaica, despite the fact that they are occurring in Jamaica. Hence, strictly speaking they do not come within the scope of the present study. In other words, we have nothing to do with modern spiritism whether regarded as a psychic study or a religious mania. We are restricting ourselves to such phenomena as are distinctively Jamaican and which have consequently come down to us from the days of slavery and beyond.

While the Ashanti formed only a comparatively small percentage of the whole slave population of Jamaica, as we have seen, from earliest days, they exercised such a dominance over the natives of all other tribes, that they forcibly imposed their culture on the entire mass, and effectively blotted out whatever manners and customs were at variance with their own. Thus we find, for example, that their system of day-names became adopted generally and that regardless of tribes it was the Ashanti nomenclature that was in common use.

This paramount influence was effected on the part of the Ashanti principally through terror of their exercise of the old tribal witchcraft which attained its purpose through fear, judiciously supplemented by secret poisoning whenever this was found necessary.

Doctor Walter Bradford Cannon, the distinguished Physiologist of the Harvard Medical School, has just written to me concerning "the-casting of a fatal spell on a person by a king or priest or voodoo doctor exerting an influence among savage and superstitious people, with the result that the person who is credulous and terrorized by the spell is said to die." Doctor Cannon, in consequence of experiments that are being conducted under his direction among the lower animals, has come to some very interesting conclusions that will no doubt be published in due course. Suffice it to say here that his explanation: "It is as if the animal bled to death within its own tissues," satisfies in every way what I have myself observed in Jamaica. Men and women literally pine away from fear of obeah which they have heard is being worked against them, and frequently death has resulted when there was no indication whatever of poisoning. I have personally come in contact with such cases and have felt convinced that death was due entirely to the state of nervous fear that haunted the victims day and night, depriving them of all nourishment and repose until they actually wasted away, and died of exhaustion.

The Ashanti believed in a Supreme Being, but their external religious rites were chiefly concerned with spirit control. They greatly feared an evil spirit, Sasabonsam, who had much in common with the Devil of Christianity, and they suppressed in Ashanti homeland and became perhaps the greatest single influence in the lives of the Ashanti descendants among the Jamaican slaves. For, substantially unchanged in form or practice, the old Ashanti witchcraft continued on to the end of slavery in the island, under the term obeah, and completely deleted all other systems of the black art that had been familiar to the slaves from other tribes back in Africa.

The Ashanti did not fare so well in the preservation of their tribal religious practices. As public functions were forbidden them, they were forced to adapt themselves to circumstances and the secretiveness of the obayifo had to be employed by the priest of religion, the okomfo. Since the Ashanti religious rites had the common good in view even as the aim of witchcraft tended primarily to the harm of the individual, the age-old antagonism of okomfo and obayifo was for a time set aside and an unholy alliance was formed between the two against the common oppressor of both-the white man. This alliance was probably facilitated if not positively coerced by the martial spirits among the slaves who acted as leaders and stirred them up to the pitch of frenzy that repeatedly led to slave uprisings and rebellions. Such leaders found it necessary to make constant use of the obayifo to keep the less belligerent slaves in a state of subserviency to the Ashanti leadership.

As a group, the Ashanti and their descendants in Jamaica clung to the old religious traditions and beliefs, even when the external ceremonies had to be disguised under the shield of an alien dance that finally caused their adopted practices to become known as myalism.

The okomfo, or myal-man as he was now called, chafed under the forced coalition with his logical arch-enemy, and no sooner had Emancipation put an end to the need of co-operation than the old antagonism broke out again and a serious effort was made on the part of the old priestly class to annihilate the servants of Sasabonsam, under the pretence of digging up obeah. The struggle, however, was a short one. The very excesses of the myal-men only accentuated the secret pretences to spiritual power affected by their adversaries, and the popular estimation of the obeah-man did not suffer in consequence. In fact it was the obeah-man who gradually came to assert the stronger influence in the life of the "bush," just as he had gained the upper hand in the days of slavery. He better satisfied the selfish aims of the individual particularly in matters of revenge, and necessarily the myal-man as such was gradually eliminated, as myalism itself gave way to revivalism.

With the waning influence of the myal-man, as time went on, the obeah-man naturally assumed to himself the rôle of his old adversary, in great part as a cloak to his own machinations, until myalism itself became regarded as a mere offshoot or modification of obeah. There was no longer any question of public good, the individual alone was to be considered whether for weal or woe. But through it all, the obeah-man never wavered in his devotion to his Sasabonsam or Devil, and the forces for evil had definitely shaken off the old religious restraint of the Ashanti.

So it is at the present time in Jamaica, we usually find the same individual exercising the functions of myal-man and obeah-man alike, digging up to-day the obeah that he himself set last night, or curing in turn the very victim of his wiles.

Moreover, having absorbed the office of myal-man, what is more natural than that our up-to-date obeah-man should seek to master the more modern forms of pretended magic that are being widely advertised by "fakers" in the Press abroad. Thus he now acquires whatever books he can on the subject and endeavours to test the formulae in practice, until many of his ilk differ but little from the charlatans throughout the world who seek an easy living by their wits at the expense of the superstitious or illiterate. But there is in reality one great difference in the practice as it goes on in Jamaica from what is customary abroad. The Jamaica obeah-man still believes that, even in the use of these new-fangled methods, it is the influence of his Sasabonsam or Devil that produces the effect. Ordinarily abroad, the magician is simply a clever impostor who is fully conscious of the fact himself.

Obeah, as practised in Jamaica to-day, especially in the Metropolis and the larger towns, might well be regarded for the most part as obtaining money under false pretences, as has been advocated. But in the "bush" there are still many of the craft who ply their trade along the time-honoured lines. If a few shillings or a pound or two is in the making, they will stoop to the sharp practices that are becoming so popular with their brethren of the city, but as a rule they take themselves seriously and weave their spells and utter their invocations to Massa Debbil without disguise, placing their unbounded confidence in him as their chief reliance, and continuing on this phase of demonolatry that has come down in direct descent from their forebears, the servants of Sasabonsam back in Ashantiland. This does not mean that the obeah-man actually has an evil-spirit at his beck and call. But whatever his power or lack of power may be, he believes that he has such a co-operating spirit, and it is his intention to attain his end through a diabolic influence.

If any constituent part of an act is evil, the act itself is morally wrong, and what might have been indifferent or even good in itself can become vitiated by the evil intention of the one who performs it. Thus, if he thinks that he is doing evil, and deliberately goes ahead, even if the act in itself might have been good or indifferent, he is actually committing the evil of his intent.

The Ashanti regards his nkabere or good-luck charm as the temporary receptacle of some spiritual influence, just as he looks on the shrines of his abosom or minor deities as the scat for the time being of these spiritual entities, without for a moment wavering in his monotheistic belief in the Supreme Being. But did he, as so many early travellers erroneously declared, intend to give to these so-called fetishes divine adoration when he sacrificed his fowl to them, then would he indeed have been guilty of the idolatry attributed to him, and that too without the slightest material change either in the object or the manner of the cult.

When, on the other hand, the Ashanti obayifo operates precisely as the servant of his Sasabonsam Devil, just as his successor the obeah-man of Jamaica places his reliance in Satan whom he personally invokes to attain his end, we have nothing more nor less than a form of demonolatry in the one as in the other. Even granting, if you wish, that both are victims of hallucination, providing only that they have sufficient use of reason to appreciate what they are doing, the culpability is there, because their intention is precisely to place themselves in communication with the Devil and through his influence they hope to effect their purposes. By this very act they have placed themselves under an obligation to their patron, and accordingly at times they surrender themselves to him in ways that are better left undescribed.

Is it, then, mere coincidence, that it is precisely in these "bush" districts where the old order of things still persists that we find the psychic phenomena which form the subject of the present study? I do not recall having ever heard of any such manifestations in Kingston or its immediate vicinity, but I would not be surprised at their occurrence in some of the slum sections where even now real obeah is worked in secret on occasions. At all events the cases that we now have under consideration all occurred at a distance from the city of Kingston and in neighbourhoods where genuine obeah was being practised.

I do not mean to infer that the obeah-man is the direct or immediate cause of the mysterious poltergeist and other happenings. Quite the contrary. As already stated, such a control of diabolic influence on the part of the obeah-man would appear to me as being repugnant to Divine Providence in the ordinary course of human events, although it might be permitted on rare occasions. For His own good purposes, God may permit at times some friend of Satan to exercise preternatural power as in the case of the Witch of Endor. But this is not the ordinary course of events. Certainly in all the phenomena in Jamaica that I have been able to study, not in a single instance have I found the slightest indication that the happenings were invoked by any human being. If the directing force was really diabolic, then his Satanic Majesty was seemingly conducting operations in person and not at the behest of any of his servants among the obeah-men. Of that I am convinced.

The Book of Job in the Old Testament recounts the severe afflictions that a holy man undergoes at the hands of Satan. God permits it all precisely to extol his virtue through the heroic patience that he manifests. God says to Satan: "Behold he is in thy hand, but yet spare his life." So that even here bounds are set to the power of the evil one. Moreover during all the trials that follow, Job is borne up and strengthened by the grace of God which eventually prevails against all the wiles of Satan.

While the Book of Job is not a strictly historical narrative, it is a didactic poem with a historical basis and written under Divine inspiration. Being an integral part of the Canon of Holy Scripture, the principles that it enunciates are all in conformity with the dictates of right reason. We have authority, then, for saying that when God permits Satan to so assail his victim that he deprives him "of all his substance" and covers him "with ulcers from head to foot," even then we are not justified in arguing as did the friends of Job that this is punishment for sin. Perhaps it is to be but a contrast to what is to come, for even in a worldly way, it may be God's will, that virtue should be rewarded with the promised hundred-fold.

Nevertheless, as a general rule, this consoling aspect is not usually connected in Holy Scripture with the assailments of the Devil, who in the words of Saint Peter, "as a roaring lion, goeth about seeking whom he may devour."

Thus, too, in the Book of Tobias, we have the case of Sara who "had been given to seven husbands, and a devil named Asmodeus had killed them, at their first going in unto her."

At times evil spirits serve as; ministers of God's wrath, as in His dealings with the Egyptians: "And He sent upon them the wrath of His indignation: indignation and wrath and trouble, which He sent by evil angels."

Among the bits of wisdom enunciated by Jesus, the son of Sirach of Jerusalem, we find: "There are spirits that are created for vengeance, and in their fury they lay on grievous torments. In the time of destruction they shall pour out their force: and they shall appease the wrath of Him that made them."

Of the examples of obsession in the New Testament, we must satisfy ourselves by quoting three that are recorded by Saint Mark in his Gospel, in each of which physical violence is done by the evil spirits.

"And there was in the synagogue a man with an unclean spirit; and he cried out, saying: What have we to do with thee, Jesus of Nazareth? Art Thou come to destroy us? I know who Thou art, the Holy One of God. And Jesus threatened him, saying: Speak no more, and go out of the man. And the unclean spirit tearing him, and crying out with a loud voice, went out of him."

"And they came over the strait of the sea into the country of the Gerasens. And as He went out of the ship, immediately there met him out of the monuments a man with an unclean spirit. Who had his dwelling in the tombs, and no man now could bind him, not even with chains. For having been often bound with fetters and chains, he had burst the chains and broken the fetters in pieces, and no one could tame him. And he was always day and night in the monuments and in the mountains, crying and cutting himself with stones. And seeing Jesus afar off, he ran and adored Him. And crying with a loud voice, he said: What have I to do with Thee, Jesus the Son of the most high God? I adjure Thee by God that Thou torment me not. For He said unto him: Go out of the man, thou unclean spirit. And He asked him: What is thy name? And he saith to Him: My name is

Legion, for we are many. And he besought Him much, that He would not drive him away out of the country. And there was there near the mountain a great herd of swine feeding. And the spirits besought Him, saying: Send us into the swine, that we may enter into them. And Jesus immediately gave them leave. And the unclean spirits going out, entered into the swine: and the herd with great violence was carried headlong into the sea, being about two thousand and were stifled in the sea. And they that fed them fled, and told it in the city and in the fields. And they went out to see what was done."

"And one of the multitude, answering, said: Master, I have brought my son to Thee, having a dumb spirit, who, wheresoever he taketh him, dasheth him, and he foameth, and gnasheth with the teeth, and pineth away; and I spoke to Thy disciples to cast him out, and they could not. Who answering them, said: O incredulous generation, how long shall I be with you? How long shall I suffer you? Bring him unto Me. And they brought him. And when He had seen him, immediately the spirit troubled him; and being thrown down upon the ground, he rolled about foaming. And He asked his father: How long time is it since this hath happened unto him? But he said: From infancy: and oftentimes hath he cast him into the fire and into waters to destroy him. But if Thou canst do any thing, help us, having compassion on us. And Jesus saith to him: If thou canst believe, all things are possible to him that believeth. And immediately the father of the boy crying out, with tears said: I do believe, Lord; help my unbelief. And when Jesus saw the multitude running together, He threatened the unclean spirit, saying to him. Deaf and dumb spirit, I command thee, go out of him; and enter not any more into him. And crying out, and greatly tearing him, he went out of him, and he became as dead, so that many said: He is dead. But Jesus taking him by the hand, lifted him up; and he arose. And when He was come into the house, his disciples secretly asked Him: Why could not we cast him out? And He said to them: This kind can go out by nothing, but by prayer and fasting."

The Reverend Simon Augustine Blackmore, S.J. has well said: "A Christian knows, on the authority of divine revelation as well as from the nature of certain phenomena, that God, by His extraordinary providence, sometimes allows evil spirits to intervene in human affairs. But he also knows that such intervention is not a regular and fixed institution by which men may communicate with spirits whensoever they will. Philosophically, the notion is contrary to the divine attributes of God, and is disproved by all moralists in the treatise on magic. Moreover, spiritistic séances are always wicked by their very nature, because of the evil intention of communicating with spirits, contrary to the Divine Law. Hence, any alleged intervention of spirits must be examined into in every instance or be judged on its own merits according to the evidence, as to its probability or certainty, as the case may be.

"That the living have at times received communications which can be explained only by the presence and activity of some intelligent agent external to our world of sense, is a proposition which no Christian will find difficult of acceptance. It may be said, indeed, to be an essential part of the dogmatic teaching of both Judaism and Christianity. From beginning to end the Bible records many interventions of angelic spirits as the messengers of God to men and hardly less emphasizes the cunning duplicity of Satan and his satellites in their conspiracy against the welfare of man." While the writer is treating directly of modern Spiritism, all that he says here may be equally applied to the question of our Jamaica phenomena.

It is to be noticed that wherever devil-worship is in vogue, as for example in various parts of Africa, the evil one is allowed considerable latitude in the way of material manifestations; and even obsessions similar to those recorded in Holy Writ, occur from time to time in many parts of the world. It is my conviction, from the viewpoint of a Catholic priest, that all this is by permission of Almighty God, perhaps as punishment for dealing with the Devil and for the usual attendant vices; or, perhaps again, merely as a timely warning to others. In every instance, too, there is a limitation set to the power of the evil one beyond which he cannot pass, and even if he has entered into physical possession of a tortured body, he cannot control the soul and its faculties without the free consent of the victim's will.

The supposititious requirements for a practitioner of witchcraft calls for "a voluntary personal surrender to the Devil and an acquiescence in his will; being endowed with the power of divination, fortune telling, horoscopy, the casting of spells, and other mysterious achievements." This assumes a certain contract with the Devil whereby the witch acquires a directive force over powerful spiritual agencies, having at beck and call one or more evil spirits with which to cast spells on persons and places. In other words, if such a state of affairs were possible, we would have an efficient medium or control, directing the external manifestations of diabolic power. Certainly as far as Jamaica is concerned, I have never seen the slightest indication of any such mediumship or control. Obeah-men may claim to have disturbed the peace of a community or of an individual by means of duppies. But, as I have already stated and now repeat by way of emphasis, every single case that I have examined of phenomena that appeared in any way preternatural was completely dissociated from any kind of mediumship or control. It simply happened nor was there even a breath of rumour connecting it with the working of obeah or any other form of magic.

When the atmosphere has been properly surcharged electrically, we may anticipate a thunderstorm with all its usual disturbances of wind and rain. So, too, once the obeah-man has created what I might call a diabolic atmosphere in a district, when his communications with the Devil has given his Satanic Majesty some standing in the spiritual life of the community, and the co-operation of the clients of the obeah-man has firmly established a practice which is nothing less than demonolatry, we need not be surprised if the Power of Evil begins to manifest material phenomena, perhaps of the poltergeist type, seeking to weaken church control and so gradually to augment the tendency to evil throughout the district.

I do not for a moment imply that such a condition of affairs is at all peculiar to Jamaica. It is the same the whole world over wherever similar conditions happen to exist. And let it be remembered that right here in these United States we are far from being free from communications with the Devil and other forms of demonolatry. There are many practices in vogue, not among the poor and illiterate of country districts, but actually within select circles of intellectual centres where proceedings are carried on that differ little from the séance that was mentioned at the opening of the present chapter. Moreover we have this statement from one of the most distinguished students of demonology, Montague Summers, F.A.S.L. in his contribution to The History of Civilization Series: "In the nineteenth century both Albert Pike of Charleston and his successor Adriatic, Lemmi have been identified upon abundant authority as being Grand Masters of societies practising Satanism, and as performing the hierarchical functions of 'the Devil' at the modern Sabbat." I do not attempt to substantiate this statement of fact in any way. I merely quote it on the authority of a distinguished scholar whose writings on witchcraft have gained for him an international reputation. My sole purpose is to show that we of the outside world cannot reproach Jamaica if among the ignorant in the heart of the "bush" obeah takes the form of demonolatry.

Furthermore, it ill becomes us to be hypercritical concerning superstitious beliefs of the Jamaica "bush." Recently glancing through a local paper, The Boston Post of October 20, 1934, I noticed more than two full columns devoted to advertisements connected with meetings of a psychic nature. Actually there were twenty-six separate attractions competing for public support. A professed "Non-Spiritualist" was to lecture on "Do the Dead Appear?" and a number of "Spirit Photographs" were to be shown upon a screen during the lecture, presumably in support of the affirmative side of the question. A "trance lecturer and message bearer" was to be supplemented during the week by other artists, and the Saturday evening reception was to be featured by "good mediums" and "refreshments." Another advertisement offered as an attraction for Friday "Extra Mediums and coffee and cake," while a rival attraction advertised a "Message Séance" which was naively enhanced by an "Oyster Supper." Still another advertisement was satisfied with the general statement "Refreshments served." And all this in the vicinity of cultured Boston!

Mr. Summers, whom we have just cited, opens the first chapter of The History of Witchcraft and Demonology by quoting from Jean Bodin, "A sorcerer is one who by commerce with the Devil has a full intention of attaining his own ends," and adds: "It would be, I imagine, hardly possible to discover a more concise, exact, comprehensive and intelligent definition of a Witch." Certainly we have this definition fully verified in the case of the Jamaica obeah-man as the direct descendant in theory and practice from the Ashanti obayifo.

Although I am reluctant to pass definite judgment on each phenomenon taken separately since the possibility of error or delusion in a single happening is admittedly great, still one particular instance of those already quoted may be chosen for special attention. Let us take the one that was given in the Introduction as Case II and which happened at All Saints Mission.

In addition to the written document of Father Emerick and my own personal experience as there related, I have at different times received verbally confirmatory evidence from Fathers Duarte, Prendergast and Magrath, besides oral statements from Father Emerick, each dealing with what came under his own observation. Except in details these relations varied little from the written account of Father Emerick, having for the most part to do with the unceremonious disappearance of a gentleman and lady who had called at the mission house late at night. I am quite certain that there was no collusion among them in their testimony. Others have also told me their stories about the same happenings, but either their evidence was only hear-say and accordingly discounted, or else the person knew of the reputation of the house before anything had happened to him there, and in consequence I have disbarred their statements from consideration as being possibly the result of overexcited imaginations.

Here then I have the evidence of four fully qualified and independent witnesses substantially agreeing in all essentials, supplemented by my own experiences which, if entirely divergent in character, supported in principle the main point at issue, that something was actually happening at the mission house that could not be explained by natural agencies. And I cannot help being forced to the conclusion that we were not all the victims of delusions, especially as I have heard of no disturbances on the premises since the reconstruction of the old mission house was undertaken some time ago.

In connexion with modern spiritism, Father Blackmore writes: "Who these invisible agents are that masquerade as the souls of the dead is clear to every Christian who knows from Sacred Scripture that the fallen angels, the outcasts of heaven, are always eager, for their own pernicious purpose, to intermeddle in the affairs of human life. By their fruits you shall know them."

So, too, in such spirit manifestations as we have been discussing, the presumption is that the spiritual influence back of them must be ascribed not to the angels but to the demons. For where the effect is evil, we must look for an evil cause--truly by their fruits you shall know them.

In conclusion, it must not be thought that these phenomena are of common occurrence in Jamaica. Needless to say, I have diligently sought out every case that was supported by first-hand information--one would never finish were he to listen to all the hear-say accounts repeated "on the best of authority." And the results of more than a quarter of a century of labour and investigation have brought to light only the instances that have been here cited, and they were actually spread out over forty years or more in the happening.

Taking them all together as a composite whole it is my unhesitating conclusion that there are times in Jamaica when phenomena occur that transcend the forces of Nature and must be attributed to spirit control, which, judged from the consequences, are of diabolic origin.

Nevertheless, I repeat again, it would be a serious mistake to stress particular instances independent of the rest and at all times in the acceptance of evidence we must play the rôle of sceptic rather than that of enthusiast, sifting carefully every word of testimony and testing out each fact as far as possible. For, it is a time-honoured proverb in Jamaica, "No ebery chain you hear a fe rollen calf," meaning, "Do not jump to conclusions too hastily."

DOCUMENTATION

CHAPTER I--ASHANTI CULTURAL INFLUENCE IN JAMAICA

W. J. Gardner, History of Jamaica, London, 1873, Preface, p. 4.

ditto, p. 184.

Edward Long, The History of Jamaica, London, 1774, Vol. II, p. 472.

ditto, p. 473.

ditto, p. 474.

ditto, p. 474.

ditto, p. 475.

Harry H. Johnston, The Negro in the New World, London, 1910, p. 111.

ditto, p. 111, Note.

ditto, p. 275.

A. B. Ellis, History of the Gold Coast, London, 1893, p. 94.

Gardner, 1.c., p. 175.

Long, 1.c., Vol. II, p. 427.

R. Sutherland Rattray, Ashanti Proverbs, Oxford, 1916, Proverb #523.

J. B. Danquah, Akan Law and Customs, London, 1928, p. 241.

J. G. Christaller, Dictionary of the Asante and Fante Language Called Tshi (Twi), Basel, 1933, p. 43.

Bedford Pim, The Negro and Jamaica, London, 1866, p. 64 f. Note:--Quamin really signifies Saturday, not Monday; and, Quaco represents Wednesday, not Thursday.

R. C. Dallas, The History of the Maroons, London, 1803, Vol. I, p. 24 f.

Long, 1.c., Vol. II, p. 340. 264

Dallas, 1.c., Vol. 1, p. 30.

ditto, p. 31.

ditto, p. 33. Note:--According to Professor Martha Warren Beckwith of Vassar College, Black Roadways, Chapel Hill, 1929, p. 176 f., even to-day the Jamaica Maroons use the old Ashanti language which she calls Kromanti as a secret code of speech. She also declares that old "Kromanti" songs are still sung among these same Maroons. (l.c., p. 192 f.)

Dallas, l.c., Vol. I, p. 34. Cfr. also Martha Warren Beckwith; "The Maroons know 'stronger obeah' than any other group; they are more cunning in herb magic; they command a secret tongue (the so-called Kromanti), and they know old songs in this speech 'strong enough to bewitch anybody'; they employ old arts which deal with spirits." (l.c., p. 191.)

Dallas, l.c., Vol. I, p. 93.

Rattray, Ashanti Proverbs, #1.

Frank Cundall, Historic Jamaica, London, 1915, p. 325.

Dallas, l.c., Vol. I, p. 58.

ditto, p. 64.

Christaller, l.c., p. 356, Onyame.

Dallas, l.c., Vol. I, p. 66.

ditto, p. 116.

ditto, p. 129.

ditto, Vol. II, p. 348 f.

ditto, Vol. I, p. 176.

J. B. Moreton, West India Customs and Manners, London, 1793, p. 133f.

Bryan Edwards, History, Civil and Commercial, of the British Colonies in the West Indies, London, 1793, Vol. II, p. 64.

R. S. Rattray, Ashanti, Oxford, 1923, p. 73. Note:--Doctor Beckwith accentuates the fact that the Maroons to-day refer their traditions back to the Kromanti, (l.c., p. 184) and further asserts that the Maroons form "in some respects a secret society . . . which preserves certain so-called Kromanti customs as a proof of their African pride of blood." (l.c., p. 184 f.)

W. F. Butler, An Autobiography, New York, 1913, p. 149.

Chambers's Journal, London, Vol. V, No. 215, p. 82.

ditto, p. 83.

Folk-lore. A Quarterly of Myth, Tradition, Institution and Custom, London, Vol. IV, p. 211. Note:--Doctor Beckwith quotes the Jamaica proverb, "If you promise senseh fowl anyt'ing, him wi' look fe it," and explains it as "a saying which warns one to keep one's promises in an obeah transaction." (l.c., p. 1200.)

Rattray, Ashanti Proverbs, #697.

ditto, #175.

Isabel Cranstoun Maclean, Children of Jamaica, Edinburgh, 1910, p. 31.

Rattray, Ashanti Proverbs, #14.

Edwards, l.c., Vol. II, p. 70.

Rattray, Ashanti, p. 215.

Rattray, Ashanti Proverbs, #56.

Herbert G. DeLisser, Twentieth Century Jamaica, Kingston, 1913, p. 110.

Edwards, l.c., Vol. II, p. 71. Note:--Professor Beckwith adopts this view of Bryan Edwards, saying: "Obeah is, I take it,

Obboney,"' and adds: "There is a tendency among the sceptical to-day to admit the powers of the obeah-man but to ascribe them to the Devil, so exchanging pagan for Christian folklore." (l.c., p. 105.)

A. W. Cardinall, In Ashanti and Beyond, Philadelphia, 1927, p. 48.

T. Edward Bowditch, Mission from Cape Coast Castle to Ashantee, London, 1819, p. 318.

Cfr. Hebrewisms of West Africa, p. 21f.

R. Sutherland Rattray, Religion and Art in Ashanti Oxford, 1927, p. 160.

ditto, p. 161.

Rattray, Ashanti, p. 82.

Barker and Sinclair, West African Folk-Tales, London, 1917, p. 24.

Rattray, Ashanti Proverbs, #175.

Cfr. Voodoos and Obeahs, p. 215 f. Note:--Had he been really making obi, he would have been surer of his privacy and would have squatted on the ground surrounded by his paraphernalia and this would have been the scene with little variation. Most of the ingredients to be used are concealed in a bag from which he draws them as he needs them. The special offering of his patron which must include a white fowl, two bottles of rum and a silver offering are on the ground beside him. Before him is the inevitable empty bottle to receive the ingredients. The incantation opens with a prolonged mumbling which is supposed to be "an unknown tongue." This is accompanied by a swaying of the body. Gradually ingredients are placed in the bottle, and a little rum is poured over them. The throat of the fowl is deftly slit and drops of blood are allowed to fall first on the silver offering, and then on the contents of the bottle to which is finally added a few feathers plucked from various parts of the fowl with a last libation of rum. During all this process the obeah-man has been drawing inspiration from frequent draughts of rum, reserving a substantial portion to be con-sumed later when he makes a meal off the flesh of the fowl.

Rattray, Ashanti, p. 311f.

ditto, p. 311.

Note:--The name Jamaica is generally derived from the old Indian name which signifies a land of springs or streams.

Rattray, Ashanti Proverbs, #14.

ditto, #85.

Anderson and Cundall, Jamaica Proverbs and Sayings, London, 1927, #979

ditto, #979.

Rattray, Ashanti Proverbs, #125.

Anderson and Cundall, #671.

Rattray, Ashanti Proverbs, #137.

Anderson and Cundall, #3.

Rattray, Ashanti Proverbs, #200.

Anderson and Cundall, #587.

ditto, #591.

Rattray, Ashanti Proverbs, #204.

Anderson and Cundall, #562.

ditto, #563.

Rattray, Ashanti Proverbs, #224.

ditto, #263.

ditto, #269.

Anderson and Cundall, #1173

Rattray, Ashanti Proverbs, #270

ditto, #288.

Anderson and Cundall, #626.

Rattray, Ashanti Proverbs, #292.

Anderson and Cundall, #1134.

Rattray, Ashanti Proverbs, #298.

ditto, #305.

Anderson and Cundall, #397.

Rattray, Ashanti Proverbs, #407.

Anderson and Cundall, #1194.

Rattray, Ashanti Proverbs, #460.

ditto, #529.

Anderson and Cundall, #1246.

Rattray, Ashanti Proverbs, #590.

Anderson and Cundall, #538.

Rattray, Ashanti Proverbs, #630.

Gardner, l.c., p. 393.

Rattray, Ashanti Proverbs, #669.

Anderson and Cundall, #511.

Rattray, Ashanti Proverbs, #677.

Anderson and Cundall, #1147.

Rattray, Ashanti Proverbs, #753

Anderson and Cundall, #1168.

Rattray, Ashanti Proverbs, #793

Anderson and Cundall, #160.

Rattray, Ashanti Proverbs, #807

Anderson and Cundall, #282a.

ditto, #888.

R. Sutherland Rattray, Akan-Ashanti Folk-Tales, Oxford, 1930, p. 149.

Anderson and Cundall, #1224.

Note:--In an appendix to his Reports of the Jamaica Assembly on the subject of the slave trade, London, 1789, Stephen Fuller gave a summary of the Negroes from Africa who were sold in Jamaica between 1764 and 1788. During this period some 50,000 slaves were imported by the five principal agents and of these nearly 15% came from the Gold Coast.

CHAPTER II--JAMAICA WITCHCRAFT

Notes and Queries, Vol. III, p. 59f.

ditto, Vol. III, p. 149f.

ditto, Vol. III, p. 150.

ditto, Vol. III, p. 309f.

ditto, Vol. III, p. 376.

The Medical Times, September 20, 1851, p. 306.

Notes and Queries, July 15, 1899, p. 47. Note:--This letter of James Platt drew forth the following reply from James Hooper of Harwich in Notes and Queries for July 29, 1899: "If the Reverend H. Goldie's etymology as quoted by Mr. Platt, is correct, Dr. Brewer's account of obiism, as he spells the word, is all wrong. 'Obiism, Serpent-worship. From the Egyptian Ob (the sacred serpent). The African sorceress is still called obi. The Greek ophis is of the same family. Moses forbade the Israelites to inquire of Ob, which we translate wizard.' Now this looks very interesting, and carries us far; but is there an Egyptian word Ob signifying the sacred serpent? And is the Hebrew word Ob identical with the Egyptian Ob; and are both susceptible of the same interpretation? Is an African witch called Obi?"

Jacob Bryant, (1715-1804) of whom his biographer wrote: "In point of classical erudition he was perhaps without an equal in the world," published in 1774-76, A New System or an Analysis of Antient Mythology, "wherein an attempt is made to divest Tradition of Fable, and to reduce Truth to its original Purity." An entire chapter is devoted to "Ob, Oub, Pytho, sive de Ophiolatria."--Cfr. (Third Edition) London, 1807, Vol. II, p. 197 ff.-- According to Bryant, a serpent in the Egyptian language was called Ob or Aub--Obion is still the Egyptian name of a serpent-- Moses, in the name of God, forbids the Israelites even to inquire of the daemon, Ob which is translated charmer or wizard, divinator aut sortilegus, etc. All this was adopted by the Report of the Lords of the Committee of the Council appointed for the consideration of all Matters relating to Trade and Foregn Plantations, London, 1789, as a basis of the etymology of the word obeah, and as this Report has since served as a starting point for all writers on the subject, the views of Bryant have prevailed until comparatively recently. Thus we find The Daily Advertiser of Kingston, Jamaica, in the issues of October 13-16, 1790, reprinting that part of the Report which refers to obeah.

In The Gentleman's Magazine, December, 1816, p. 502f., there is a letter addressed to the Editor, Sylvanus Urban, dated Penzance, June 1, and signed C. V. L. G., wherein, without reference to the above Report, the writer calls attention to Bryant's derivation of the word Ob, and adds: "The curious coincidence which I mean to remark is, that the witchcraft practised by the Blacks in the West Indies at this day is called Ob or Obi; the ignorant Negroes are under the most superstitious dread of those who profess the art."

The New Dictionary on Historical Principles. Edited by Sir James A. H. Murray, Oxford, 1909, Vol. VII.

Harry H. Johnston, l.c., p. 253, Note 1.

Hugh Goldie, Dictionary of the Efik Language, Glasgow, 1874, p. 300.

ditto, p. 118.

Rattray, Ashanti, p. 104.

Rattray, Religion and Art in Ashanti, p. 45.

R. Sutherland Rattray, Ashanti Law and Constitution, Oxford, 1929, p. 313.

Christaller, l.c., p. A

ditto, p. 429.

Rattray, Ashanti Proverbs, #56.

Rattray, Religion and Art in Ashanti, p. 28.

Rattray, Ashanti Proverbs, #56.

Christaller, l.c., p. 11.

ditto, p. 588.

British Museum MS. 12405, p. 463.

Rattray, Religion and Art in Ashanti, p. 39.

ditto, p. 28.

J. Leighton Wilson, Western Africa, Its History, Condition and Prospects, London, 1856, p. 211.

H. G. DeLisser, Twentieth Century Jamaica, Kingston, 1913, p. 108 ff.

Acts of Assembly, passed in the Island of Jamaica, from 1681 to 1737, inclusive, London, 1743, p. 55.

Rattray, Ashanti, pp. 242-286.

ditto, p. 266.

ditto, p. 265.

Acts of Assembly, l.c., p. 108.

Acts of Assembly, passed in the Island of Jamaica, from 1770 to 1783, inclusive, Kingston, 1786, p. 256 ff.

John Lunan, Abstracts of the Laws of Jamaica relating to Slaves, St. Jago de la Vega, 1819, p. 118.

Christaller, l.c., p. 301.

Voodoos and Obeahs, p. 145f.

The Annual Register, 1760, p. 124

C. O. 139/21. Note:--Conditions in Jamaica at the time may be judged from contemporaneous Publications in England. Thus in The London Chronicle, Vol. VIII (1760), No. 569, a letter dated Kingston, Jamaica, June 14, 1760, mentions: "On Thursday afternoon two Negroes, named Quaco and Anthony, concerned in the late insurrection in St. Mary's, were executed at Spring Path, according to sentence. The former was burnt at a stake, and the latter hanged, his head cut off, and fixed on a pole on the Greenwich road etc." The Annual Register, under date of August 1, 1760, gives (p. 124 f.) extracts of a letter from Jamaica dated May 8, 1760: "They cut off the overseer's head put his blood in a calabash, mixed gun-powder with it, and eat their plantains dipped in it, as they did by every white man they killed. I was last Saturday at Spanish Town before which time one, who had not been in the rebellion actually was burnt alive, for having sworn to cut his master and mistress's heads off, and to make punch bowls of them." A second letter, dated May 21, 1760, states, (l.c., p. 124): "The sentence against the rebel Negroes was put into execution. One of them lived nine days, wanting six hours, without a drop of water, hanging in an excessive hot place, though they complained of the cold in the night."

Long, l.c., Vol. II, p. 416.

Charles Leslie, A New History of Jamaica, London, 1740, p. 308.

Robert Renny, An History of Jamaica, London, 1807, 169 f. Note:--Professor Beckwith remarks: "It is true that as the Negroes become better educated and more intelligent, the spiritist beliefs (upon which obeah practices depend) lose their hold upon the mind; hence a larger and larger number of obeah practitioners become such for mercenary reasons or for the opportunity the trade gives them to satisfy sensual desires. But the fact that the trade remains lucrative proves the persistence of the belief, and there is no reason-to suppose that the practitioner is in every case more intelligent than the great mass of the people who employ his skill." (1.c., p. 107 f.)

J. Stewart, An Account of Jamaica and its Inhabitants, London, 1808, p. 256 ff.

J. Stewart, A View of the Past and Present State of the Island of Jamaica, Edinburgh, 1823, p. 276f.

John Williamson, Medical and Miscellaneous Observations relative to the West India Islands, Edinburgh, 1817.

ditto, Vol. I, p. 361.

ditto, Vol. I, p. 359 f.

ditto, Vol. I, p. 114 ff.

Voodoos and Obeahs, p. 191 f.

R. R. Madden, A Twelvemonths' Residence in the West Indies, during the Transition from Slavery to Apprenticeship, London, 1835, Vol. I, p. 93.

Benjamin Luckock, Jamaica: Enslaved and Free, New York, 1846, p. 126.

Charles Rampini, Letters from Jamaica, Edinburgh, 1873, p. 132.

T. Banbury, Jamaica Superstitions: or The Obeah Book, Kingston, 1894, p. 5.

ditto, p. 6.

ditto, p. 7 f.

ditto, p. 18.

W. p. Livingston, Black Jamaica, London, 1899, p. 19 ff.

Abraham J. Emerick, Obeah and Duppyism: in Jamaica, Woodstock, 1915, p. 191 ff.

ditto, p. 81.

Voodoos and Obeahs, p. 214f.

Chambers's Journal, Vol. V, No. 215, p. 81.

ditto, p. 81.

ditto, p. 82.

ditto, p. 84.

Claude McKay, Banana Bottom, New York, 1933, p. 132.

ditto, p. 134.

Folk-Lore. A Quarterly Review of Myth, Tradition, Institution and Custom, London, Vol. IV, p. 207 ff.

ditto, p. 210.

Rules and Regulations for the Jamaica Constabulary Force, Spanish Town, 1867, p. 26.

Harry McCrea, The Sub-Officers' Guide, Kingston, 1908, p. 83.

J. E. R. Stephens, Supreme Court Decisions of Jamaica and Privy Council Decisions, from 1774-1923, London, 1924, p. 1538.

Banbury, l.c., p. 9.

Note:--According to Doctor Beckwith: "By whatever natural means the obeah-man may achieve his ends, there is no doubt whatever as to the faith of the Negroes im his spiritual power. . . . One of the strongest arguments against the honesty of the obeah-man is the fact that he actually does excite a man to crime as a condition laid down by the spirit to make his obeah work." (l.c., p. 140.)

Voodoos and Obeahs, p. 218.

CHAPTER III--APPLIED MAGIC

The Universal Dictionary of the English Language. Edited by Henry Cecil Wyld, London, 1932, p. 787.

British Museum Library, 6005 . k . 5 .

ditto, p. vii.

Cfr. Jacques-Charles Brunet, Manual du Libraire et de l'Amateur de Livres, Paris, 1860, Vol. I, col. 139, Albertus Magnus.

Marius Decrespe, Les Secrets Admirables du Grand Albert, Paris, 1885, Preface, p. vi.

ditto, Preface, p. vii.

The Jamaica Mercury and Kingston Advertiser, Kingston, Jamaica, Vol. II, p. 458.

ditto, Vol. II, p. 698.

ditto, Vol. II, p. 747.

The Royal Gazette, Kingston, Jamaica, Vol. III, No. 89, p. 13.

ditto, Vol. III, No. 93, p. 79.

Benjamin Moseley, A Treatise on Sugar, London, 1:800, p. 197 ff.

William Burdett, Life and Exploits of Mansong, Sommers Town, 1800, p. 17.

CHAPTER IV--POPULAR BELIEF IN GHOSTS

Hesketh J. Bell, Obeah; Witchcraft in the West Indies, London 1889, p. 122 ff.

Rattray: Religion and Art in Ashanti, p. 152.

ditto, p. 152.

Rattray, Ashanti Proverbs, #34, p. 36.

ditto, p. 37.

ditto, p. 38.

Banbury, l.c., p. 27.

Christaller, l.c., p. 100.

Banbury, l.c., p. 27. Note:--Writing of the period prior to the great Earthquake of 1692, Gardner says of the slaves: "Great lamentation was made over the graves of the departed, and the spirit, or 'duppy', was supposed to hover for some days about the spot before it took its final departure for Africa, food and rum was placed upon the grave, and the supply renewed from day to day." (Gardner, l.c., p. 99.)

Banbury, l.c., p. 31.

ditto, p. 31.

Abraham J. Emerick, Jamaica Duppies, Woodstock, 1916, p. 339.

ditto, p. 340.

ditto, p. 341.

ditto, p. 345.

Christaller, l.c., p. 424.

Banbury, l.c., p. 23f. Note:--Charles Rampini in his Letters from Jamaica, Edinburgh, 1873, p. 83, states: "A very mischievous ghost is that known by the name of 'rolling calf,' a spirit who haunts the city by night with a flaming eye, trailing a long chain behind him. To speak to, or to touch the chain of a rolling calf will cause him to turn and rend you. The only way to escape is to stick an open penknife in the ground and run without looking behind you.

Banbury, l.c., p. 25. Note:--According to Professor Beckwith, (l.c., p. 100f.): "Whatever the origin of the rolling calf it is looked upon to-day as the animal form assumed by especially dangerous duppies. Obeah-men often become tolling calves and they 'set' rolling calves upon people. Murderers and butchers and I know not how many other reprobates become rolling calves when they die, and go to live not only at the roots of cottonwood trees and in clumps of bamboos but also in caves and deserted houses, whence they emerge at night to follow sugar wains because of their fondness for molasses, or to break into cattle pens."

Banbury, l.c., p. 26. Note:--A writer in Chambers's Journal, January 11, 1902, asserts: "The rolling calf . . . This is a quadruped with blazing eyes and having a clanking chain round its neck. Like the loup-garou, it prowls at night, and the man whom it touches dies. The only way to escape--so the Negroes say--is to stick a penknife in the ground and turn your back on the monster. Like Mephistopheles held back by the sign of the Cross, it cannot then advance, however malevolent it may be."

Banbury, l.c., p. 23.

Rattray, Religion and Art in Ashanti, p. 153.

Rattray, Ashanti, p. 152.

Banbury, l.c., p. 19. Note:--Isabel Cranstoun Maclean, (l.c., p. 30 tells us: "Sometimes a man gets the obeah-man to bottle his enemy's shadow for him. So long as it is tightly corked, he has power over that poor enemy and can make him do anything he likes."

Banbury, l.c., p. 20.

ditto, p. 23.

ditto, p. 21.

Rattray, Religion and Art in Ashanti, p. 154. Note:--The Daily Gleaner of Kingston, of March 17, 1934, contained an article entitled "With West Indian Duppies," by L. C. Quinlan, wherein it is asserted: "That every man is accompanied by two duppies, a good and a bad one, is a general belief. When a man sleeps, the good duppy remains on watch beside him, while the other goes walking, nor can the sleeper wake until the evil spirit has returned. When you go on a journey, be sure the bad duppy precedes you, as if it doesn't it is likely to harm you. just how you can insist on the bad duppy keeping ahead of you I am at a loss to say." While the writer implies that there is a general belief in this "dream-soul" or bad duppy as he calls it, from my own experience, as related in the text, I could find only vestiges of the belief.

Banbury, l.c., p. 33.

Christaller, l.c., p. 11.

Banbury, l.c., p. 32 f. Note:--It is Doctor Beckwith's opinion that "Ole Hige is still a menace to infants in Jamaica, and it is from fear of her visit that they are guarded by a blue cross on the ninth night after birth and that a cross is put on the door of dwellings, or grain is strewn before the door. But I do not think her name carries otherwise much fear with it. She is the skin-changing witch of European folk tale, and the story is commonly told of the child who watches the witch slip out of her skin and, while she is away, burns or peppers it so that she cannot resume it again at her return. The lively recital of the hag's consternation, her cry of 'Kin, you no know me?' never fails to win a roar of merriment from the delighted audience. Equally uproarious mirth accompanies the recital of her way of counting when grain or rice is scattered at the door or an X marked on the sill--'One, two, t'ree, an' deh a da!' she reiterates, because, since she can never count beyond the number 'three' and has then to go back and repeat the reckoning, the tale is never told. Why the poor old thing has to count at all is part of the mystery."

Banbury, l.c., p. 35.

Rattray, Ashanti. p. 54.

ditto, p. 145f.

ditto, p. 146.

Martha Warren Beckwith, Jamaica Folk-Lore, New York, 1928, Jamaica Proverbs, #257.

Rattray, Ashanti Proverbs, #41.

CHAPTER V--FUNERAL CUSTOMS

DeLisser, l.c., p. 93. Note:--The Negro tribes that had not been contaminated by Mohammedan contacts had a degree of morality that shamed the Whites who first had dealings with them. Cfr. J. H. Driberg, The Lango, London, 1923, p. 209 f., especially the Notes. Here we find the death penalty prescribed for those sensual acts which are usually classified as being "against nature."

M. Malte-Brun, Universal Geography, Philadelphia, 1827, Vol. III, p. 23.

Charles W. Thomas, Adventures and Observations on the West Coast of Africa, and its Islands, New York, 1860, p. 129.

Rattray, Religion and Art in Ashanti, p. 151.

ditto, p. 151. Note:--T. Edward Bowditch, (l.c., p. 364) relates in connexion with the Ashanti funeral customs: "The singing is almost all recitative, and this is the only part of the music in which the women partake; they join in the choruses, and at the funeral of a female sing the dirge itself; but the frenzy of the moment renders it such a mixture of yells and screeches, that it bids defiance to all notation."

Rattray, Religion and Art in Ashanti, p. 158.

ditto, p. 159.

ditto, p. 159.

ditto, p. 190.

ditto, p. 160.

Rattray, Ashanti Proverbs, #77.

Rattray, Religion and Art in Ashanti, p. 167.

ditto, p. 167 ff.

ditto, p. 170.

ditto, p. 170.

ditto, p. 161 f. Note:--As will be shown later on, this Ashanti use of the word hole as meaning a grave perseveres in Jamaica where every clergyman soon becomes familiar with the request: "Me beg you one hole, sah!"

Rattray, Religion and Art in Ashanti, p. 163.

ditto, p. 163.

ditto, p. 165f.

ditto, p. 166.

ditto, p. 184.

J. B. Danquah, l.c., p. 234.

Charles Leslie, 1.c., p. 308 ff. Note:--Sir Hans Sloane, Natural History of Jamaica, London, 1707, Vol. 1, Introduction, p. xlviii, writing from personal observation had previously reported: "The Negroes from some countries think that they return to their own country when they die in Jamaica, and therefore regard death but little, imagining they shall change their condition by that means from servile to free, and so for this reason often cut their own throats. Whether they die thus or naturally, their country people make great lamentations, mournings, and howlings about their expiring, and at their funeral throw in rum and victuals into their graves, to serve them in the other world. Sometimes they bury it in gourds, at other times spill it in the graves."

Edward Long, 1.c., Vol. II, p. 421 f. Note:--In describing the Koromantyn funerals as he had witnessed them in Jamaica, Bryan Edwards l.c., Vol. II, p. 850, reported: "At the burial of such among them as were respected in life, or venerable through age, they exhibit a sort of Pyrrhic or warlike dance, in which their bodies are strongly agitated by running, leaping, and jumping, with many violent and frantic gestures and contortions. Their funeral songs too are all of the heroic or martial cast"--he has just mentioned that the songs of the Eboes are soft and languishing, those of the Koromantyns heroic and martial--affording some colour to the prevalent notion that the Negroes consider death not only as a welcome and happy release from the calamities of their condition, but also as a passport to the place of their nativity; a deliverance which, while it frees them from bondage, restores them to the society of their dearest, long-lost and lamented relatives in Africa. But I am afraid that this, like other European notions concerning the Negroes, is the dream of poetry; the sympathetic effusion of a fanciful or too credulous an imagination." Then after showing the Negro's fear of death, he declares: "We may conclude, therefore, that their funeral songs and ceremonies are commonly nothing more than the dissonance of savage barbarity and riot; as remote from the fond superstition to which they are ascribed, as from the sober dictates of a rational sorrow." The Reverend James M. Phillippo, a Baptist missionary in Jamaica of twenty years' experience, in his Jamaica, its Past and Present State, (London, 1843, p. 244 ff.), relates concerning the slaves: "Their practices at funerals were unnatural and revolting in a high degree. No sooner did the spirit depart from the body of a relative or friend, than the most wild and frantic gesticulations were manifested, accompanied by the beating of drums and the singing of songs. When on the way with the corpse to interment, the bearers, who were often intoxicated, practised the most strange and ridiculous manoeuvres. They would sometimes make a sudden halt, put their ears in a listening attitude against the coffin, pretending that the corpse was endued with the gift of speech--that he was angry and required to be appeased, gave instructions for a different distribution of his property, objected to his mode of conveyance, or refused to proceed farther towards the place of burial until some debts due to him were discharged, some slanderous imputation on his character removed, some theft confessed, or until they (the bearers) were presented with renewed potations of rum: and the more effectually to delude the multitude, and thereby enforce their claims, to some of which they were often instigated by the chief mourners, they would pretend to answer the questions of the deceased, echo his requirements, run back with the coffin upon the procession, or jerk it from side to side of the road; not unfrequently, and under the most trivial pretence, they would leave the corpse at the door or in the house of a debtor or neighbour indiscriminately, and resist every importunity for its removal, until his pretended demands were satisfied. On estates these ceremonies were generally performed in a manner which was, if possible, still more revolting. They took place at night by the light of torches, amidst drumming, dancing, singing, drunkenness, and debauchery. The coffin was usually supported on the heads of two bearers, preceded by a man carrying a white flag, and followed by the intoxicated multitude. They went to each. house of the Negro village ostensibly to 'take leave,' but really for exaction and fraud . . . The corpse being deposited in the grave and partially covered with earth, the attendants completed the burial (for a time) by casting the earth behind them, to prevent the deceased from following them home. The last sad offices were usually closed by sacrifices of fowls and other domestic animals, which were torn to pieces and scattered over the grave, together with copious libations of blood and other ingredients, accompanied at the same time with the most violent and extravagant external signs of sorrow; they stamped their feet, tore their hair, beat their breasts, vociferated, and manifested the most wild and frantic gestures. No sooner, however, did the party return to the house of their relatives and friends than every sign of sadness vanished; 'the drums resounded with a livelier beat, the song grew more animated, dancing and festivity commenced, and the night was spent in riot and debauchery.' Were the deceased a female, the reputed husband for about a month afterwards was negligent in his person and dress. At the close of this period he proceeded with some of his friends to the grave with several articles of food, and sung a song congratulating the deceased on her enjoyment of complete happiness. This was supposed to terminate their mutual obligations. Each of the party then expressed his wishes of remembrance to his kindred, repeated benedictions on his family, promised soon to return to them, repeated promises to take care of her children, and bade the deceased an affectionate farewell. An additional quantity of earth was now thrown over the grave, and the party partook of the repast they had provided, concluding the ceremony with dancing, singing, and vociferation, regarding death as a welcome relief from the calamities of life, and a passport to the never-to-be-forgotten scenes of their nativity."

Gardner, l.c. p. 186 f. Note:--Matthew Gregory Lewis, more familiarly known as "Monk" Lewis, recorded in his Journal of a West India Proprietor, (London, 1834, p. 97 f.), under date of January 13, 1816: "The Negroes are always buried in their own gardens, and many strange and fantastical ceremonies are observed on the occasion. If the corpse be that of a grown person, they consult it as to which way it pleases to be carried; and they make attempts upon various roads without success, before they hit upon the right one. Till that is accomplished, they stagger under the weight of the coffin, struggle against its force, which draws them in a different direction from that in which they had settled to go; and sometimes in the contest the corpse and the coffin jump off the shoulders of the bearers. But if, as is frequently the case, any person is suspected of having hastened the catastrophe, the corpse will then refuse to go any road but the one which passes by the habitation of the suspected person, and as soon as it approaches his house, no human power is equal to persuading it to pass. As the Negroes are extremely superstitious and very much afraid of ghosts (whom they call the duppy), I rather wonder at their choosing to have their dead buried in their gardens; but I understand their argument to be, that they need only fear the duppies of their enemies, but have nothing to apprehend from those after death, who loved them in their lifetime; but the duppies of their adversaries are very alarming beings, equally powerful by day as by night, and who not only are spiritually terrific, but who can give very hard substantial knocks on the pate, whenever they see fit occasion, and can find a good opportunity."

Gardner, l.c., p. 386 ff. Note:--J. Stewart who reported conditions as he found them in Jamaica in 1823, mentions a rather amusing incident, (A View of the Past and Present State of the Island of Jamaica, p. 276): "A Negro who was to be interred in one of the towns, had, it was pretended by some of his friends, a claim on another Negro for a sum of money. The latter denied any such claim; and accordingly, at the funeral of the deceased the accustomed ceremonies took place opposite to the door of his supposed debtor; and this mummery was continued for hours, till the magistrates thought proper to interfere, and compelled the defunct to forego his claim, and proceed quietly on to his place of rest." Cynric R. Williams who visited Jamaica in this same year, 1823, in his Tour through the Island of Jamaica, London, 1826, p. 104 ff., relates: "I did not attend the funeral of the Negro above mentioned, as I thought my presence might be unwelcome, but my two lacqueys were of the party; and Ebenezer, as I suspected, did not lose so excellent an opportunity of endeavouring to edify his brethren, and displaying his progress in religious knowledge. He objected to the heathen ceremony of throwing a fowl into the grave, and said that the yams which they would have buried with the corpse had no more business there than a hog in the Gibna's (Governor's) garden. The son, in the law, of the deceased, described the scene to me, or rather the speech made by Ebenezer, on the occasion, which I shall endeavour to relate in his own words. The corpse was buried by moonlight with the help of torches, and after the Negro fashion; but Ebenezer, seeing that the business was to end there, had called out to know if they would not 'read ober him, and if they were not going to sabe his soul?' The Negroes, very accommodating, told him he might read if he would; on which he took a book from his pocket, and held it the wrong way upward (which did not much signify, as he does not know his letters) and began as follows: 'Dea belubb'd, we gather tigether dis face congregation, because it horrible among all men not to take delight in hand for wantonness, lust, and appetite, like brute mule, dat hab no understanding. When de man cut down like guinea grass, he worship no more any body, but gib all him world's good to de debbil; and Garamighty tell him soul must come up into heab'n, where notting but glorio. What de use of fighting wid beast at Feesus? Rise up all and eat and drink, because we die yesterday, no so tomorrow. Who shew you mystery? Who nebba sleep, but twinkle him yeye till de trumpet peak? Who baptize you, and gib you victory ober der debbil's flesh? Old Adam, belubb'd!--he bury when a child, and de new man rise up when he old. Breren, you see dat dam rascal Dollar;--he no Christian; he no Jew, no missionary, no Turk, for true. You see him laugh (Abdallah denied it)--when he go to hell be die, and nebba gnash him teeth, and worms can't nyam him. Breren, all Christians, white and black man, all one colour--Sambo and mulatto--no man bigger dan another, no massa, and no fum fum--plenty o' grog.--So, breren! Garamighty take de dead man, and good night!'" Rattray, Religion and Art in Ashanti, p. 104 ff.

ditto, p. 106.

ditto, p. 108.

ditto, p. 2.

ditto, p. 2. Note:--W. D. Weatherford, The Negro from Africa to America (New York, 1924, p. 45), offers the following suggestion as the African viewpoint of the food offered to spirits: "When a man dies his spirit adds itself to that innumerable company of spirits which fill the world about us. The spirit needs the food and care just as it did in its human incarnation, save that it now only consumes the essence of the food, leaving the visible or material food which is eaten by the natives."

Martha Warren Beckwith, Black Roadways, Chapel Hill, 1929, p. 70.

ditto, p. 71.

ditto, p. 71.

ditto, p. 73.

ditto, p. 74.

ditto, p. 75.

ditto, p. 76 f.

ditto, p. 77 f.

ditto, p. 80 f.

ditto, p. 82.

DeLisser, 1.c., p. 120 ff.

Voodoos and Obeahs, p. 152f.

Whisperings of the Caribbean, p. 235 f.

ditto, p. 238 f.

CHAPTER VI--POLTERGEIST

Voodoos and Obeahs, p. 220.

Rattray, Religion and Art in Ashanti.

Rattray, Ashanti Proverbs, #57.

Rattray, Ashanti, p. 163.

Rattray, Religion and Art in Ashanti, p. 25 ff.

A. W. Cardinall, In Ashanti and Beyond, Philadelphia, 1927, p. 224.
Note:--In Chambers's Journal, January 11, 1902, p. 81 ff. there appeared an article entitled "'Obeah' To-day in the West Indies," wherein the writer makes this statement: "Just as I was writing, the following curious 'duppy' story came under my notice. It is believed by hundreds of black people in the district of Lamb's River, Jamaica: A boy who was wanted to give evidence in a criminal case was missed a few months ago. It was

supposed that he had run away; but it is now darkly rumoured that he was murdered by a young woman, who has ever since been tormented by his 'duppy.' The ghost stones her every night. People say they see the stones hurtling through the air, and the bruises on her body; but they never see anybody throw them. Hundreds of people--so the story goes--follow the luckless young woman about every night to see where the stones come from, but it remains a mystery. The young woman has had her head broken by them, and it is feared that she will lose her reason."

Bell, 1.c., p. 93 ff. Note:--Andrew Lang in The Making of Religion, (London, 1898, p. 366), includes an Appendix, entitled, "The Poltergeist and his Explainers," where, after discussing a number of cases, he concludes: "It seems wiser to admit our ignorance and suspend our belief. Here closes the futile chapter of explanations. Fraud is a vera causa, but an hypothesis difficult of application when it is admitted that the effects could not be caused by ordinary mechanical means. Hallucination, through excitement, is a vera causa, but its remarkable uniformity, as described by witnesses from different lands and ages, knowing nothing of each other, makes us hesitate to accept a sweeping hypothesis of hallucination. The case for it is not confirmed, when we have the same reports from witnesses certainly not excited. This extraordinary bundle, then, of reports, practically identical, of facts paralyzing to belief, this bundle made up of statements from so many ages and countries, can only be 'filed for reference.'" It is interesting, then, to record that I received a letter from the Most Reverend Arthur Hinsley, Apostolic Delegate, in East Africa, dated Mombasa, February 11, 1933, wherein he states: "The stone-throwing propensity of the Jamaica Duppies is extraordinary! I heard from missionaries in Uganda or in Kavirondo (Kenya) of two or three cases of such mysterious stone-throwing." Perhaps one of the most remarkable cases that have been recorded on excellent authority is that reported in Rome of January 23, 1909, by Monsignor Delalle, Vicar Apostolic in Natal, which concerns the exorcism of a possessed girl named Germana at St. Michael's Mission, Natal in May, 1907. We have here extraordi-nary strength, as well as knowledge of what is going on at a distance. The girl was sixteen years of age, utterly ignorant of Latin, and yet the Bishop addressed her only in that tongue, while she answered usually in Zulu, but sometimes in Latin.

CHAPTER VII--CONCLUSIONS

Job ii. 6.

I Peter v.8.

Tob. iii. 8.

Ps. lxxvii. 49.

Eccl. xxxix. 33, 34.

Mark i. 23-26.

Mark v. 1-14

Mark ix. 16-28.

Simon Augustine Blackmore, Spiritism. Facts and Frauds. New York, 1924, p. 208 f. Note --Cfr. also Alexius M. Lepicier, The Unseen World, London, 1909 p. 3: "Very many of the so-called spiritistic manifestations reported in books and journals have, under closer examination, been proved to be the result of mere trickery and fraud. It is nevertheless admitted that there are certain phenomena which, after rigid examination, cannot possibly be accounted for by these means, and that it would be an arbitrary and highly unscientific proceeding were we to deny the operation of the invisible spiritual world in connexion with them."

J. W. Wickwar, Witchcraft and the Black Art, London, 1925, p. 188.

Montague Summers, The History of Witchcraft and Demonology, London, 1926, p. 8.

Jean Bodin, De la Demonomanie des Sorciers, Paris, 1580.

Summers, l.c., p. 1.

Blackmore, l.c., p. 158.

BIBLIOGRAPHY

SPACE restricts us to such works as may be found in the Boston College Library, Chestnut Hill, Mass.

ANONYMOUS.

Acts of Assembly, passed in the Island of Jamaica from 1681 to 1737, inclusive, London, 1743.

Acts of Assembly, passed in the Island of Jamaica from 1681 to 1754, inclusive, London, 1756.

Acts of Assembly, passed in the Island of Jamaica from 1770 to 1783, Kingston, 1786.

Act to Remedy the Evils arising from irregular Assemblies of Slaves, etc. Passed by the Assembly of Jamaica in December, 1760. (Photostatic copy in the Boston College Library.)

Consolidated Slave Law, passed 22 December 1826 London, 1827.

Hints respecting Christian Education of the Negro Population in the British Colonies, London, 1833.

Religious Instruction of the Coloured and Slave Population of Jamaica, London, 1832.

Report of the Jamaica Royal Commission of Inquiry respecting certain Disturbances in the Island of Jamaica and the Measures taken in the Course of their Suppression, London, 1866.

Report of the Lords of the Committee of the Council appointed for the Consideration of all Matters relating to Trade and Foreign Plantation, London, 1789,

Re-view of Hamel, the Obeah Man, London, 1827.

Slave Law of Jamaica and Documents relative thereto, London, 1828.

ANDERSON AND CUNDALL.

Jamaica Proverbs and Sayings, London, 1927, 296

ARMISTEAD, WILSON.

Tribute for the Negro, Manchester, 1848.

ARNAUD, ODETTE.

Mer Caraïbe, Paris, 1934.

BACON, EDGAR MAYHEW.

The New Jamaica, New York, 1890.

BANBURY, R. THOMAS.

Jamaica Superstitions or The Obeah Book, Kingston, 1894.

BARCLAY, ALEXANDER.

A Practical View of the Present Stage of Slavery in the West Indies, London, 1828.

BASTIAN, ADOLF.

Der Fetisch an der Küste Guineas, Berlin, 1884.

BAYLEY, F. W. N.

Four Years' Residence in the West Indies, London, 1830.

BECKFORD, WILLIAM.

A Descriptive Account of the Island of Jamaica, London, 1790.

BECKWITH, MARTHA WARREN.

Folk-Games of Jamaica, Poughkeepsie, 1922.

Christmas Mummings in Jamaica, Poughkeepsie, 1923.

The Hussey Festival in Jamaica, Poughkeepsie, 1924.

Jamaica Anansi Stories, New York, 1924.

Jamaica Folk-Lore, New York, 1928.

Black Roadways; a Study of Jamaica Folk-Lore, Chapel Hill, 1928.

BELL, HESKETH J.

Obeah; Witchcraft in the West Indies, London, 1889.

BICKNELL, R.

West Indies as they are, or a Real Picture of Slavery, but more particularly as it exists in the Island of Jamaica, London, 1825.
BIGELOW, JOHN.

Jamaica in 1850, New York, 1851

BLEBY, HENRY.

Death Struggle of Slavery, London, 1853.

Scenes in the Caribbean Sea, London, 1868.

The Reign of Terror, London, 1868.

BLOME, RICHARD.

Description of the Island of Jamaica, London, 1678

BOSMAN, WILLIAM.

A New and Accurate Description of the Coast of Guinea, London, 1705.

BOWDITCH, T. EDWARD.

Mission from Cape Coast Castle to Ashantee, London, 1819.

Essay on Superstitions, Customs and Acts, Common to the Ancient Egyptian, Abyssineans and Ashantee, Paris, 1821.

BOWLER, LOUIS P.

Gold Coast Palava: Life on the Gold Coast, London, 1911.

BRAWLEY, B. G.

Short History of the American Negro, New York, 1913.

Social History of the American Negro, New York, 1921.

BRIDGES, GEORGE WILSON.

A Voice from Jamaica; in reply to William Wilberforce, London, 1823.

Annals of Jamaica, London, 1828.

BROWNE, PATRICK.

Civil and Natural History of Jamaica, London, 1756.

BRYMNER, D.

The Jamaica Maroons, London, 1895.

BUCHANAN, CLAUDIUS.

Colonial Ecclesiastical Establishment, London, 1812.

BURDETT, WILLIAM.

Life and Exploits of Mansong, commonly called Three-finger Jack, the Terror of Jamaica, Sommers Town, 1800.

BURKHARDT, G. E.

Die Evangelische Mission unter den Negern in Westindien und Sued-Amerika, Leipzig, 1876.

CALDECOTT, A.

The Church in the West Indies, London, 1898.

CAMERON, NORMAN EUSTACE.

The Evolution of the Negro, Georgetown, Demerara, 1929.

CARDINALL, A. W.

In Ashanti and Beyond, London, 1927.

CARMICHAEL, MRS. A. C.

Domestic Manners and Social Conditions of the White, Coloured and Negro Population of the West Indies, London, 1834.

CHRISTALLER, J. G.

Dictionary of the Asante and Fante Language Called Tshi (Twi), Basel, 1933.

CLARIDGE, W. WALTON.

History of the Gold Coast and Ashanti, London, 1915.

CLARK, A. H.

Ingenious Method of Causing Death Employed by the Obeah Men of the West Indies,--American Anthropologist, 1912.

CLARKE, JOHN.

Memoir of Richard Merrick, Missionary in Jamaica, London, 1850.

COKE, THOMAS.

History of the West Indies, Liverpool, 1808-11.

COLERIDGE, HENRY NELSON.

Six Months in the West Indies in 1825, New York, 1826.

COOK, E. M.

Jamaica: The Lodestone of the Caribbean, Bristol, 1924.

COOPER, THOMAS.

Facts, illustrative of the Condition of the Negro Slaves in Jamaica, London, 1824.

Correspondence Relative to the Condition of the Negro Slaves in Jamaica, London, 1824.

CROWNINSHIELD, MRS. SCHUYLER.

West Indian Tales, New York, 1898.

CUNDALL, FRANK.

Historic Jamaica, London, 1915.

Chronological Outlines of Jamaica History, 1492-1926, Kingston, 1927.

Studies in Jamaica History, London, 1900.

DALLAS, ROBERT CHARLES.

History of the Maroons, London, 1803.

DANQUAH, J. B.

Akan Laws and Customs, London, 1928.

DELANY, FRANCIS X.

History of the Catholic Church in Jamaica, New York, 1930.

DeLISSER, HERBERT G.

In Jamaica and Cuba, Kingston, 1927.

Twentieth Century Jamaica, Kingston, 1913.

Revenge: a Tale of Old Jamaica, Kingston, 1919.

White Witch of Rosehall, London, 1929.

DENNETT, R. E.

At the Back of the Black Man's Mind, London, 1906.

DODSWORTH, FRANCIS.

Book of the West Indies, London, 1904.

DOWD, JEROME.

The Negro Races, New York, 1907.

DUNCAN, PETER.

Narrative of the Wesleyan Mission to Jamaica, London, 1849.

DUPUIS, JOSEPH.

Journal of a Residence in Ashantee, London, 1824.

EDWARDS, BRYAN.

History, Civil and Commercial, of the British Colonies in the West Indies, London, 1793.

Proceedings of the Governor and Assembly of Jamaica in regard to the Maroon Negroes, London, 1796.

ELLIS, ALFRED BURTON.

The Land of Fetish, London, 1883.

The Tshi-Speaking Peoples of the Gold Coast of West Africa, London, 1887.

History of the Gold Coast of West Africa, London, 1893.

West African Folklore--Popular Science Monthly, 1894.

EMERICK, ABRAHAM J.

Obeah and Duppyism in Jamaica (Printed Privately) Woodstock, 1915.

Jamaica Mialism, (Printed Privately) Woodstock, 1916.

Jamaica Duppies, (Printed Privately) Woodstock, 1916.

EVANS, H. B.

Our West Indian Colonies, London, 1855.

EVES, CHARLES WASHINGTON.

West Indies, London, 1889.

FISKE, Amos KIDDER.

The West Indies, New York, 1899.

FOULKES, THEODORE.

Eighteen Months in Jamaica, London, 1833.

FOX-BOURNE, H. R.

Story of the Colonies, London, 1869.

FRANK, HARRY A.

Roaming through the West Indies, New York, 1920.

FREEMAN) RICHARD AUSTIN.

Travel and Life in Ashanti and Jaman, Westminster, 1898.

FREEMAN, THOMAS B.

Journal of Various Visits to the Kingdoms of Ashanti, etc., London, 1844.

FROUDE, JAMES ANTHONY.

England in the West Indies or the Bow of Ulysses, London, 1888.

FULLER, STEPHEN.

New Act of Assembly of the Island of Jamaica . . . commonly called the New Consolidated Act, London, 1789.

Two Reports from the Committee of the Honourable House of Assembly of Jamaica, London, 1789.

Proceedings of the Honourable House of Assembly of Jamaica, on the Sugar and Slave Trade, London, 1793.

GARDNER, WILLIAM JAMES.

History of Jamaica from its Discovery by Christopher Columbus to the Present Time, London, 1873.

GAUNT, MARY.

Where the Twain Meet, New York, 1922.

Reflection--In Jamaica, London, 1932.

GRAINGER, JAMES.

The Sugar-Cane; a Poem, London, 1766.

GREEN, SAMUEL.

Baptist Mission in Jamaica, London, 1842.

GROS, JULES.

Voyages, Aventures et Captivitié de J. Benet chez les Achantis, Paris, 1884.

GURNEY, JOHN JOSEPH.

Familiar Letters to Henry Clay of Kentucky, Describing a Winter in the West Indies, New York, 1840.

HARVEY, THOMAS.

Jamaica in 1866, London, 1867,

HAWTAYNE, G. H. ("X. BEKE").

West Indian Yarns, Demerara, 1890.

HAY, J. DALRYMPLE.

Ashanti and the Gold Coast, London, 1874.

HAYFORD, CASELY.

Gold Coast Native Institutions, London, 1874,

HERSKOVITS, MELVILLE J.

On the Provenience of New World Negroes, Evanston, 1933.

The Second Northwestern University Expedition for study of the Suriname Bush-Negroes, 1929, The Hague, 1929.

HILL, ROBERT T.

Cuba and Porto Rico with the Other Islands of the West Indies, New York, 1898.

HINE, JOHN B.

Jamaican Obeah texts, Miskatonic University Press, 1886

HOLFORD, G.

Observations on the Necessity of Introducing a Sufficient Number of Respectable Clergymen into Our Colonies in the West Indies, London, 1808.

HOVEY, SYLVESTER.

Letters from the West Indies: relating especially to Jamaica, New York, 1838,

HOWE, E. W.

The Trip to the West Indies, Topeka, 1910.

JAY, CHARLES.

Observations on the Present State and Future Prospects of the West Indies, London, 1847.

JAY, E. A. HASTINGS.

Glimpse of the Tropics, or, Four Months Cruising in the West Indies, London, 1900.

JECKYLL, WALTER.

Jamaica Song and Story; Anancy Stories, Digging Songs, Ring Tunes and Dancing Tunes, London, 1907.

JOHNSTON, HARRY H.

The Negro in the New World, London, 1910.

JONES, CHESTER LLOYD.

Caribbean Backgrounds and Prospects, New York, 1931.

KEMP, DENNIS.

Nine Years at the Gold Coast, London, 1898.

KINGSLEY, CHARLES.

At Last: a Christmas in the West Indies, London, 1871.

KINGSLEY, MARY H.

Travels in West Africa. London, 1897.

West African Studies, London, 1899.

KNATCHBULL-HUGESSON, E. H.

Immigrants and Liberated Africans admitted into each of the British West India Colonies, London, 1872.

KNIBB, WILLIAM.

Facts and Documents connected with the late Insurrection in Jamaica and the Violations of Civil and Religious Liberty arising out of it, London, 1832.

LABAT, PÈRE.

Nouveau Voyage aux Isles de l'Amérique, La Haye, 1724.

LESLIE, CHARLES.

New History of Jamaica, London, 1740.

LEWIS, MATTHEW GREGORY.

Journal of a West Indian Proprietor, kept during a Residence in the Island of Jamaica, London, 1834.

LINDBLOM, GERHARD.

Africanische Relikte und Indianische Entelehnungen in der Kultur der Busch-Neger Surinams, Göteborg, 1924.

LIVINGSTON, WILLIAM PRINGLE.

Black Jamaica: a Study in Evolution, London, 1899.

LLOYD, WILLIAM.

Letters from the West Indies, London, 1837.

LONG, EDWARD.

History of Jamaica, London, 1774.

LOWE, JOSEPH.

Inquiry into the State of the British West Indies, London, 1807.

LUCKOCK, BENJAMIN.

Jamaica: Enslaved and Free, New York, 1846.

LUNAN, JOHN.

Abstract of the Laws of Jamaica relating to Slaves, St. Jago de la Vega, 1819.

McCREA, HARRY.

Sub-Officers' Guide, Kingston, 1903.

MAC DONALD, GEORGE.

The Gold Coast, Past and Present, New York, 1898.

McKAY, CLAUDE.

Banana Bottom, New York, 1933.

MAC LEAN, ISABEL CRANSTOUN.

Children of Jamaica, Edinburgh, 1910.

McMAHON, BENJAMIN.

Jamaica Plantership, London, 1839.

MADDEN, RICHARD ROBERT.

A Twelvemonths' Residence in the West Indies, during the Transition from Slavery to Apprenticeship, London, 1835.

MANNINGTON, GEORGE.

West Indies with British Guiana and British Honduras, New York, 1925.

MARRYAT, JOSEPH.

Thoughts on the Abolition of the Slave Trade, London, 1816.

More Thoughts occasioned by two Publications, London, 1816.

More Thoughts Still on the State of the West India Colonies, London, 1818.

MARTIN, ROBERT MONTGOMERY.

History of the West Indies, London, 1836-37.

MEREDITH, HENRY.

Account of the Gold Coast of Africa, London, 1812.

MILNE-HOME, MARY PAMELA.

Mamma's Black Nurse Stories, Edinburgh, 1890.

MILNER, T. H.

Present and Future State of Jamaica Considered, London, 1839.

MONTAGNAC, NOEL DE.

Negro Nobodies, London, 1899.

MOORE, J. HAMPTON.

With Speaker Cannon through the Tropics, Philadelphia, 1907.

MORAND, PAUL.

Magie Noire, Paris, 19,28.

MORETON, J. B.

West India Customs and Manners, London, 1793.

MOSELEY, BENJAMIN.

A Treatise on Sugar, London, 1800.

NASSAU, ROBERT HAMMILL.

Fetishism in West Africa, London, 1904.

Where Animals Talk, London, 1914.

NUGENT, LADY MARIA.

Journal of a Voyage to, and Residence in, the Island of Jamaica from 1801 to 1805, London, 1839.

OLDMIXON, JOHN.

History of Jamaica, London, 1708.

OLIVER, VERE LANGFORD.

Caribbeana, London, 1910-19.

PARSONS, ELSIE CLEWS.

Folk-Lore of the Antilles, New York, 1933.

PHILLIPPO, JAMES MURCEL.

Jamaica: Its Past and Present State, London, 1843,

PIM, BEDFORD CLAPPERTON THEVELYAN.

The Negro and Jamaica, London, 1866.

PITMAN, FRANK WESLEY.

Development of the British West Indies 1700-1763, New Haven, 1917.

PITTARD, EUGÈNE.

Contribution à l'Étude Anthropologie des Achanti,-- L'Anthropolie, Paris, 1925.

PULLEN-BURRY, BESSIE.

Jamaica as it is, 1903, London, 1903.

Ethiopia in Exile: Jamaica Revisited, London, 1905.

RAGATZ, LOWELL JOSEPH.

Fall of the Planter Class in the British Caribbean, 1763-1833, New York, 1928.

RAMPINI, CHARLES.

Letters from Jamaica, Edinburgh, 1873.

RATTRAY, R. SUTHERLAND.

Ashanti Proverbs, Oxford, 1916.

Ashanti, Oxford, 1923.

Religion and Art in Ashanti, Oxford, 1927.

Ashanti Law and Constitution, Oxford, 1929.

Akan-Ashanti Folk-Tales, Oxford, 1930.

REGNAULT, ELIAS.

Histoire des Antilles, Paris, 1849.

RENNY, ROBERT.

History of Jamaica, London, 1807

RILAND, JOHN.

Memoir of a West India Planter, London, 1827,

ROBERTS, HELEN H.

Three Jamaica Folk Stories,--Journal of American Folklore, 1922.

A Study of Folksong Variants based on Field Work in Jamaica,-- Journal of American Folklore, 1925.

RODWAY, JAMES.

West Indies and the Spanish Main, London, 1896.

ROSE, G. H.

Letter on the Means and Importance of Converting the Slaves in the West Indies to Christianity, London, 1823.

ROSNY, LUCIEN DE.

Les Antilles, Paris, 1886.

ROUGHLEY, THOMAS.

The Jamaica Planter's Guide, London, 1823.

ST. JOHNSTON, T. R.

West India Pepper-pot, or Thirteen "Quashie" Stories, London, 1928.

SAMUEL, PETER.

Wesleyan-Methodist Missions in Jamaica and Honduras London, 1850.

SCOTT, MICHAEL.

Tom Cringle's Log, Edinburgh, 1833.

Cruise of the Midge, Paris, 1836.

Captain Clutterbuck's Champagne, Edinburgh, 1862.

SCOTT, SIBBALD DAVID.

To Jamaica and Back, London, 1876.

SELIGMAN, C. G.

Races of Africa, London, 1930.

SENIOR, BERNARD MARTIN.

Jamaica as it was, as it is, and as it may be, London, 1835.

SEWELL, WILLIAM G.

Ordeal of Free Labour in the British West Indies, New York, 1861.

SHERLOCK, P. M.

Jamaica Superstitions, Empire Review, 1924.

SHORE, JOSEPH.

In Old St. James, Kingston, 1911.

SINCLAIR, AUGUSTUS CONSTANTINE.

Parliamentary Debates of Jamaica, Vol. XIII, Spanish-Town, 1866.

Chronological History of Jamaica, Jamaica, 1889.

SINGLETON, J.

Description of the West Indies: a Poem, London, 1776.

SLOANE, HANS.

Voyage to the Islands . . . and Jamaica, London, 1707-25.

SPENCER, HERBERT.

Descriptive Sociology: African Races: Compiled and abstracted by Prof. Duncan, London, 1875.

Reissue, entirely rewritten by E. Torday, London, 1930.

STEPHEN, JAMES.

The Slavery of the British West India Colonies, delineated, London, 1824.

STERNE, HENRY.

A Statement of Facts, London, 1837.

STEWART, J.

Account of Jamaica and Its Inhabitants, London, 1808.

View of the Past and Present State of the Island of Jamaica, Edinburgh, 1817.

STODDARD, CHARLES AUGUSTINE.

Cruising among the Caribbees, New York, 1895.

STUART, VILLIERS.

Jamaica Revisited, London, 1891.

STURGE, JOSEPH.

West Indies in 1837, London, 1838.

TALBOYS, W. P.

West India Pickles, New York, 1876.

TAYLOR, R.

Negro Slavery Especially in Jamaica, London, 1823.

THOMAS, HERBERT T.

Untrodden Jamaica, Kingston, 1890.

TREVES, FREDERICK.

Cradle of the Deep, New York, 1920.

TROLLOPE, ANTHONY.

West Indies and the Spanish Main, London, 1857.

TROWBRIDGE, WILLIAM R. H.

Gossip of the Caribbies. Sketches of Anglo-West Indian Life, London, 1895

TRUMAN, GEORGE.

Narrative of a Visit to the West Indies in 1863-64, Philadelphia, 1867.

TURNBULL, DAVID.

The Jamaica Movement, London, 1850.

UDAL, J. S.

Obeah in the West Indies, Folk-Lore, London, 1915.

UNDERHILL, EDWARD BEAN.

West Indies: their Social and Religious Condition, London, 1862.

VAN DYKE, JOHN C.

In the West Indies, New York, 1932.

VERRILL, ALPHEUS HYATT.

Book of the West Indies, New York, 1917.

WALKER, H. DE R.

West Indies and the Empire, London, 1901.

WALKER, JAMES.

Letters on the West Indies, London, 1818.

WALKER, WILLIAM.

On the Social and Economic Position and Prospects of the British West India Possessions, London, 1873.

WATSON, RICHARD.

Defence of the Wesleyan Methodist Missions in the West Indies, London, 1817.

WEATHERFORD, WILLIS DUKE.

The Negro from Africa to America, New York, 1924.

WENTWORTH, TRELAWNEY.

West India Sketch Book, London, 1834.

WERNER, ALICE.

Natives of British Central Africa. London, 1906.

WHITEHEAD, HENRY S.

Obi in the Caribbean, The Commonweal, 1927.

WHITELEY, HENRY.

Three Months in Jamaica in 1832, London, 1833.

WILBERFORCE, WILLIAM.

An Appeal to the Religion, Justice, and Humanity of the Inhabitants of the British Empire, in behalf of the Negro Slaves in the West Indies, London, 1823.

WILCOX, ELLA WHEELER.

Sailing Sunny Seas, Chicago, 1909.

WILLIAMS, CYNRIC R.

Tour through the Island of Jamaica from the Western to the Eastern End, in the Year 1823, London, 1826.

WILLIAMS, JAMES.

Narrative of Events since the First of August, 1834, London, 1837,

WILLIAMS, JOSEPH JOHN.

Whisperings of the Caribbean, New York, 1925.

Hebrewisms of West Africa, New York, 1930.

Voodoos and Obeahs, New York, 1932.

WILSON, J. LEIGHTON.

Western Africa, Its History, Condition and Prospects, London, 1856.

WILSON, MRS. W. E. (WONA).

Selections of Anancy Stories, Kingston, 1899.

YOUNG, ROBERT.

View of Slavery in connection with Christianity, London, 1825.

ZELLER, RUDOLF.

ENDNOTES

[1] As shown in Voodoos and Obeahs Myalism is a residue of the old Ashanti religious rites as found in Jamaica just as obeah is a continua-tion of Ashanti witchcraft. (p. 3)

[2] The Reverend Abraham J. Emerick, S.J., was born at Falmouth, Pennsylvania, November 211, 1856, and died at Woodstock, Maryland, February 4, 1931. After missionary work in Jamaica from 1895 to 1905, he laboured for a time among the coloured people of Philadelphia and subsequently spent more than a dozen years in Saint Mary's County, Maryland, where he devoted himself especially to his beloved Negroes whom he had come to know so well. (p. 5)

[3] Numerals in the text indicate references to be found in the Documentation towards the end of the volume. (p. 19)

[4] Sir Hans Sloane who came to Jamaica in 1687 as Physician to the Governor, Christopher, Duke of Albemarle, in his Voyage to the Islands, London, 1707, Vol. 1, Introduction, p. lii, gives Pequenos Ninnos (little tots) as the origin of piganinnies. This in turn has been transformed into piccaninnies or as we have it in the "bush" picknies. The word however is not of Jamaica origin. Ligon shows that it was in common use in Barbados before the seizure of Jamaica by the English. It was probably brought to the island by the Barbadians who accompanied the army of invasion in 1655. (p. 28)

[5] I am deeply indebted to the officials of the Record Office for courteously giving me free access to their files as well as for furnishing me with photostatic copies of the Act of 1760. (p. 64)

www.ingramcontent.com/pod-product-compliance
Lightning Source LLC
Chambersburg PA
CBHW051243020426
42333CB00025B/3027